Multinational Companies from Japan

T0303997

Since the bursting of Japan's bubble economy, from 1990 onwards, its multinational companies (MNCs) have faced new competitive challenges and questions about the management practices on which they had built their initial success in global markets.

Japanese engagement in the international economy has undergone a number of phases. Historically, Japanese MNCs learnt from foreign companies, frequently through strategic alliances. After the post-war 'economic miracle', Japanese manufacturers in particular converted themselves into MNCs, transferred their homegrown capabilities to overseas subsidiaries and made an impact on the world economy. But the period after 1990 marked declining Japanese competitiveness and raised questions about the ability of Japanese MNCs to be more responsive and global in their strategies, organization and capabilities. It has been argued that the established management practices of Japanese MNCs inhibited adaptation to recent demands of global competition.

This volume presents new case evidence on how Japanese MNCs have responded to the new challenges of the global marketplace, and it provides examples of how they have transformed strategies and competitive capabilities. This book was originally published as a special issue of *Asia Pacific Business Review*.

Robert Fitzgerald is a Reader in Business History and International Management at Royal Holloway, University of London, UK. He specializes in business history, Asia Pacific business and multinational enterprise, and he has recently published *Rise of the Global Company: Multinational Enterprise and the Making of the Modern World* (2015).

Chris Rowley is Inaugural Professor of Human Resource Management at the Cass Business School, City University, London, UK, and Adjunct Professor at Griffith University, Brisbane, Australia. He is the editor of the book series *Working in Asia* and *Asian Studies*, and has published widely, with over 500 journal articles, books and chapters and other contributions in practitioner journals, magazines and newsletters.

Multinational Companies from Japan

Capabilities, competitiveness, and challenges

Edited by
Robert Fitzgerald and Chris Rowley

LONDON AND NEW YORK

First published 2016
by Routledge
2 Park Square, Milton Park, Abingdon, Oxon, OX14 4RN, UK

and by Routledge
711 Third Avenue, New York, NY 10017, USA

First issued in paperback 2017

Routledge is an imprint of the Taylor & Francis Group, an informa business

British Library Cataloguing in Publication Data
A catalogue record for this book is available from the British Library

ISBN 13: 978-1-138-29498-1 (pbk)
ISBN 13: 978-1-138-94632-3 (hbk)

Typeset in TimesNewRomanPS
by diacriTech, Chennai

Publisher's Note
The publisher accepts responsibility for any inconsistencies that may have arisen
during the conversion of this book from journal articles to book chapters, namely
the possible inclusion of journal terminology.

Disclaimer
Every effort has been made to contact copyright holders for their permission to
reprint material in this book. The publishers would be grateful to hear from any
copyright holder who is not here acknowledged and will undertake to rectify any
errors or omissions in future editions of this book.

Contents

CONTENTS

Citation Information

The chapters in this book were originally published in the *Asia Pacific Business Review*, volume 21, issue 3 (July 2015). When citing this material, please use the original page numbering for each article, as follows:

Chapter 1
Japanese multinationals in the post-bubble era: new challenges and evolving capabilities
Robert Fitzgerald and Chris Rowley
Asia Pacific Business Review, volume 21, issue 3 (July 2015) pp. 279–294

Chapter 2
Global value chains and the lost competitiveness of the Japanese watch industry: an applied business history of Seiko since 1990
Pierre-Yves Donzé
Asia Pacific Business Review, volume 21, issue 3 (July 2015) pp. 295–310

Chapter 3
Do Japanese electronics firms still follow traditional vertical integration strategies? Evidence from the liquid crystal display industry
Derek Lehmberg
Asia Pacific Business Review, volume 21, issue 3 (July 2015) pp. 311–332

Chapter 4
Strategic capabilities and the emergence of the global factory: Omron in China
Robert Fitzgerald and Jiangfeng Lai
Asia Pacific Business Review, volume 21, issue 3 (July 2015) pp. 333–363

Chapter 5
Boundary-crossing and the localization of capabilities in a Japanese multinational firm
Jacky F.L. Hong and Robin Stanley Snell
Asia Pacific Business Review, volume 21, issue 3 (July 2015) pp. 364–382

Chapter 6
Do Japanese MNCs use expatriates to contain risk in Asian host countries?
Jean-Pascal Bassino, Marion Dovis and Pierre van der Eng
Asia Pacific Business Review, volume 21, issue 3 (July 2015) pp. 383–402

For any permissions-related enquiries please visit
http://www.tandfonline.com/page/help/permissions

Notes on Contributors

Richa Awasthy is an Assistant Professor at the International Management Institute in New Delhi, India. Her specialization is in organizational behaviour and human resources.

Jean-Pascal Bassino is Professor of Economics and Director of the Institut d'Asie Orientale, at l'École Normale Supérieure de Lyon, France. His research interests include historical trends in living standards and regional inequalities in Asia; the relationship between human capital accumulation, income and biological well-being; and the international strategy of Japanese companies. He is the editor (with Andreosso-O'Callaghan and Jaussaud) of *Changing Economic Environment in Asia* (2001).

Pierre-Yves Donzé is an Associate Professor in the Graduate School of Economics at Kyoto University, Japan. He specializes in the history of the watch industry, the economic and social history of Switzerland and Japan and the history of medicine. He is the author of *A Business History of the Swatch Group* (2014).

Marion Dovis is an Assistant Professor in the Faculty of Economics and Management at Aix-Marseille University, Aix-en-Provence, France. She has published articles in a number of journals, including *Canadian Journal of Economics, Journal of International Trade and Economic Development*, the *Economics of Transition*, and *Revue d'Economie Politique*.

Robert Fitzgerald is a Reader in Business History and International Management at Royal Holloway, University of London, UK. He specializes in business history, Asia Pacific business and multinational enterprise, and he has recently published *Rise of the Global Company: Multinational Enterprise and the Making of the Modern World* (2015).

Jacky F.L. Hong is Associate Professor in Management and Director of the MBA Program in the Faculty of Business Administration at the University of Macau, Macau. His research interests include organizational learning, knowledge management, strategic management and management of Chinese enterprise. He has published articles in a number of journals, including *Multinational Business Review, Organization Studies, Management Learning* and *Global Economics and Management Review*.

Jiangfeng Lai holds a PhD from the University of London, and is the director of arts business based in Hong Kong. He has an expertise and academic interest in multinational enterprise, Chinese business, and knowledge transfer.

Derek Lehmberg is Assistant Professor of Management at North Dakota State University, Fargo, North Dakota, USA. His research interests are in Japanese management, competitive strategy and strategic investments in times of technological uncertainty.

NOTES ON CONTRIBUTORS

Kalpana Narain is a Managing Partner at Full Spectrum Consulting, a business and strategy consulting firm, based in Gurgaon, India. She has 25 years of experience working in investment banking, publication relations and leadership development.

Rishika Nayyar is an Assistant Professor in the Department of Commerce at Delhi University, New Delhi, India.

Chris Rowley is Inaugural Professor of Human Resource Management at the Cass Business School, City University, London, UK, and Adjunct Professor at Griffith University, Brisbane, Australia. He is the editor of the book series *Working in Asia* and *Asian Studies*, and has published widely, with over 500 journal articles, books and chapters and other contributions in practitioner journals, magazines and newsletters.

Robin Stanley Snell is Professor in the Department of Management at Lingnan University, Hong Kong. His current research projects focus on the authenticity of organizational citizenship behaviour, gender and performance management and business ethics in China. He is the author of *Developing Skills for Ethical Management* (1993).

Pierre van der Eng is an Associate Professor in the Crawford School of Public Policy at the Australian National University, Canberra, Australia. He is an economist and historian with academic interests in economic history and development economics as well as business history and international business. Much of his research relates to various aspects of long-term economic growth, and development in Indonesia and in Southeast Asia.

Sumati Varma is Associate Professor of Commerce at Sri Aurobindo College, University of Delhi, New Delhi, India. She has been a consultant to several Indian and international organizations, including the World Bank Group and the National Council for Educational Research and Training (NCERT), where she has been a member of the Textbook Development Committee.

Megan Min Zhang is a PhD candidate in the Ivey Business School at Western University, London, Canada.

Japanese multinationals in the post-bubble era: new challenges and evolving capabilities

Robert Fitzgerald[a] and Chris Rowley[b,c,d]

[a]*Royal Holloway, University of London, UK;* [b]*Cass Business School, City University, London, UK;* [c]*HEAD Foundation, Singapore;* [d]*Griffith Business School, Griffith University, Australia*

Since the bursting of Japan's bubble economy, from 1990 onwards, Japanese multinational companies (MNCs) have faced new competitive challenges and questions about the management practices on which they had built their initial success in global markets. Japanese engagement in the international economy has undergone a number of phases. In the period before the Second World War, Japanese companies learnt from foreign MNCs in trading, shipping, and manufacturing, frequently through strategic alliances, and leveraged their capabilities to succeed in overseas and largely Asian markets. In the immediate post-war decades, during the Japanese 'economic miracle', there were notable examples of MNC investment in raw materials and labour intensive production, but both inward and outward foreign direct investment were not significant. Japanese companies achieved leadership in management and technology, in order to support a strategy of export-orientated industrialization. Changes in government policies in the developed economies of the US and Western Europe forced leading Japanese manufacturers to convert themselves into MNCs and to transfer their home-grown capabilities to overseas subsidiaries. The period after 1990 marked declining Japanese competitiveness and it asked questions about the ability of Japanese MNCs to be more responsive and global in their strategies, organization and capabilities.

Introduction

Much of the writing on Japanese business has focused on its unique, national or culturally determined characteristics. Yet, the influence of multinational enterprises or corporations (MNCs) goes beyond Japan's interaction with the international economy and their activities have shaped the strategies, capabilities and organization of Japanese business. From the nineteenth century onwards, alliances with foreign MNCs and the overseas operations of Japanese companies have been noteworthy in their impact. The story of the post-war 'economic miracle' (from 1950 to 1973) and the 'lost decades' (since 1990) are better known than the earlier periods of Japan's engagement with the international economy. As the country recovered from the Second World War, licensing foreign technology and learning from leading foreign and notably US companies, Japan established a range of enterprises that exploited their particular combination of core capabilities through exports to overseas markets. Japanese levels of outward foreign direct investment (FDI) during the 1950s and 1960s were not significant, and the securing of raw materials to underpin industrialization at home and for the textile sector the attractions of cheaper labour in Asia were the principal motives; it was in the 1980s that these capital flows grew dramatically.

As is well known, capital and exchange controls had been formally lifted for some time before Japanese manufacturers decided to transform themselves, from the 1980s onwards, into MNCs, defined as owning or managing operating subsidiaries in foreign markets. Considering the timing of the surge in outward FDI, their motive was to overcome the imposition of tariffs and import quotas in the developed markets of the US and Western Europe, or, in other words, to protect the large export trade they had created. An additional reason was the rising value of the Yen, which favoured FDI over international strategies based on exports. As well as the strategies of individual companies, we have to account for the broader issues of international political economy to explain the motivations and strategies of Japanese MNCs. There are, too, matters of comparative economic development: post-war FDI followed the development of the Japanese economy and moved from the founding of overseas subsidiaries in light manufacturing to the building of an international presence in heavy industrial goods, complex machinery, consumer durables and automobiles. Japanese companies had achieved higher levels of managerial and technological capability in their home market. They were, as a result, able to make an impact outside Japan by boosting capital, output and jobs in host economies and, critically, by seeking to transfer their leading management methods and technologies to their subsidiaries. US and European businesses attempted, from the 1980s, to upgrade their failing competitiveness by adopting or adapting Japanese management methods. For a period, 'globalization', global 'best practice' and 'Japanization' all became synonymous.

As they established their presence in the developed markets of the US and Western Europe, Japanese MNCs showed an increasing bias towards wholly owned overseas operations, and frequently, in manufacturing, towards 'greenfield' sites and developments. Perhaps the most famous example of this approach, Toyota, linked their preferred entry strategy in host markets to their ownership of highly competitive management and production methods that they sought, with success and adaptations, to transfer to subsidiaries (Toyota 2012). Overseas plants that it owned or controlled facilitated the transfer of methods and protected proprietary knowledge and technology. This model of MNC strategy and organization was marked by high levels of managerial centralization, strong cross-border control by the parent enterprise and marked reliance on the know-how, technologies and senior personnel of the main business in Japan. To assist in the maintenance of MNC parent control and in the overseas installation of home country practices, Japanese companies relied extensively on the sending of expatriate engineers and managers to their subsidiaries.

Once Japanese MNCs had met their initial strategic motivations for overseas investments in developed economies (to secure export markets), it followed that they would have to consider the next stage of subsidiary development. To be more competitive and more responsive to national or regional markets, the enhancement of local capabilities would gain priority and centralized, cross-border control would consequently have to recede in favour of subsidiary level decision-making in product development, research, or employment policies. By the mid-1990s, Japanese business practices seemed no longer able to provide the means of sustaining and improving competitiveness. The top-down parent–subsidiary relationship did not facilitate the ability to absorb lessons in managerial practices from overseas markets, unlike flatter federative structures, in which capabilities were not concentrated in Japan but spread more evenly throughout the MNC. Slow or negative growth rates in Japan emphasized the search for growth in overseas markets and made the case for subsidiaries having an enhanced role in relation to the parent business. From the 1990s, Japanese MNCs had to give increased consideration to FDI strategies of efficiency seeking (in overseas R&D networks, or through access to lower production or labour costs) and asset seeking (acquiring foreign firms and attempting to utilize their capabilities).

Three questions arise from the post-1990 period, following the bursting of the Japanese 'bubble', which exposed weaknesses in business practices and ended decades of rapid growth. First, how different were the strategies and organization of Japanese MNCs in the post-bubble period to those utilized previously? Second, in what ways did the strategies and organization of Japanese MNCs change after 1990? Third, how effective were Japanese MNCs in responding to new competitive challenges and evolving new or improved capabilities? We address these questions next.

The long-view: Japan and the multinational before 1950

The role of MNCs in the Japanese economy before 1950 underwent three phases: 1875–1914, 1914–1937 and 1937–1950. From 1875 to 1914, and through their interactions with foreign businesses, Japanese trading and shipping firms increasingly established themselves overseas, and many of them built their success on the expansion of Japan's leading industry at the time, cotton textiles. From 1914 to 1937, the Japanese industrial base broadened and the examples of notable FDI by foreign firms in Japan increased, speeding the transfer of managerial and technological know-how. As in the case of trading companies, Japanese manufacturers showed a strategic pattern of leveraging lessons from foreign MNCs and exploiting their own growing capabilities in Asia and in its colonies. Another pattern was the active involvement of government in protecting the emergence of Japanese businesses and in assisting their evolution in international markets. The strains created by worldwide economic depression after 1929 and international criticism of Japanese policy in Manchuria from 1931, began to turn the government against inward FDI. With the invasion of China in 1937, nationalist–militarist policies were confirmed, and the attack on Pearl Harbour in 1941 brought Japan into the Second World War (Fitzgerald 2015).

As soon as the US had forced open Japanese ports to trade, in 1858, foreign trading firms and banks began to exploit the new opportunities given to them: amongst the many firms that came to Japan were the British-owned Jardine Matheson, and Adamson, Bell, plus the Hongkong Bank (the forerunner to HSBC); Walsh, Hall, from the US; Germany's E. Fischer & Co. and Deutsche-Asiatische Bank (part of Deutsche Bank); and the Banque Franco-Japonaise, a joint venture. Thomas Blake Glover arrived as a Jardine Matheson representative and stayed to find his own trading house. He enabled the 'Choshu Five', some of whom would come to dominate politics in Meiji Japan, to tour and learn from the West. Glover supplied armaments to the Choshu and Satsuma clans of South West Japan, whose intervention in the Meiji Restoration of 1868 was pivotal. Amongst his commercial activities, Glover's dealings with what became the Mitsubishi conglomerate (then one of Japan's newest but fastest expanding *zaibatsu*) fundamentally shaped that business and especially its trading entity (the origins of the modern Mitsubishi Corporation).

In reforming its economy and staving off colonization, the first commercial aim of the government was not industrialization but taking control of its trade, dominated by foreign merchants and shipping lines. From 1875, the government sought to establish its own trading firms, assisting them through the founding of the Tokyo Marine Insurance Company (in 1879) and the Yokohama Specie Bank (1880), which provided exchange and credit. Leading general trading companies (*sogoshosha*) were often arms of business conglomerates (*zaibatsu*) and government sponsorship and contacts were central to their growth and success [a model that would be replicated in Korea, with their general trading companies and *chaebol*. See Jun and Rowley (2014)]. European and especially British trading companies were commercially powerful in Asia and active participants in the spread of imperialism in the region. They and US companies also served as business models for Japanese trading houses. The *sogoshosha* developed and provided the overseas expertise and knowledge other parts of Japanese business lacked and by dealing in many products and acting for many clients, their scale became a source of advantage against international competitors that remained at this point more experienced and better connected. By 1911, Japan directly controlled 51% of its exports and 64% of its imports (Fitzgerald 2015; Kawabe 1989).

Mitsui Bussan, from 1876, challenged Walsh, Hall for the rice trade, although to achieve its aims it had to rely on the cooperation of another foreign trader, E.B. Watson (Kawabe 1987). It had links with Carnegie Steel, the American Locomotive Company and the world leader in cotton textile machinery, Britain's Platt Brothers, and it founded cotton spinning enterprises and flour milling in Shanghai. With the help of R.W. Irwin, Mitsui Bussan established a New York office in order to organise its valuable silk exports and it worked with the London-based Ralli Brothers in India. By 1908, it had representative offices throughout Asia (especially in China), Siberia, the US, Australia and Germany. Like other Japanese traders, it was instrumental to the economic development and integration of Japan's own colonies through their investments in natural resources and manufacturing. Sugar plantations in Taiwan ranked amongst the largest joint stock businesses in Japan (Suzuki 1990). After the Russo-Japanese War in 1904–1905, Japan forcibly took possession of the Liaotong Peninsula (containing Dalian and Port Arthur), where it established the South Manchuria Railway, which depended heavily at the time on the trade in soybeans and products (Patrikeff and Shukman 2007; Allen and Donnithorne [1954] 2003; Fitzgerald 2015).

By 1899 and as soon as the Japanese government had permitted inward FDI, the American Bell Telephone Company's manufacturing subsidiary, Western Electric, bought a controlling interest in Nippon Electric Company (today's NEC). Western Electric had the guarantee of government orders given to NEC and it was required to fulfil a national project to connect the Japanese archipelago and to facilitate imperial expansion into Korea and Manchuria through long-distance telephone communications. Western Electric brought its technology and production methods and supervised the training of managers, supervisors and engineers. General Electric of America, by 1910, was a major shareholder in the Tokyo Electric Company (Tokyo Denki) and in the Shibaura Engineering Works (Shibaura Seisakusho), in alliance with Mitsui Bank (Shibaura later acquired the name of Toshiba). The well-known engineering firm of Armstrong Whitworth assisted the establishment of shipyards. One early example of outward FDI, from 1916 to 1918, was the South Manchurian Railway establishing the Anshan Iron and Steel Works, which became part of an industrial complex making ceramics, oil, fats, flour, sugar, chemicals, shale oil and electricity. In the inter-period, Japan maintained or reaffirmed its openness to inward FDI, but as an industrializing country, its government used import licensing, tariffs and quotas to foster domestic manufacturing. It especially encouraged joint ventures with foreign investors in the expectation that they would promote the transfer of technology and management. In 1923, Siemens & Halske (now simply Siemens) founded Fuji Denki Seizo, in later years simply Fuji Electric, in association with Furukawa Electric, itself part of a large *zaibatsu*. Fuji's Kawasaki factory became a classic example of transferred technological and managerial capabilities (Kudo 1994; Udagawa 1990; Fitzgerald 2015; Wray 1984; Mason 1990; Wilkins 1986).

Mitsubishi Electric was incorporated during 1921 with the US MNC, Westinghouse, as a shareholder. On the back of a government commission and using broadcasting equipment made by its US partner, NEC introduced radio to Japan between 1924 and 1930. The companies that made up Germany's I.G. Farben had a central role in the emergence of the Japanese chemical industry from the late 1920s onwards. With the invasion of Manchuria and Japan's decision to leave the League of Nations, an increasingly nationalist-militarist government sought to reduce the influence of overseas capital. Western Electric had sold its interest to International Standard Electric (ISE) – a subsidiary of International Telephone and Telegraph – and the Japanese government forced ISE to increase the shares controlled by the Sumitomo *zaibatsu*. Legislation forced Ford and General Motors to withdraw from their cooperation with Toyota and Nissan motors, which in any case turned their attention to producing military trucks. During the Second World War, the various trading enterprises, banks, NEC and the Nissan new *zaibatsu* acquired large interests throughout Japan's colonies and occupied territories (Kudo 1994; Fitzgerald 2015; Mason 1987, 1990).

Post-war economic 'miracle' and multinational business

The history of Japan and MNCs in the post-war period is divided by a fundamental watershed. Under the Foreign Exchange and Foreign Trade Control Law of 1949 and the Foreign Investment Control Law of 1950, inward and outward flows of FDI were not possible without official approval and both became strictly limited. Exceptions were investments overseas in raw materials and supplies, often led by trading companies, since these were needed to further industrialization and economic growth at home. Investments in essential manufacturing components or in components used for re-export in finished products were accepted. With rising production and labour costs in Japan, textiles firms could relocate, largely in East Asia and they received tax assistance and subsidies to assist their transformation (Solis 2003). From 1980 onwards, some ten years after the relaxation of overseas investment and currency regulations, large Japanese manufactures led the dramatic surge in outward FDI. The ownership advantages and core capabilities that enabled Japanese companies to become successful MNCs were built during the earlier period of rapid growth. By the 1980s, Japanese companies were perceived as having acquired and developed superior managerial methods (Dore 1973; Vogel 1979; Thurow 1981).

In the post-war era and critically from the outbreak of the Korean War in 1950, the US actively sought to build Japan as a Cold War ally in a turbulent region of the world. After years of experimentation, Fujitsu produced Japan's first commercial computer, but the Japanese government realized that, to avoid falling further and further behind in the international technology race, it would need access to US patents. In 1961, Fujitsu made an agreement with IBM, in return for the government allowing the US company to manufacture locally, as IBM Japan. In parallel, Japan restricted imports, subsidized native producers and curtailed needless competition in the interests of stimulating innovation in computing. After a period, the government forced Fujitsu to devote itself to mainframes and integrated circuits. Product successes were forthcoming, but could not match those of IBM Japan. The Ministry of International Trade and Industry (MITI) decided to reorganize the nation's computing sector and paired Fujitsu with the computing division of a major rival, Hitachi. In 1972, a small investment in the US's Amdahl Corporation, founded by an ex-IBM engineer, gave access to the new firm's technological insights and Fujitsu traded limitless capital from the Japanese government and the captive sales market of NTT (Nippon Telegraph and Telephone). The Fujitsu-Hitachi M-series was the result and by 1980 it was outselling IBM in the Japanese home market, if not in overseas markets.

For policy-makers, the Fujitsu-IBM story was a clear case of how engagement in the international economy could be combined with government-led industrial strategy if a developing country wanted to close the gap with global leaders rather than just exposing itself to advanced competition. Once its economic miracle was under way and Japan had joined the group of developed countries, it was another logical destination for overseas manufacturing investment. Yet, the government maintained regulations curtailing imports and legislation forbade outward and inward FDI with the aim of keeping all capital for the industrialization of the Japanese home economy by Japanese companies (Fitzgerald 2015).

For the US administration that ruled Japan after 1945, the family-owned *zaibatsu* conglomerates had been part of the nationalist military regime that had provoked war in the Pacific. It was determined to replace the controlling families and it ended the economic power of the conglomerates by breaking them up into unconnected companies. The Japanese government from 1949 began to ease such anti-monopoly regulations and went further with the relaxation of rules after the Korean War, deeming business groups as important to its post-war policy objectives. Former *zaibatsu* reconvened after 1954 as *kigyo shudan* (often called, mistakenly, *kigyo keiretsu*), this time looser groupings of independent businesses with their own professional managers; other major *kigyo shudan* coalesced around major banks. By pooling capital and spreading commercial risks, they could assist bold plans in investment and labour power, as made by MITI, to bring about Japan's rapid industrialization. As well as being suspicious of the *zaibatsu*, the US administration had objected to the size and reach of the *sogoshosha*. It split them up, in 1947: Mitsui Bussan ended up as 233 separate enterprises, Mitsubishi Shoji as 139. From 1950, the Japanese government allowed them to re-group, with Mitsubishi Shoji being re-established in 1950 and Mitsui & Co. likewise in 1958. In the 1960s and amongst many varied activities, including the procurement of technology and raw materials for the home economy, Mitsui & Co. was active in copper mining in Mexico, Chile, Canada and Australia, and from 1971 it allied with three Japanese chemical firms and the National Iranian Oil Company (NIOC) to form the Iran Japan Petroleum Company. Mitsubishi Shoji worked on LNG production with Royal Dutch Shell, operated iron-ore and coal mines in Canada and Australia and marketed Mitsubishi cars in alliance with Chrysler in the US. It re-incorporated itself as Mitsubishi Corporation in 1971 (Fitzgerald 2015).

Japanese government initiatives and subsidies from 1947 and throughout the 1950s were essential to creating both the shipbuilding and shipping industries, assisting the securing of raw materials, technology and equipment, and supporting the official strategy of export-orientated industrialization. Tokyo Automobile Industries Company became known as Izusu, in 1949. Under licence from the Rootes Group from 1953, the company made the Hillman Minx and from 1961 it produced its own car, the Bellel. In 1971, Izusu signed a deal with General Motors, which took 34% of its shares and the flow in design and product development went in both directions. The Izusu Faster inspired the Chevrolet LUV or pick-up truck, which appeared first in 1972, in the US and later in Latin America; the Kadett, made by GM's German subsidiary, Opel, transmuted into Izusu's Gemini, launched in 1974, and into Buick's Opel, for the US market. Japanese *kaisha* created the leadership in management, products and technology (often combining low price and rising quality) that could be a foundation for future MNC investment. Fujitsu Fanuc (Fuji Automatic Numerical Control) – a wholly owned subsidiary of Fujitsu spun-off as a separate enterprise in 1972 – dominated the factory automation business in Japan. In 1975, it licensed its technology to Pratt and Whitney, the US aerospace engineering company and to Siemens, which also took a shareholding in the Japanese firm. Furukawa

Aluminium Company – founded in 1959 with technical assistance from Alcoa – built two plants in Romania during 1966 (Fitzgerald 2015).

We know, furthermore, that the engineering conglomerate Hitachi Zosen established a chemical fertilizer plant for the Gujarat State Fertilised Company of India in 1957, in a record 33 months. The construction company, Kajima – with its expertise in earthquake technologies – took up the challenges of overseas projects throughout Asia in the 1960s, before, in the decade that followed, undertaking major and diplomatically sensitive contracts in East Berlin and entering the US. Japan's rapid industrialization and urbanization created construction and engineering companies with experience of managing large projects. While preferring for the time being to export to the developed markets of Western Europe and North America, where it set up sales offices, Toyota did establish its first overseas operation, in 1958, an assembly plant in Brazil and then two more in South Africa in 1964 and Ghana in 1969, in part as responses to government pressure. Fuller FDI strategies followed some examples of MNC apprenticeship, encouraged by the rising value of the Yen and by the relaxing of government controls on outward flows of capital in 1971 (Interview, Toyota executives, January 2012). Nippon Seiko – adopting a strategy of providing enhanced customer service in its export markets – founded its first overseas factory in Sao Paolo in 1970, another in Michigan in 1973 and one in Peterlee, Scotland in 1976. Japan's second largest bearing maker, NTN Corporation, was similarly manufacturing in the US and additionally in Canada and Germany by 1980. Sony – building its reputation in the electronics industry as an innovator – opened its first US plant in 1971 and another in South Wales in the UK by 1974 (Fitzgerald 2015; Mason and Encarnation 1994).

Outward FDI surge and capability transfer

The take-off in Japanese FDI and, therefore, in Japanese manufacturing FDI occurred during the 1980s, when governments in the US and Western European governments imposed quotas and tariffs that threatened the overseas markets so successfully won through exports. Therefore, before the take-off, some 66% of Japanese FDI could be found in developing countries, against 27% by US MNCs and 20% by those from Britain (Kojima 1978). By 1970, outward Japanese FDI was only significant in mining, timber, pulp and textiles and by 1975 Mitsubishi Corporation, Mitsui & Co., Marubeni and C. Itoh accounted for 40% of outward FDI stocks (Ozawa 1979). In 1977, Japan provided approximately 6% of total global FDI flow and at its peak in 1989 it was the largest provider with 30%. Japanese FDI flow amounted to $4693 million in 1980, with manufacturing composing 36% of this total; in 1989, the figures were $67,540 million and 24%. By 1988, Japan had overtaken the European Community and the US as the largest supplier of outward FDI flows. In 1980, some 34% of FDI flows from Japan went to North America, 12% to Europe and 25% to Asia; by 1989, the figures were 50, 22 and 12% respectively, witnessing the new determination of Japanese MNCs to invest in North America and Europe and less in Asia (UNCTAD 1994, 1998; Fitzgerald 2015).

As we have noted, the capabilities owned by Japanese MNCs account for the success of their overseas operations but do not explain their strategic motivation for establishing foreign subsidiaries. The rising value of the Yen undermined the policies of export-orientated industrialization and changes in the structures of international political economy were determinant. Japan had abided by Voluntary Export Restrictions, as early as 1957 in cotton goods, followed by others in steel in 1969 and in woollens and colour televisions in the 1970s. Britain limited Japanese automobile imports from 1975. From

1981, the US began to impose import restrictions in automobiles and machine tools and the European Economic Community began a range of controls from 1986 onwards (Farrell 2008).

From the 1980s, outward FDI was led by the automobile and electrical-electronic sectors. They, and the general trading enterprises, featured amongst the largest of Japan's MNCs. Toyota, Sony and Panasonic became important MNCs, as well as owners of international brands. Moreover, new Japanese manufacturing affiliates overseas brought with them the management and production techniques that had made them such highly successful exporters and Western firms tried to restore their dwindling competitive position by imitating them (with mixed results). Their methods had acquired the reputation of global 'best practice'. Japan was home to eight of the top 50 non-financial MNCs, as ranked by assets, in 1992, seven in manufacturing, one in trading; it could claim eight manufacturers and six trading companies in the top 100 by 1998, although some sliding down the table rankings by individual companies was an early hint that their comparative competitiveness had already peaked (Rugman and Brewer 2001; UNCTAD 1998).

During the post-war decades, Toyota had developed home-based 'ownership advantages' in management and production systems, human resource management and distribution, and an expertise in R&D. Its FDI policy rested on setting up overseas plants rested on a desire to transfer the internationally acclaimed 'Toyota Way', led by the parent business in Japan. The company began production in the US from 1983 and in Britain by 1992 (Toyota 2012). From 1988, Sanyo began manufacturing in the US and in Europe (Panasonic-Sanyo 2010). Sony Corporation's acquisition of Columbia Pictures was both an investment opportunity and a chance to diversify by product range and geographically. There were acquisitions as well as greenfield developments, as instanced by Bridgestone's acquisition of Firestone, which made it an international leader in the industry. In Europe, some Japanese companies quickly founded regional enterprises. Panasonic Europe was established in 1988 and Toyota had a European headquarters from 1990. In 1998, Toyota launched the Yaris, the first car it designed in and for the European market. Despite, however, acknowledgement of the need to develop managerial and product development capabilities in overseas subsidiaries, Japanese MNCs generally retained their reputation for being tightly controlled from Japan and by Japanese management (Ando 2004; Mason and Encarnation 1994; Abo 1994; Kenney and Florida 1993).

The post-bubble challenge for Japanese MNCs

From 1990, the Japanese economy entered its years of low and even negative growth; as the internationally praised success story came to an end, the identification of Japanese management methods with global 'best practice' similarly ended. The difficulties that Japan faced raised questions about the efficacy of imitating Japanese firms and of Japanese MNCs transferring their capabilities to their subsidiaries. When economic growth did not return, as might have been expected, it suggested that the Japanese political and business systems needed reform and forced Japanese companies to re-assess their competitiveness and core capabilities (Schaede 2008). Japanese MNCs have had to tackle the problems of poor growth rates in their home economy. This deteriorating economic performance occurred, moreover, during years in which the pace and nature of internationalization or globalization increased significantly.

The surge in global FDI was especially noteworthy, as were the unprecedented expansion of cross-border mergers and acquisitions; the off-shoring of production to locations of low costs and wages; a greater tendency towards FDI strategies of efficiency-seeking and asset-seeking; the forging of cross-border, vertical production or value chains; a rise in the use of strategic alliances and the contracting out of production and key activities; the redirection of FDI to developing countries and ultimately the arrival of 'dragon multinationals' or developing economy MNCs; the growth in service FDI relative to manufacturing and resource extraction; and a tendency towards federative, flatter MNC organisation and the enhancement of subsidiary capabilities, instead of the hierarchical and established parent-subsidiary relationship (Fitzgerald 2015). While the international competitiveness of Japanese MNCs was adversely affected by the prolonged economic slowdown of their home economy, their continued preference for established strategies, organisation and capabilities has impaired their adaptation to changes in global markets (Black and Morrison 2012; Collinson and Rugman 2008; Itagaki 2009; Marukawa 2009; Numagami, Karube, and Kato 2010). The continued reliance on the knowledge and experience of home country personnel has been a block on such a transformation and inhibited the development of overseas subsidiaries and host country personnel (Black and Morrison 2012; Collinson and Wilson 2006; Byun and Ybema 2005; Hong and Snell 2008; Hong, Snell, and Easterby-Smith 2006; Beechler and Bird 1999; Busser 2008; Lam 2003; Marukawa 2009).

The end of Japan's fast growth era from 1990 hurt general traders whose fortunes were tied to the country's import-export trade. With little scope for growth at home, the *sogoshosha* needed to foster business worldwide and they abandoned their traditions of a fully comprehensive service and maximum sales for the profit testing of every commercial activity. They became more involved in business solutions, consultancy, project management, IT, communications, venture capital, investments and technology acquisition, as well as logistics and chain management. Four *sogoshosha* could be found, moreover, in the list of the world's top 100 non-financial MNCs for 2008, measured by overseas assets, with Mitsubishi the largest in 32nd place, followed by Mitsui & Co., Sumitomo Corporation and Marubeni.

As the growth of Japanese manufacturing MNCs slowed, service sectors outside trading found it difficult to build an overseas presence (UNCTAD 2008). Japan's 'Big Bang', in 1994–1997, initiated a series of mergers leading to the emergence of 'mega-banks' better able to compete globally, including the Bank of Tokyo Mitsubishi, in 1996, which through a succession of further amalgamations created Mitsubishi UFJ Financial Group, in 2005, as the world's largest bank by assets. Yet, overall, Japanese banks did not evolve into globally competitive MNCs. Japanese retailers – Seven & I Holdings, owner of Ito-Yokada, and Aeon – expanded within Asia, but remained highly reliant on their home market. The most impressive entrant was Uniqlo, which took GAP as its model and shared Zara's mix of good design, high quality, low price and fast logistics. The company opened its first store in Tokyo in 1984, going international in London and Shanghai by 2002 and operating in 10 overseas countries by 2012 (Fitzgerald 2015).

Japanese manufacturers had traditionally favoured greenfield developments, but, as asset seeking became a more common MNC strategy, they too adapted. Asahi Glass bought Pilkington for its proprietorial knowledge and market access; Toshiba bought Westinghouse for its patents and technology in nuclear energy; Japan Tobacco bought UK Gallagher for its brands and market presence; and Takeda too gained market access, patents and R&D. Asset seeking enabled Japanese firms to expand quickly as MNCs and to obtain capabilities they did not possess. Nonetheless, while Toyota and Honda retained international competitiveness, other automobile enterprises such as Nissan came under the control of foreign MNCs. Japanese MNCs had succeeded through faith in their home-grown capabilities, strong parental or HQ control and the transfer of capabilities to its subsidiaries. By the end of the 1990s, Japanese business practices seemed no longer able to provide the means of sustaining and improving competitiveness and top-down parent-subsidiary relationships appeared less appropriate. The growth of global production chains and contracted production; the need to empower subsidiaries in faster growing markets and the consequent advantages of federated MNC organisation and the gains from more open organisational structures that could absorb lessons from global competition created challenges for Japanese companies that found change difficult or slow to achieve (Farrell 2008; Fitzgerald 2015).

To what extent did Japanese MNCs seek to adapt their strategies, organization and capabilities since the 1990s? How successful were they in their policies? These questions are answered by our collection's contributions. A quick overview of these is presented in Table 1. In terms of the logic of our structure, the contributions address a number of themes central to the study of Japanese MNCs. The first two authors, Donze and Lehmberg, take a business history or long term perspective on the nature of changes in global competition since the 1990s, and assess to what Japanese MNCs in two industries have adjusted strategically and organisationally to that change over two decades. The next two contributions – Fitzgerald and Lai, and Hong and Snell – consider how effectively Japanese MNCs have transferred their home grown capabilities to overseas and localized them with their overseas subsidiaries. In both cases, they evaluate a major Japanese MNC and its investment in China. The last group of authors – Bassino, Marion Dovis and Pierre van der Eng; Zhang; Varma, Awasthy, Narain and Nayyarm – look at the organisational and managerial issues within Japanese MNCs that inhibit cross-border capability transfer and the effective management of subsidiaries, and they suggest potential solutions.

Donzé takes a long-term, business history approach to analyze the declining international competitiveness of Seiko and the Japanese watch industry since 1990. He argues that Seiko found it difficult to adjust to the new character of global value chains, retaining the producer-driven strategy that had underpinned its earlier success, despite having lost its technological advantage. The overall industrial organisation moved to a buyer-driven global value chain, but Seiko failed to undertake the necessary changes in strategy and management in response to changes in international markets.

Lehmberg also offers a long-term view with his evaluation of the Japanese liquid crystal display industry. He argues that Japanese electronics firms have been known for applying vertical integration strategies, consistent with Japanese managerial preferences, traditional relationships and institutions. Outside Japan, however, changes in the technological and competitive environment have brought increasing vertical specialization in the electronics industry. The picture he presents is a complex one: he uncovers evidence of Japanese electronics firms de-integrating and developing cooperative relationships in technology transfer and outsourcing with overseas firms, but conflicts between the retention of traditional methods and needed competitive responses made change a difficult process. Despite operating in the rising diversity of overseas operations, in its subsidiaries, and through alliances and contracted partners, the strength of well-entrenched Japanese business approaches made the strategic and organisational transformation partial.

The transfer of electronics production to lower cost locations, in developing economies, has been a pronounced feature of the global economy since the 1990s. Fitzgerald and Lai provide a case study of Omron's subsidiary in China in order to explore the long-term evolution of a Japanese-owned subsidiary. They explore, first, the origins of the Omron Shanghai subsidiary and the parent company's ability to transfer its capabilities and leading Japanese methods within a traditional parent-subsidiary relationship. Second,

Table 1. Overview: content, themes, methods, findings and implications.

	Content	Themes	Methods	Findings	Implications
1	Japanese multinationals in the post-bubble era: new challenges and evolving capabilities	• Long history of MNCs engaging with foreign businesses • Global challenges	Historical literature survey	MNCs historically adopted variety of international strategies other than those associated with FDI since the 1980s	MNC difficulties adjusting to global competition, but show capacity to adapt or build on established management practices
2	Global value chains & the lost competitiveness of the Japanese watch industry: Seiko since 1990	• Production emphasis • Decline in global competitiveness • Rise of buyer-driven global value chains	Longitudinal case study	Production emphasis and specific nature of home market inhibited ability to compete through contemporary global value chains	Difficulties of transforming home nation strategic emphasis and established management practices in response to global markets and technological change
3	Do Japanese electronics firms still follow traditional vertical integration strategies? Evidence from the LCD industry	• Declining production competitiveness • Technological change • Cross-border vertical de-integration strategies	Industry event database analysis	Varied firm-level responses to adjusting established management practice to product life cycle, standardization and vertical de-integration	Difficulties of transforming home nation strategic emphasis and established management practices in response to global markets and technological change
4	Strategic capabilities and the emergence of the global factory: Omron in China	• Capability transfer • Economic development • Parent-subsidiary relations • The global factory	Longitudinal case study	Move from joint venture to wholly owned subsidiary facilitated capability transfer and influence of parent MNC	Manufacturing MNCs can adapt established practices and organization to contemporary global competition
5	Boundary crossing and the localization of capabilities in a Japanese multinational firm	• Capability transfer • NC parent-subsidiary relations	Case study and questionnaire	Pragmatic and knowledge barriers in MNCs inhibit capability transfer and engagement of local management	MNCs need to develop space to enable knowledge transfer, knowledge acquisition and building of trust
6	Do Japanese MNCs use expatriates to contain risk in Asian host countries?	• Effect of expatriation in MNCs on capability transfer	Quantitative analysis of database of subsidiaries	MNCs in risky host environments utilize local managers to alleviate risks and firm specific factors affect outcomes	MNCs undergo transitory phase of expatriate control to boost sustainability and efficiency of subsidiaries with higher ownership levels compensating for expatriate decline

(Continued)

Table 1 – *continued*

	Content	Themes	Methods	Findings	Implications
7	Cross-national distance and insidership within networks: Japanese MNCs' ownership strategies in their overseas subsidiaries	• Interaction of home and host country factors and internal dimensions of management, organisation, knowledge and power relations within MNCs	Quantitative longitudinal analysis of databases	Insider networks within MNCs reduce cross-border administrative distance, but cultural distance reduces effectiveness of insider networks	Companies can build on existing internal capabilities to overcome divisions within MNCs and between home and host countries
8	Cultural determinants of alliance management capability – an analysis of Japanese MNCs in India	• Institutional and strategic factors determining entry mode of MNCs	Case studies	Established MNCs management practices inhibit building of trust relations	Established MNC techniques in consultation, consensus formation and planning used to found joint venture trust relations, mutual understanding and cooperation
9	Conclusion: Japanese MNCs: competitiveness, management and subsidiaries	• Long term perspective • Capability transfer • Organisational problems and solutions	Literature survey	Contribution of business history to evaluating strategic change and clash between established home grown MNCs and contemporary demands of global competition	MNCs can adapt traditional management strengths and capabilities to new demands of global competition

they look at Omron's attempt to turn their Chinese subsidiary into a 'global factory', utilizing global, as opposed to Japanese, 'best practice', within, in principle, a more federative structure in which subsidiaries possess particular capabilities and exercise greater degrees of managerial autonomy. They additionally consider the implications of ownership – the shift from a joint venture to a wholly-owned subsidiary – for management control and capability transfer. With the important exception of employment matters, it is the strategic intent of the parent MNC that is determinant in both phases of Omron Shanghai's development and there appears a continuation of established Japanese practices.

Hong and Snell similarly conducted a case study to explore the challenges encountered by the subsidiary of a Japanese MNC in localizing its capabilities in China. They draw on the concepts of knowledge boundaries and boundary crossing, they examine how power relations and politics between a Japanese MNC headquarters and a foreign subsidiary can potentially impede the transfer of capabilities to the host country. They also identify how the continued reluctance of Japanese MNCs to allow host country employees to cross pragmatic and cultural knowledge boundaries have slowed down the process of localizing capabilities, slowing organisational adaptation and improvisation.

Bassino, Dovis and van der Eng consider studies of the localization of Japanese practices and the role of expatriate management in that process, plus the lack of consensus over those studies. They investigate 13 Japanese MNC subsidiaries in Asia and conclude that levels of expatriation are weakly correlated to measures of host country risk. Expatriates have been seen as a means of retaining parent MNC coordination and control and obviating the risk of opportunistic behaviour with joint ventures or subsidiaries. Another view is that expatriates can be a resource for building subsidiary management and localizing decision-making in the long term. They argue that expatriation can help deal with host country risks, but that the factors specific to the MNC and the subsidiary (capital intensity, the ownership share of the parent firms and the age of the venture) generate varied outcomes in the attempts to maximize returns and align objectives.

Zhang evaluates Japanese MNC approaches to equity ownership in and control over subsidiaries and the relationship to strategic objectives. She utilizes ideas on cross-national distance, but adds participation in 'insider networks' within the business that can compensate for a sense of foreignness. Cross-national difference and 'insider-ship' vie with each other to determine the levels of equity ownership. Her research suggests the importance of companies taking into account multiple factors in the management of overseas subsidiaries in the achievement of strategic objectives. Cultural and administrative distances – plus economic, geographic, knowledge and connectedness distances – influence Japanese MNC ownership levels. The tacitness of cultural knowledge shapes insider-ship within networks to adjust negatively MNC ownership levels, improving local responsiveness; the codifiability of administrative knowledge within insider networks alleviates the influence of administrative distance on MNC ownership levels, improving internal consistency.

Varma, Awasthy, Narain and Nayyarm look at how effectively Japanese MNCs have competed in India, by assessing their capability in forging local alliances. It uses case studies of three joint ventures and considers the role of national and organisational culture in determining the nature of alliance management and creating diverse outcomes. The authors assess the capabilities of Japanese MNCs in alliance management. Success stories highlight mutual trust, communication, consensus in decision-making, an understanding of cultural differences in culture and an overall adherence to the Japanese style of management. They infer that trust and relational capital are important instruments of collaboration. Failure results from cultural differences, lack of common vision and strategic goals and different perceptions about the industry dynamics, time horizons and risks.

Conclusion

The contributions to this volume offer a number of overlapping themes (whose implications will be discussed further in the conclusion). Several of them adopt a long-term or business history approach that can track how the international competitive landscape has changed for Japanese business in general or for specific industries and assess how effectively Japanese MNCs have responded since the peak of their success by the mid-1990s. Overall, the authors have looked at a number of significant changes in the nature of cross-border competition and identified topics of strategy and capability by which to assess the nature and extent of the response by Japanese MNCs. They have emphasized, furthermore, the frequently uneasy clash between established Japanese management practices (typically home-grown) and the new demands of global competition for MNCs. The contributors note the switch from production to buyer-driven global value chains; management responses to the growing incidence of cross-border vertical specialization; the emergence of global factory strategies and the role assumed by parent MNCs and their capabilities; and the rising incidence of strategic alliances and cooperative relationships, alongside their effective management. They evaluate, finally, which factors might affect the ability of Japanese MNCs to make competitive and organisational adjustments: parental MNC intent and capability in the cross-border transfer of management practices; degrees of host country risk; measures of institutional difference, and gaps in economic development between home and host nations; parent firm-subsidiary and subsidiary-subsidiary power relations and knowledge boundaries; and the evolution of insider networks that overcome institutional and cultural distances.

Disclosure statement

No potential conflict of interest was reported by the authors.

References

Abo, T. 1994. *Hybrid Factory: The Japanese Production System in the United States*. New York: Oxford University Press.
Allen, G. C., and A. G. Donnithorne. (1954) 2003. *Western Enterprise in Far Eastern Economic Development*, Reprint. London: Routledge.
Ando, K. 2004. *Japanese Multinationals in Europe*. Basingstoke: Edward Elgar.
Beechler, S., and A. Bird. 1999. *Japanese Multinationals Abroad: Individual and Organizational Learning*. New York: Oxford University Press.

Black, J., and A. Morrison. 2012. "The Japanese Global Leadership Challenge: What It Means for the Rest of the World." *Asia Pacific Business Review* 18 (4): 551–566. doi:10.1080/13602381. 2012.690300.

Busser, R. 2008. "'Detroit of the East'? Industrial Upgrading, Japanese Car Producers and the Development of the Automotive Industry in Thailand." In *Multinationals, Technology and Localization in Automotive Firms in Asia*, edited by R. Rajah, Y. Sadoi, and R. Busser, 29–45. New York: Routledge.

Byun, H., and S. Ybema. 2005. "Japanese Business in the Dutch Polder: The Experience of Cultural Differences in Asymmetric Power Relations." *Asia Pacific Business Review* 11 (4): 535–552. doi:10.1080/13602380500135836.

Collinson, S., and A. Rugman. 2008. "The Regional Nature of Japanese Multinational Business." *Journal of International Business Studies* 39 (2): 215–230. doi:10.1057/palgrave.jibs.8400347.

Collinson, S., and D. Wilson. 2006. "Inertia in Japanese Organizations: Knowledge Management Routines and Failure to Innovate." *Organization Studies* 27 (9): 1359–1387. doi:10.1177/0170840606067248.

Dore, R. 1973. *British Factory, Japanese Factory*. Los Angeles: University of California Press.

Farrell, R. 2008. *Japanese Investment in the World Economy*. Basingstoke: Edward Elgar.

Fitzgerald, R. 2015. *Rise of the Global Company: Multinationals and the Making of the Modern World*. Cambridge: Cambridge University Press.

Hong, J., and R. Snell. 2008. "Power Inequality in Cross-Cultural Learning: The Case of Japanese Transplants in China." *Asia Pacific Business Review* 14 (2): 253–273. doi:10.1080/13602380701314750.

Hong, J., R. Snell, and M. Easterby-Smith. 2006. "Cross-Cultural Influences on Organizational Learning in MNCs: The Case of Japanese Companies in China." *Journal of International Management* 12 (4): 408–429. doi:10.1016/j.intman.2006.09.005.

Itagaki, H. 2009. "Competitiveness, Localization and Japanese Companies in China: Realities and Alternate Approaches." *Asia Pacific Business Review* 15 (3): 451–462. doi:10.1080/13602380802667502.

Jun, W., and C. Rowley. 2014. "Change and Continuity in Management Systems and Corporate Performance: Human Resource Management, Corporate Culture, Risk Management and Corporate Strategy in South Korea." *Business History* 56 (3): 485–508. doi:10.1080/00076791. 2013.809522.

Kawabe, N. 1987. "Development of Overseas Operations by General Trading Companies, 1868–1945." In *Business History of General Trading Companies*, edited by S. Yonekawa and H. Yoshihara, 71–103. Tokyo: Tokyo University Press.

Kawabe, N. 1989. "Japanese Business in the United States Before the Second World War: The Case of Mitsui and Mitsubishi." In *Historical Studies in International Corporate Business*, edited by A. Teichova, M. Levy-Leboyer, and H. Nussbaum, 65–83. Cambridge: Cambridge University Press.

Kenney, M., and R. Florida. 1993. *Beyond Mass Production: The Japanese System and Its Transfer to the US*. New York: Oxford University Press.

Kojima, K. 1978. *Direct Foreign Investment: A Japanese Model of Multinational Business Operations*. London: Croom Helm.

Kudo, A. 1994. "IG Farben in Japan: The Transfer of Technology and Managerial Skills." *Business History* 36: 159–183.

Lam, A. 2003. "Organizational Learning in Multinationals: R&D Networks of Japanese and US MNEs in the UK." *Journal of Management Studies* 40 (3): 673–703. doi:10.1111/1467-6486. 00356.

Marukawa, T. 2009. "Why Japanese Multinationals Failed in the Chinese Mobile Phone Market: A Comparative Study of New Product Development in Japan and China." *Asia Pacific Business Review* 15 (3): 411–431. doi:10.1080/13602380802667387.

Mason, M. 1987. "Foreign Direct Investment and Japanese Economic Development, 1899–1931." *Business and Economic History* 16: 93–107.

Mason, M. 1990. "With Reservations: Pre-War Japan as Host to Western Electric and ITT." In *Foreign Business in Japan Before World War II*, edited by T. Yuzawa and M. Udagawa, 35–47. Tokyo: Tokyo University Press.

Mason, M., and D. Encarnation. 1994. *Does Ownership Matter? Japanese Multinationals in Europe*. Oxford: Clarendon Press.

Numagami, T., M. Karube, and T. Kato. 2010. "Organizational Deadweight: Learning from Japan." *Academy of Management Perspectives* 24 (4): 25–37.

Ozawa, T. 1979. *Multinationalism, Japanese Style: the Political Economy of Outward Dependency*. Princeton, NJ: Princeton University Press.

Panasonic-Sanyo. Interviews, Sanyo Europe, February 2010.

Patrikeff, F., and H. Shukman. 2007. *Railways and the Russo-Japanese War: Transporting War*. New York: M.E. Sharpe.

Rugman, A. M., and T. Brewer, eds. 2001. *The Oxford Handbook of International Business*. Oxford: Oxford University Press.

Schaede, U. 2008. *Choose and Focus: Japanese Business Strategies for the 21st Century*. Ithaca, NY: Cornell University Press.

Solis, M. 2003. "Adjustment Through Globalization: The Role of State FDI Finance." In *Japan's Managed Globalization: Adapting to the 21st Century*, edited by U. Schaede and W. Grimes, 24–43. London: M.E. Sharpe.

Thurow, L. 1981. *Dangerous Currents: the State of Economics*. New York: Random House.

Toyota., Interviews, Toyota Europe, January 2012.

Udagawa, M. 1990. "Business Management and Foreign-Affiliated Companies in Japan Before World War II." In *Foreign Business in Japan Before World War II*, edited by T. Yuzawa and M Udagawa, 199–223. Tokyo: Tokyo University Press.

UNCTAD. 1994. *World Investment Report*. New York: United Nations.

UNCTAD. 1998. *World Investment Report*. New York: United Nations.

UNCTAD. 2008. *World Investment Report*. Paris: United Nations.

Vogel, E. 1979. *Japan as No.1*. Tokyo: Charles Tuttle.

Wilkins, M. 1986. "Japanese Multinational Enterprise Before 1914." *Business History Review* 60.

Wray, W. D. 1984. *Mitsubishi and the NYK, 1870–1914*. London: Routledge.

Global value chains and the lost competitiveness of the Japanese watch industry: an applied business history of Seiko since 1990

Pierre-Yves Donzé

Graduate School of Economics, Kyoto University, Kyoto, Japan

An applied business history approach offers particular insights into the lost competitiveness of the Japanese watch company Seiko and its causes. Although Seiko was the world's largest firm in the watch industry in the mid-1980s, the company experienced a huge decrease in sales during the next decade and became unable to compete effectively against Swiss watch companies that had repositioned themselves in luxury business. The focus on the evolution of global value chains (GVC) in the industry, which saw a shift from producer-driven GVC to buyer-driven GVC, highlights a major change in the 1990s. Seiko did not change its strategy despite this paradigm shift and has continued to run its foreign subsidiaries according to the producer-driven model.

Introduction

United Nations Conference on Trade and Development (UNCTAD) data on the 100 largest non-financial transnational corporations, ranked by foreign assets, illuminate the major changes that Japanese multinational corporations (MNC) encountered between 1995 and 2013. While petroleum and manufacturing remain major sectors on a worldwide scale, the last two decades have been characterized by the emergence of new fields, including telecommunications, public utilities, and diversified businesses, that are dominated by global companies. Japanese MNCs, however, have not engaged in these new sectors and have thus dropped significantly down the rankings.

In 1995, Japanese MNC were among the most globalized companies in the world. The UNCTAD top 100 included a total of 18 Japanese companies in the automotive (Toyota, Nissan, Honda, and Mitsubishi Motors), trading (Mitsubishi Corporation, Mitsui, Itochu, Nisso Iwai, Marubeni, and Sumitomo), electronics (Sony, Hitachi, Matsushita, Fujitsu, Toshiba, and NEC), metal (Nippon Steel), and precision instruments (Canon) industries. By 2013, however, this number had dropped to a mere 10 firms in the automotive (Toyota, Honda, and Nissan), trading (Mitsubishi, Mitsui, Sumitomo, Itochu, and Marubeni), electronics (Sony), and tobacco (JT) industries. While trading companies have maintained their competitive advantages due to their special functions in supplying natural resources to the Japanese economy via overseas investments (Tanaka 2012), manufacturing industry has nearly disappeared from this ranking – with the exceptions of three automobile companies and Sony – but still draws the most scholarly attention (Sako 2004; Kawabe 2011; Motoyama 2012).

17

Literature review

A growing number of authors have emphasized the decline of the Japanese manufacturing industry since the late 1990s (Shiomi and Kikkawa 2008; Aoshima, Takaishi, and Cusumano 2010). According to Ozawa (2007), the flying-geese theory explains the gradual transfer of production to neighbouring East Asian nations, a move that forced Japan to innovate permanently and reposition constantly in more value-added products. Several scholars have also stressed the difficulties that firms confront in shifting product architectures from the integral model to modularization (Gawer and Cusumano 2002; Fujimoto 2004) and new innovation strategies in the American IT industry (Arora, Branstetter, and Drev 2013).

However, some scholars in management and business history have recently shown that the Japanese manufacturing industry reorganized at the regional level rather than simply declining and transferring to South Korea, Taiwan, Hong Kong, and China (Shioji 2008; Kikkawa and Kubo 2010; Kikkawa 2011). Since the late 1990s, the shift from production systems that were largely integrated within Japanese manufacturing companies to global value chains (GVC) led to a strong regionalization of production, especially in electronics and machines, with high-value parts made in Japan, semi-finished products realized in South Korea and Taiwan, and final assembly performed in China. Consequently, the rise and generalization of GVC are the key phenomena in explaining the lost competitiveness of most Japanese manufacturing firms in the electronic appliance industry. Industrial competitiveness has shifted from Japan to East Asia as a whole, and competitive Japanese manufacturing companies have involved themselves in the development of new materials for the IT industry rather than in finished goods (Kikkawa and Hirano 2011).

However, most of the Japan-related literature focuses on so-called "producer-driven GVC" – industrial organizations where manufacturers of core technologies control the chain, secure profits, and secure supplies of parts in low-wage countries. Yet, as Gereffi (1994a) emphasized, another feature of the evolution of both GVC and the global manufacturing industry is an organizational structure in which technology does not form a barrier to entry and enterprises involved in design and marketing constitute the locus of power and profit: the 'buyer-driven GVC', which represents the approach in the consumer goods, fashion, and textile industries (Lane and Probert 2009).

The consumer goods industry in Japan can be broken down into two main categories. The first group comprises the traditional sectors such as food, beverages, and tobacco. As Porter, Takeuchi, and Sakakibara (2000) argued, most of the companies in this area have very limited international competitiveness due to what the authors call the 'misalignment between Japanese home customer needs and the needs of the global market'. Companies that pursued global expansion strategies through M&A, such as the beverage company Kirin (Da Silva Lopes and Casson 2007) or Japan Tobacco (Fujikawa et al. 2012) are mostly exceptions to the predominant trends.

The other group covers sectors like textiles or watches – areas where competitive advantages once hinged on technological issues and shifted in the 1980s and 1990s to marketing, design, and distribution, creating the need for firms to build and manage buyer-driven GVC in order to remain competitive in the global market. Analyses of such cases in Japan are very rare and usually focus on successful enterprises like the fashion company Fast Retailing and its Uniqlo brand (Choi 2011), but these sorts of companies are largely exceptions and not representative of the difficulties that most Japanese consumer goods manufacturers face in trying to reposition successfully in GVC. The major change in GVC governance – a shift from producer-driven GVC to buyer-driven GVC in the 1980s and

1990s – is what sapped Japanese consumer goods MNC, unable to cope with the mutation, of their competitiveness.

The existing literature in management studies lacks a diachronic perspective, making it difficult to analyse this change properly. Scholars have tended to look at GVC as if they were stable systems in which various actors positioned themselves to secure their competitive advantages. The idea of evolution is essentially restricted to the mutation from the Chandlerian model of the large enterprise – the concentration of production and distribution within a firm – to the emergence of GVC (Gereffi 1994b). Raikes, Jensen, and Ponte (2000) criticized this absence of historical grounding and especially questioned the specificities of buyer-driven and producer-driven GVC, arguing that this distinction was 'too rigid and uncontextualized time-wise to be used uncritically'. They argued that the lack of a diachronic perspective makes it impossible to highlight the major changes of governance within GVC, some of which moved from the producer-driven model to the buyer-driven model over time. Gereffi, Humphrey, and Sturgeon (2005) also attempted to refine the typology of GVC and integrate organizational change over time into their model, but the insufficient contextualization of the cases in their analysis makes it difficult to understand the nature of the change fully.

The example of the watchmaker Seiko can contribute to a better understanding of the reasons behind the lost competitiveness of the Japanese consumer goods industry. It follows the applied business history approach, which gives attention to organizational change over time.

Research questions and methodology

As the competitive advantages of watch firms moved from technological innovation to marketing in the 1990s, the industry – and the case of Seiko, specifically – provides a good example for analysing the impact that the emergence of buyer-driven global value chains has had on the management of firms positioned until then in producer-driven GVC. Seiko became the world leader of the watch industry at the beginning of the 1980s thanks to process (mass production of high-quality goods) and product (quartz watch) innovations (Shintaku 1994 and Donzé 2011). Moreover, from the late 1960s to the early 1980s, Seiko opened production subsidiaries abroad in order to access specific markets like the United States and benefit from low wages in the manufacture of low value-added parts, especially in Southeast Asia. This period witnessed Seiko's transformation into an MNC.

However, the advent of electronic watches opened the doors to buyer-driven GVC. By using an applied business history approach, we will be able to see how Seiko faced and dealt with this paradigm shift. As Kikkawa 2013 stressed, 'business history is an academic discipline that focuses on using the historical method to perform empirical analyses of changes in organizational management'. In the context of other social sciences, history adheres to an *ex ante* perspective: analysing events from the past to the present rather than looking back on the past from a present perspective. This mode allows historians to provide timely contextualized analyses and focus on evolutionary processes, thereby avoiding the deterministic risks of a path dependency approach (Bucheli and Wadhwani 2013). Situating his views among the various fields of this discipline, Kikkawa (2006) proposed a specific approach – "applied business history" – that strives to show history can help elucidate a given firm's current ability to compete. An advocate of a historical approach that extends up to the present, Kikkawa defines his approach as follows:

> The study of applied business history is about identifying the dynamism of industrial and corporate growth through an examination of business history; then, based on the findings, such studies explore solutions to the contemporary problems encountered by relevant industries and companies. (Kikkawa 2012)

Data analysis

The analysis of Seiko's business history in this section evaluates the development of the firm since the 1980s within its changing environment. However, fully understanding the evolution of the firm's organization and product innovation requires a look at the industry level in order to underline the major business changes and the changing conditions of global competition. Production and trade statistics for the major watchmaking nations (Japan, Switzerland, and Hong Kong), as well as government and trade association reports, provide a clear overview of this evolution. Furthermore, annual reports of the main Japanese watch companies shed light on the changes of their relative competitiveness. The second part of the analysis examines Seiko itself through primary sources and company-published documents. This two-level historical approach helps delineate the reasons behind the Japanese watch industry's lost competitiveness.

The transformation of the production system

Until the mid-1950s, the production of watches occurred in highly concentrated and vertically integrated production systems either within single firms (in Japan and the United States) or within an industrial district (Switzerland) (Donzé 2012a). In the latter case, the producers of finished watches relied on independent companies for their parts supplies, but institutional rules forbade them from purchasing parts outside Switzerland; thus, it is impossible to assert that global value chains existed at that time. The growing competition between American, Swiss, and Japanese firms after World War II led them to reorganize their production systems gradually and implement producer-driven value chains during the 1960s.

In order to cut production costs, the major watch companies opened subsidiaries in East Asia, concentrating especially on Hong Kong, to procure low value-added parts (such as cases and straps) and assemble finished products (Donzé 2012b). American, Japanese, and Swiss companies relocated portions of their production activities there; this transfer was made possible not only by the low cost and abundance of cheap domestic labor (the pull factor) but also by evolving watch production technology (the push factor). The spread of mass production for mechanical watches propelled the standardization of parts and models, facilitating the relocation of some assembly operations abroad. In the specific case of Switzerland, an institutional factor came into play: with the country phasing out the cartel system and enforcing strict controls on exports from 1961 to 1965, Swiss manufacturers took advantage of the international division of labour.

The 1960s saw the number of watch enterprises in Hong Kong grow from 61 in 1960 to 229 in 1970 (Hong Kong Government Industry Department 1996). These firms were highly dependent, both economically and technologically, on the world's leading watch groups. They had no access to the market of finished watches because they could not produce movements. The emergence of a watch industry in Hong Kong represents an international division of work that took the form of a producer-driven value chain. However, the emergence of electronic watches in the early 1970s provided an opportunity to sever these ties of dependency and shift towards a new form of value chain.

The advent of quartz watches had a major impact on power relations within the global watch industry: by facilitating and ensuring broad access to watch movements, it considerably weakened the position of established firms and supported the emergence and subsequent growth of newcomers (Stephens and Dannis 2000). Developed in the late 1960s, the first analogue quartz watches were launched in 1969–1972, followed shortly thereafter by digital models (from 1972–1973 onward). These first quartz watches were still relatively expensive, and prices fell only after the mid-1970s (Shintaku 1994).

The Hong Kong watch industry experienced a boom within this new technological context. The assembly and subsequent production of quartz watches began in 1975. The shift to electronic watches happened very quickly: they already accounted for 68.3% of the total value of Hong Kong's watch exports in 1980 and then leapt to 94.8% by 1990 (Hong Kong Government Industry Department 1996). Above all, electronic watches made it possible for Hong Kong to establish itself as a leading watchmaking nation. The total value of its watch and clock exports was USD 285.8 million in 1975 and USD 3.8 billion in 1990 (Hong Kong Census Department 1975–1990).

Moreover, electronic watches liberated Hong Kong entrepreneurs from their historical reliance on large foreign watch firms. Although their new suppliers of chips and digital displays were still foreign companies, these providers were not watch industry players but rather electronic component manufacturers. In addition, electronic watches also played a key role in the emergence of Hong Kong's watchmakers by giving the companies direct access to markets. In 1987, they made their first appearance at the Basel Fair, the largest watch distribution event in the world.

The Hong Kong watch industry entered a new phase in the late 1980s. Companies relocated production to China and began constructing a new type of value chain in which they could enjoy stronger bargaining power, with Hong Kong entrepreneurs becoming intermediaries between cheap labour in China and global markets (Berger and Lester 1997). Consequently, this transfer of production resulted in a very high rate of growth among re-exports from Hong Kong, which increased from 36.1% in 1990 to 75.5% by 1995 and has amounted to more than 90% since 2000. The ability to design watches for customers from throughout the world, especially from the fast fashion business, allowed Hong Kong manufacturers to establish their community as a hub for watchmaking. The best example is undoubtedly the American company Fossil, founded in Texas in 1984 and the fourth-largest watch company in the world in 2012. The firm focuses exclusively on design, marketing, and distribution and does not have any watch production facilities in the United States. Fossil based its global extension on its 1992 acquisition of a Hong Kong-based firm that took the name 'Fossil (East) Ltd.' and responsibility for supplying the US headquarters with watches. According to group financial reports, Fossil sourced watches from a total of 38 watchmaking companies in Hong Kong and nearby China in 2000 and eventually 48 companies in the area by 2011.[1]

As long as the manufacture of mechanical movements was the core competitive advantage in the watchmaking industry, Swiss and Japanese watchmakers dominated the global market and continued to do so despite the relocation of external parts manufacturing and assembly activities to Hong Kong. Even so, the shift from producer-driven to buyer-driven GVC that occurred in the 1980s was a challenge for these firms. However, Switzerland and Japan exhibited different reactions to the changes. The main sources of profit shifted from the mastery of technology and production of watch movements to the marketing and sale of finished goods. Repositioning within GVC was thus a common issue for players in both Switzerland and Japan, but, as Figure 1 illustrates, companies in the two countries took divergent paths in response.

Although there are no production data for Switzerland, the relatively small size of the domestic market (estimated at less than 10% of gross sales) means that export statistics provide an adequate picture of the industry's evolution. After a severe crisis in 1975–1985, Switzerland recovered: its exports grew from USD 1.5 billion in 1985 to USD 5.8 billion in 1995 and, after few years of stagnation, peaked at USD 14.8 billion in 2008. This comeback and dramatic growth came out of a major marketing innovation under which

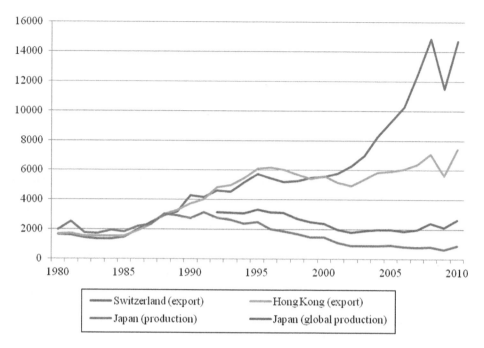

Figure 1.   Watch exports (Switzerland and Hong Kong) and production (Japan), in millions of USD, 1980–2010. *Source: Statistique annuelle du commerce extérieur de la Suisse*, Berne: Administration fédérale des douanes (1980–2010); *Kikai tokei nenpo*, Tokyo: MITI/METI (1980–2010); *Hong Kong Trade Statistics Export & Re-Export*, Hong Kong: Census Department (1980–2010); *Nihon no tokei sangyo tokei*, Tokyo: Nihon tokei kyokai, 1995–2010.

most Swiss watch companies made the shift towards luxury (Jeannerat and Crevoisier 2011; Donzé 2014). The core competitiveness of these firms changed from technological excellence to marketing strategy. The companies succeeded in controlling the new buyer-driven GVC through the support of the Swiss Made law, which specifies that a substantive proportion of work (more than half of the value of the movement and final assembly) must be realized in Switzerland.[2] By making the Swiss origin of their products the key determinant of product 'luxury', companies thus secured their positions in luxury watch GVC and established Switzerland as the main node of profit (Kebir and Crevoisier 2008). Moreover, the verticalization of distribution that has coloured the luxury business as a whole since the 1990s also bolsters these companies' standing.

Japan followed a completely different path and entered a phase of stagnation – and eventually decline – in the late 1980s. It became the world leader in the watch industry between 1980 and 1985 but was unable to deal with the emergence of buyer-driven GVC. In order to stay competitive, Japanese companies adopted a strategy typical of producer-driven GVC. Going back to 1992, data from the Japanese Clock & Watch Association underline the general trends and highlight two main features.

First, Japanese companies focused on high-tech parts, namely electronic movements. The proportion of movements relative to total national watch production (movements and finished watches) went from 41.4% in 1983 to 69.7% in 1990 and more than 90% in 2010.

Second, Japanese firms gradually relocated production to other locations in Asia, mainly in China. The proportion of watches (including movements) produced at the foreign plants of Japanese companies shot up from 17.8% in 1995 to 45.8% in 2010. However, this transfer of production to low-wage countries was still not enough to stave off declines for Japanese watch companies: after global production peaked respectively at USD 3.4 billion in 1995, it sagged and eventually stagnated at USD 2.1 billion in 2000–2010. Consequently, one can argue that the transfer of Japanese production, especially the final assembly stage, to East Asian nations – particularly China – is the major reason behind the growth and maintenance of exports from Hong Kong. Some Hong Kong watches include China-made products from Japanese companies; the high level of Hong Kong exports would thus seem to express the global competitiveness of Japanese companies. Yet, this assumption is contradicted by the fact that Japanese watch companies experienced declines in their watch sales beginning in the 1990s, as I will show below through the case of Seiko. Although there is no data available to prove this hypothesis, it actually appears that most Hong Kong watch exports include China-made products from Hong Kong watchmakers for global customers, like the case of Fossil discussed above. These watches may contain Japanese movements, but most of the product's value comes from design and conception – as a result, Japanese watch companies do not benefit so much from the high level of Hong Kong watch exports.

The next key topic for discussion is the impact of this dynamic on the competitiveness of different Japanese watch companies. Table 1 uses annual report data to show how the gross sales of the watch divisions at the three major watchmaking firms (Seiko, Citizen, and Casio) changed from 1990 to 2010. The table also indicates the ratio of watch sales to gross sales, as the firms in question are active in other production (mostly electronics, clocks, and machine tools). The figures point to two main trends.

First, the three companies experienced decreases in watch sales in the 1990s and early 2000s, precisely when the Swiss watchmakers had repositioned themselves in luxury. Strengthening the relocation of production in low-wage countries obviously had no effect on their competitiveness. Seiko, still the uncontested leader in 1990, had the largest losses: watch sales dropped 47% from 1990 to 2005. Citizen, despite rising to the top during the late 1990s, was not really growing until 2005. For all three companies, diversification outside watchmaking represented the solution. The contributions of watches to gross sales declined sharply between 1990 and 2005.

Second, in 2005 (2010 for Seiko), the Japanese watch companies entered a new phase of growth that saw increases in the percentage of watch sales relative to gross sales. Of course, in the long-term perspective, the 2013 data correspond to a recovery from the global financial crisis and the Tohoku earthquake and tsunami, not necessarily real growth. Seiko is still under the 1990 benchmark, and Citizen is only 15% above the data from 2000.

Table 1.   Watch sales of the main watchmaking companies in Japan, 1990–2013.

	Seiko		Citizen		Casio	
	Billion JPY	% of gross sales	Billion JPY	% of gross sales	Billion JPY	% of gross sales
1990	183.3	60	124.8	51	70.2	25
1995	111.3	52	107.3	53	84.1	26
2000	125.2	48	141.5	37	68.2	15
2005	107.6	50	125	37	71	12
2010	106.9	33	137.4	48	78.1	18
2013	150.7	47	162	52	n/a	n/a

Note: Casio has not published data for watches since 2010. *Source*: Annual reports.

Evolution of Seiko since 1990

Next, in order to shed light on the difficulties that Japanese watch companies have faced since the 1990s, we take the example of Seiko – the former leader. I base my analysis on annual reports, production statistics, the company's official website (www.seiko.co.jp), and an interview with Mr. Yoshino Shu, general manager at the Seiko Holdings corporate communication department (12 September 2014). My discussion focuses on two main points: first, the organization of the company and the role of foreign affiliates; and second, product development and markets.

Organization of the firm

Figure 2 shows the organization of the Seiko Group in 2014 and the orientation of watch business within the larger framework. It does not include other divisions (electronics, optical products, clocks, jewellery, or leisure goods) or distribution.

The structure has roots in the long, fifty-year (1947–1997) ban on holding companies in Japan (Shishido 2007). Beginning 1881, the Hattori family founded several companies active in watch business without establishing any official link between them (Seiko 1996). Most of the operating companies were merged into Seiko Holdings during the late 1990s; the primary exception was Seiko Epson, which remains independent and specializes in electronics and peripheral devices for computers. Indeed, the Seiko Group diversified

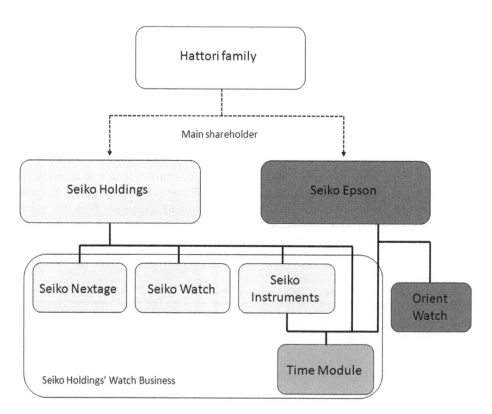

Figure 2.   Organization of watch business within the Seiko Group in 2014. *Sources*: The Seiko corporate website (www.seiko.co.jp) and an interview with Mr. Yoshino Shu, general manager of Seiko Holding's corporate communication department (12 September 2014).

gradually into electronics to grow in new fields thanks to the knowledge it had internalized to develop quartz watches. For Seiko Holdings, watches went from 90% of gross sales in 1980 to 65.6% of gross sales in 1995.[3] From 2000 to 2013, watches amounted to about 45% of gross sales. However, analysing the level of profits (operating income/net sales) makes it clear that the watch division is the most profitable division (6.5% on average from 2002 to 2013), far outstripping 'precision products and electronic components' (1.1%), 'clocks' (− 6.8%) and 'other businesses' (− 1.0%). Seiko's diversification into electronics cannot be seen as a strategy to find new growth outside of watchmaking, which still represents the company's core competency.

Seiko's relatively complex watch business is divided between Seiko Holdings and Seiko Epson. Seiko Instruments (SII), a company that was founded in 1937 and made into a wholly owned subsidiary of Seiko Holdings in 2009, and Seiko Epson handle the production of complete watches, movements, and parts. Sales activities, meanwhile, are separated among three main operating companies: Seiko Watch (spun off from Seiko Holdings in 2001) for complete watches, Seiko Nextage (founded in 2012) for licensing business, and Time Module (a joint subsidiary of Seiko Holdings, SII, and Seiko Espon that was founded in 1987) for movements. Seiko Epson, which provides movements to Time Module and watches to Seiko Watch and Seiko Nextage, has also owned Orient Watch – a small watch company founded in 1950 – since 2001. Consequently, the watch turnover that Seiko Holdings lists in its annual reports includes the group's entire watch business except for Orient Watch's sales.

Seiko became an MNC during the 1960s and 1970s when it invested in East Asia to transfer low-value added activities. Seikosha (now Seiko Holdings) opened subsidiaries for watch assembly in Hong Kong (1968) and parts manufacturing in Taiwan (1969), as well as a joint venture for case manufacturing in Singapore (1969). SII had developed its own network of subsidiaries in Asia with the opening of Singapore Time (1975) and Asian Precision in Singapore (1980). These foreign plants aimed at producing cheap parts and exporting them to Japan for assembly into watches; only a small proportion of watches were assembled outside Japan in 1980. Although specific data on Seiko are not available, the proportion of watches finished abroad for the entire Japanese watch industry amounted to a mere 6.3% of production in 1980 – when Seiko held 42% of national production. The company thus built a production-driven value chain to benefit from lower manufacturing costs and sharpen its competitive edge.

Seiko then strengthened the transfer of production to East Asia in the late 1980s, a move that obviously came as a consequence of the appreciation of the yen following the Plaza Accord (1985). In 1988, SII's Hong Kong subsidiary, Precision Engineering, transferred the assembly of watches to a new subcontract company in Guangzhou (China) and later opened new production subsidiaries in Thailand (1988), China (Dailan, 1989), and Malaysia (1990). The company also reorganized production in Singapore in the early 1990s and centralized the group's former Singaporean production centres in Johor, a region of neighbouring Malaysia. Thailand became the centre for the final assembly of watches for the world market. In 1994, the Thai subsidiary employed 770 workers and exported watches to 60 countries (Seiko 1996). Finally, in 2002, the Guangzhou factory became a wholly owned subsidiary of SII; the factory now realizes most of the group's assembly work. According to annual reports, the two largest foreign plants involved in watchmaking as of March 2013 were Dalian SII Inc. (622 employees) and SII Singapore Pte. Ltd. (515 employees).

Besides implementing this production system in East Asia, Seiko engaged actively in watch movement sales – the core technology of watch business and one that requires mass

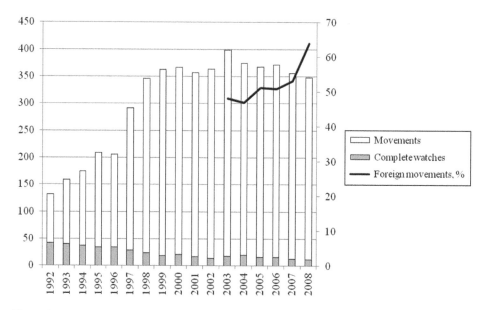

Figure 3. Production of watches and watch movements by the Seiko Group, in millions of units, 1992–2008. *Source*: Seiko Holdings production statistics, Note: Data for 2009 onward not available.

production in order to achieve low unit prices. Figure 3 effectively captures the trends of the mid-1990s, when Seiko decided to engage more in the movement business. Their production went from 90 million units in 1992 to an average of 351 million units from 2000 to 2008. While complete watches accounted for 32.3% of total production in 1992, this proportion dropped to 5.7% in 2000 and 3.3% in 2008.

Moreover, the shift to movement production drew on expanded transfers to Asian plants for support. The only data available on the production of foreign plants show that 90.1% of Seiko's complete watches were made outside Japan from 2003 to 2008, and that figure stayed roughly constant over the same six-year period. However, the proportion of movements made abroad grew from 48.2% in 2003 to 64% in 2008.

It is also important to note that in 1987, Seiko Holdings, SII, and Seiko Epson opened a joint company, Time Module, with a subsidiary in Hong Kong. Specializing in the sale of movements to private customers, the joint company provides key components to the numerous independent, Hong Kong-based designers and assembly makers of fast-fashion watches for global customers (Nakamoto 2003). In 2013, Seiko also opened a new subsidiary called 'Seiko Nextage' to further the sale of movements and engage in private label watches.

Product development strategy

There are several public documents for evaluating the extent to which the production system implemented during the mid-1990s affected Seiko sales. Based on annual reports, Figure 4 shows how Seiko Holdings watch sales changed from 1990 to 2013. The figures require close attention, however, as the complex structure of the group makes it difficult to interpret the composition of the numbers. The data on 'watch sales' includes values from three operating companies. Overall, the data point to the existence of three main phases.

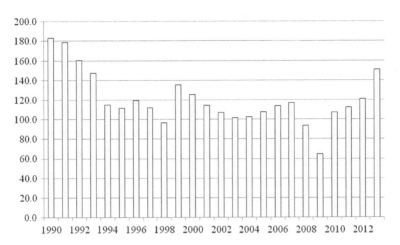

Figure 4.   Seiko Holdings, watch sales, in billions of yen, 1990–2013. *Source*: Annual reports.

First, from 1990 to 1998, Seiko published only the direct sales of Seiko Holdings (named Seiko Corporation at that time) – the division that would eventually become Seiko Watch in 2001 – and did not include the sales of related companies and subsidiaries (Time Module and the Wako department store, etc.). However, Seiko Holdings formed the core watch business of the group, as Seiko Epson and SII sold basically all their production to the company. During these nine years, sales dropped dramatically from 183.3 billion yen in 1990 to 96.7 billion yen in 1998. Assessing this decline requires a longer-term perspective. Annual sales peaked at an average of 268 billion yen in 1980–1985 and then began to decrease gradually until 1998 as Seiko lost its competitiveness against Swiss watch companies that had repositioned in luxury (Donzé 2014). The company's decision to shift mass production of movements abroad in the mid-1990s was an attempt to regain cost competitiveness. As most of these movements were sold by Time Module, one of the companies not consolidated in Seiko's published data, it is impossible to evaluate the efficiency of this strategy.

During the second period, from 1999 to 2009, Seiko Holdings published consolidated watch sales figures that included sales from all the operating companies – including Time Module – but not Seiko Epson and SII, which were legally independent. Although comparing the 1999 data with the data for the previous period has its challenges, the numbers reveal that the mass production of movements had a weak financial impact for three reasons. First, the 1999 Figure (135.3 billion yen) is lower than the annual sales total for 1993 (147.5 billion yen); this means that the strategy adopted in the mid-1990s did not halt the overall slide from the mid-term perspective. Second, the decline continued through 2003 despite increases in movement volume from 1999 to 2003 (see Figure 3). Third, stiff competition with Citizen Watch and the Swatch Group – the two other big companies engaged in the mass production of movements – led to a constant decline in unit prices, which came in at approximately USD 90 cents in 1999 and continued to fall thereafter.[4] This lack of profitability led the Swatch Group to close down its movement plant in China around 2005 and focus instead on the sale of fashion and luxury watches (Donzé 2014).

In 2001, Seiko Holdings worked to overcome this decline by spinning off its watch division into the independent Seiko Watch, which had more autonomy and the ability to make watch business-related decisions more quickly (Farhoomand and Hout 2007). The brand strategy changed, especially with the launch of new mechanical watches on the domestic market. The year 2004 saw Seiko set up the Seiko Boutiques, a global network of selective retailers, with about 40 points of sale in 2014 – most of them in China. These measures helped get sales back on the growth track – albeit only a slight increase – in 2004, but the world financial crisis put an end to the comeback.

The third period covers the years since 2010 and includes the sales of SII, which became a wholly owned subsidiary in 2009. However, as SII hardly sold watches outside Seiko Holdings, this consolidation had no consequence on the overarching trend in watch sales since 1999. The apparent growth spurt in 2010 was only an outcome of post-crisis recovery; the first real increase occurred in 2013 as the Japanese watch – and luxury – market expanded across the board under the economic policies of Prime Minister Abe.[5] Still, it remains too early to know if this expansion will last or not.

Discussion

The development of Seiko and the international expansion of its production facilities since the 1960s transformed the Japanese firm into an MNC. The first plants that the company opened in East Asia focused on low value-added activities such as assembly or the manufacture of simple parts (cases, dials, and straps), signifying an effort to reduce production costs in a competitive global environment. Swiss and American watch companies adopted the same strategy through the 1980s. The global watch industry consequently experienced a deep organizational change and witnessed the emergence of producer-driven global value chains, where companies holding the core technologies (here, the production of the watch movements) control the chain.

A major mutation then occurred in the 1980s and 1990s after the advent of electronic watches. Traditional watchmakers such as Seiko lost their competitive advantages as core technologies became easily and cheaply accessible for any independent assembly maker. As was the case in the textile and apparel industries (Lane and Probert 2009), marketing became the new basis for competition. Swiss and Hong Kong watch companies began to invest heavily in design and distribution, internalizing these functions through takeovers (Yu 1998; Davies and Ma 2003; Tuschman 2000; Donzé 2014). The overall industrial organization moved to a buyer-driven global value chain (Gereffi 1994a, 1994b).

However, Seiko's supply chain management has exhibited rather strong continuity from the 1960s onwards. The company's foreign investments from 1987 to 1990 and since 2000 have taken place via the same established model and aimed at cutting production costs and relocating low value-added activities in China and elsewhere in Asia. This clear focus on production issues does not mean that Seiko has no interest in marketing, design, and distribution, but these elements are limited to the domestic market. Indeed, Seiko demonstrates a twofold strategy: it has used one for the national market, where marketing has a strong influence, since the 1980s and another for the global market, where the control of production costs remains the main objective.

In Japan, Seiko launched a special brand for luxury jewel watches (Credor) and re-branded its mechanical Grand Seiko model in the 1990s to compete domestically against Rolex and Omega. However, these Seiko brands are rarities in the company's distribution sphere outside Japan. Moreover, Seiko has actively focused on distribution and retailing in the Japanese market. The department store Ginza, a Hattori family asset since the beginning of the 20th century, underwent renovations in 2008 and today has eight branches throughout Japan. In 1985, Seiko also founded a subsidiary – Cronos Ltd. – that specializes in the management of watch stores in other department stores and holds some

46 points of sale in Japan as of 2014. Also deserving of mention is that the private label company Nextage, founded in 2013, has contracts with the domestic apparel industry and foreign companies with a strong presence in Japan (e.g. Agnès B., Asics, Michel Klein, Issey Miyake, and Tsumori Chisato) instead of global firms (http://www.seiko-nextage. com). Viewed from Japan, then, Seiko's value chain management is very similar to the approaches that global companies like the Swatch Group or the American firm Fossil Ltd. embrace (Donzé 2014).

However, Seiko has a completely different strategy for the global market. There are very few Seiko luxury brands that can compete, and the company has not developed its own worldwide network of distributors and retailers. The family of Seiko Boutiques, launched in 2004, includes only 44 stores – 20 of which are in Greater China – as of 2014. In comparison, the global network of Omega Boutiques comprised 292 stores, with 123 in Greater China, as of that same year.[6] Nor has Seiko engaged actively in the management of distribution at the regional level. The Thong Sia Group, a company that started up in 1967 and held the sole distribution rights for Seiko watches in Hong Kong, Malaysia, and Singapore, was taken over in 2005 by the Hong Kong-based Stelux Group, a company that has operated in watch design, assembly, and retail in Asia since the early 1960s.

Seiko's strategic paths in the global and domestic markets have thus remained divergent since the 1980s. While the basis of power and profit shifted from movement production to design and distribution in the global watch industry, the company's two-pronged approach explains why the decision to focus more on the mass production of movements in the mid-1990s did not generate a significant financial outcome.

Implications

In addition to contributing to the academic discussion on global production systems and specifically to the process of organizational change within GVC over time, the Seiko case offers implications for a better understanding of Japanese MNC and management practice. The struggles that numerous Japanese firms have faced in global markets since the 2000s go beyond just technological issues and the challenges of staying competitive against other firms from South Korea, Taiwan, and China, which benefit from differences in production costs. A major weakness that obviously applies by extension to most Japanese manufacturers lies in Seiko's marketing strategy. The inability to communicate to global customers and develop products according to a marketing strategy is undoubtedly one of the biggest fetters on the company's global competitiveness. Future research should look at unsuccessful and uncompetitive firms to pinpoint the exact reasons behind these weaknesses by venturing beyond the traditional standpoint, which centres on the negative effects of State protectionism (Porter, Takeuchi, and Sakakibara 2000).

As for management practice, the analysis of Seiko clearly exposes the need for deep changes in company organization. Giving more attention to marketing, distribution, and communication in the global context is not only a matter of adopting new plans or a new strategy; firms need to reallocate their financial and human resources to achieve this goal. In terms of financial resources, Seiko and other Japanese watchmakers currently use watch business profits to keep unprofitable divisions – such as clocks for Seiko – operating. A better distribution of watch division profits would be to shut failing divisions down and invest in watch business, including distribution abroad. In terms of human resources, it seems essential to shift power from engineering to marketing. Swiss watchmakers reallocated resources in this way during the 1990s, paving the way for the industry's successful comeback (Donzé 2014).

Conclusions

This applied business history of Seiko shed light on the difficulties that the firm has faced since the 1990s. From its perch atop the watch industry in the mid-1980s, the company lost its competitiveness against Swiss and Hong Kong enterprises that built and managed new kinds of GVC that cultivated profits through marketing and distribution. The evolution of Seiko's organization and product development strategy between 1990 and the present day highlights two important incongruities.

First, there is a huge gap between Seiko and foreign companies regarding the management of GVC. Since the 1960s, the Japanese watchmaker has adhered to a stability- and continuity-oriented strategy. Seiko's global presence rests largely on the company's efforts to relocate production facilities to East Asia in hopes of cutting manufacturing costs. This strategy led the company to invest heavily in the mass production of movements. However, it did little in the way of moving up to luxury and fashion through distribution and rebranding.

Second, the Seiko strategy itself presents a rather surprising difference between domestic and foreign markets. Looking exclusively at the Japanese market, slight changes have occurred since 2000 as the company has devoted more attention to marketing, branding, and distribution after the spinoff of Seiko Watch in 2001. In Japan, the company sells more mechanical watches, manages spaces in department stores directly, and operates a subsidiary for private label watches aimed especially at fashion companies active on the domestic market. If we shift our focus to foreign markets, however, all these elements disappear – Seiko sticks to its strategy of manufacturing high-quality and cheap quartz movements and watches at its Chinese and South-East Asian plants for a global consumer audience. Hence, Seiko runs two different value chains at the same time: a buyer-driven chain at the local level and a producer-driven chain at the global level.

These characteristics apply to more than just Seiko and the watch industry, however. Very similar features are evident in most Japanese consumer goods companies and explain a great deal about their inability to adopt proper strategies for competing effectively in global markets. The shift from national to foreign markets, which represents a crucial step in combating the effects of Japan's shrinking population and domestic demand, is a far more difficult task than a simple geographical reorientation.

Disclosure statement

No potential conflict of interest was reported by the author.

Notes

1. Fossil Inc., annual reports (www.fossilgroup.com, last accessed 10 December 2014).
2. *Ordonnance réglant l'utilisation du nom «Suisse» pour les montres du 23 décembre 1971*, Berne: RS 232.119.
3. *Kaisha yoran*, Tokyo: Nikkei shimbun, 1980–1995.
4. *Nihon keizai shimbun*, 29 May 2001.
5. "Abenomics" led to a high growth of stock prices at the Tokyo Stock Exchange and consequently triggered increases in luxury good consumption among individual investors who made some gains. *Financial Times*, 18 June 2013.
6. http://www.omegawatches.com/stores (last accessed 20 September 2014).

References

Aoshima, Y., A. Takeishi, and M. A. Cusumano. 2010. *Made in Japan ha owaru no ka ? kiseki to shuen no saki ni arumono* [End of 'Made in Japan'?]. Tokyo: Toyo keizai shinposha.

Arora, A., L. G. Branstetter, and M. Drev. 2013. "Going Soft: How the Rise of Software-Based Innovation Led to the Decline of Japan's IT Industry and the Resurgence of Silicon Valley." *Review of Economics and Statistics* 95 (3): 757–775. doi:10.1162/REST_a_00286.

Berger, S., and R. K. Lester, eds. 1997. *Made by Hong Kong*. Oxford: Oxford University Press.

Bucheli, M., and R. D. Wadhwani, eds. 2013. *Organizations in Time: History, Theory, Methods*. Oxford: Oxford University Press.

Choi, E. K. 2011. "The Rise of Uniqlo: Leading Paradigm Change in Fashion Business and Distribution in Japan." *Entreprises et histoire* 64 (3): 85–101. doi:10.3917/eh.064.0085.

Da Silva Lopes, T., and M. Casson. 2007. "Entrepreneurship and the Development of Global Brands." *Business History Review* 81 (04): 651–680. doi:10.2307/25097419.

Davies, H., and C. Ma. 2003. "Strategic Choice and the Nature of the Chinese Family Business: An Exploratory Study of the Hong Kong Watch Industry." *Organization Studies* 24 (9): 1405–1435. doi:10.1177/0170840603249003.

Donzé, P. -Y. 2011. "The Hybrid Production System and the Birth of the Japanese Specialized Industry: Watch Production at Hattori & Co. (1900–1960)." *Enterprise & Society* 12 (2): 356–397.

Donzé, P. -Y. 2012a. *History of the Swiss Watch Industry from Jacques David to Nicolas Hayek*. Berne: Peter Lang.

Donzé, P. -Y. 2012b. "The Changing Comparative Advantages of the Hong Kong Watch Industry (1950–2010)." *Kyoto Economic Review* 169: 28–47.

Donzé, P. -Y. 2014. *A Business History of the Swatch Group: The Rebirth of Swiss Watchmaking and the Globalization of the Luxury Industry*. Basingstoke: Palgrave Macmillan.

Farhoomand, A., and T. M. Hout. 2007. *Seiko Watch Corporation: Moving Upmarket*. Hong Kong: Hong Kong University, case study no. 107C.

Fujikawa, Y., T. Ito, Y. Li, and A. Hirose. 2012. *Japan Tobacco: Domestic Giant Going Global*. Tokyo: Hitotsubashi University, case no. 112-019-8.

Fujimoto, T. 2004. *Nihon no monozukuri tetsugaku* [The Philosophy of Japanese Manufacturing]. Tokyo: Nihon keizai shimbunsha.

Gawer, A., and M. A. Cusumano. 2002. *Platform Leadership: How Intel, Microsoft, and Cisco Drive Industry Innovation*. Cambridge: Harvard University Press.

Gereffi, G. 1994a. "Introduction." In *Commodity Chains and Global Capitalism*, edited by G. Gereffi and M. Korzeniewicz, 1–13. Westport: Praeger.

Gereffi, G. 1994b. "The Organization of Buyer-Driven Global Commodity Chains: How U.S. Retailers Shape Overseas Production Networks." In *Commodity Chains and Global Capitalism*, edited by G. Gereffi and M. Korzeniewicz, 95–122. Westport: Praeger.

Gereffi, G., J. Humphrey, and T. Sturgeon. 2005. "The Governance of Global Value Chains." *Review of International Political Economy* 12 (1): 78–104. doi:10.1080/09692290500049805.

Hong Kong Trade Statistics Export & Re-Export,. Hong Kong: Census Department 1975–1990.

Hong Kong's Manufacturing Industries. Hong Kong: Hong Kong Government Industry Department 1996.

Jeannerat, H., and O. Crevoisier. 2011. "Non-Technological Innovation and Multi-Local Territorial Knowledge Dynamics in the Swiss Watch Industry." *International Journal of Innovation and Regional Development* 3 (1): 26–44. doi:10.1504/IJIRD.2011.038061.

Kawabe, N. 2011. *Tai Toyota no keieishi: kaigai kogaisha no jiritsu to tojokoku sangyo no jiritsu* [Business History of Toyota Motor Thailand]. Tokyo: Yuhikaku.

Kebir, L., and O. Crevoisier. 2008. "Cultural Resources and Regional Development: The Case of the Cultural Legacy of Watchmaking." *European Planning Studies* 16 (9): 1189–1205. doi:10.1080/09654310802401607.

Kikkawa, T. 2006. "Keieishi no jidai: oyo keieishi no kanosei [Contemporary Application of Business History]." *Keieishi gaku* 40 (4): 28–45.

Kikkawa, T. 2011. "Beyond Product Lifecycle and Flying Geese: International Competitiveness of East Asian Region and the Japanese Position Within." *Hitotsubashi Journal of Commerce and Management* 45 (1): 89–97.

Kikkawa, T. 2012. "International Competitiveness of Japan's Petroleum Industry: A View from Applied Business History." *Kyoto Economic Review* 81 (1): 4–13.

31

Kikkawa, T. 2013. "Fifty Years of Business History in Japan." *Japanese Research in Business History* 30 (): 11–29. doi:10.5029/jrbh.30.11.

Kikkawa, T., and S. Hirano. 2011. *Kagaku sangyo no jidai: nihon ha naze sekai wo oinukeru no ka* [The Era of Chemical Industry: Why Japan Overcame the World]. Tokyo: Kagaku kogyo nippo.

Kikkawa, T., and F. Kubo, eds. 2010. *Gurobaruka to nihon gata kigyo shisutemu no henyo, 1985–2008* [Globalization and the Transformation of Japanese Business System, 1985–2008]. Kyoto: Minerva.

Lane, C., and J. Probert. 2009. *National Capitalisms, Global Production Networks: Fashioning the Value Chain in the UK, USA, and Germany*. Oxford: Oxford University Press.

Motoyama, Y. 2012. *Global Companies, Local Innovations: Why the Engineering Aspects of Innovation Making Require Co-location*. Burlington: Ashgate.

Nakamoto, D. 2003. "Seihin no mojuruka no shinten to kohatsu kigyo no keiei senryaku: Seiko gurupu wo jirei toshite [Modularity and Competitive Strategy as Follower: A Case Study on SEIKO GROUP]." *Yokohama kokusai shakai kagaku kenkyu* 8 (4): 147–164.

Ozawa, T. 2007. *Institutions, Industrial Upgrading, and Economic Performance in Japan: The Flying-geese Paradigm of Catch-up Growth*. Northampton: Edward Elgar Publishing.

Porter, M., H. Takeuchi, and M. Sakakibara. 2000. *Can Japan Compete?* New York: Basic Books.

Raikes, P., M. F. Friis jensen, and S. Ponte. 2000. "Global Commodity Chain Analysis and the French Filière Approach: Comparison and Critique." *Economy and Society* 29 (3): 390–417. doi:10.1080/03085140050084589.

Sako, M. 2004. "Supplier Development at Honda, Nissan and Toyota: Comparative Case Studies of Organizational Capability Enhancement." *Industrial and Corporate Change* 13 (2): 281–308. doi:10.1093/icc/dth012.

Seiko. 1996. *Seiko tokei no sengoshi*. Tokyo: Seiko Institute.

Shintaku, J. 1994. *Nihon kigyo no kyoso senryaku* [The Competitive Strategy of Japanese Enterprises]. Tokyo: Yuhikaku.

Shioji, H., ed. 2008. *Higashi Ajia yui sangyo no kyoso ryoku: sono yoin to kyoso bungyo kozo* [The Competitive Advantage of East Asian Industry]. Kyoto: Minerva.

Shiomi, H., and T. Kikkawa. 2008. *Nichibei kigyo no gurobaru kyoso senryaku: nyueconomi to ushinawareta junen no saikento* [The Global Competitive Strategy of Japanese and US Firms]. Nagoya: Nagoya University Press.

Shishido, Z. 2007. "The Turnaround of 1997: Changes in Japanese Corporate Law and Governance." In *Corporate Governance in Japan: Institutional Change and Organizational Diversity*, edited by M. Aoki, G. Jackson, and H. Miyajima, 310–329. Oxford: Oxford University Press.

Stephens, C., and M. Dennis. 2000. "Engineering Time: Inventing the Electronic Wristwatch." *The British Journal for the History of Science* 33 (4): 477–497. doi:10.1017/S0007087400004167.

Tanaka, A. 2012. *Sengo nihon no shigen bijinesu: genryo chotatsu shisutemu to sogo shosha no hikaku keieishi* [Resource Business in Postwar Japan]. Nagoya: Nagoya University Press.

Tuschman, M. L. 2000. *Rebirth of the Swiss Watch Industry, 1980–1992*. Cambridge: Harvard Business School (case study series).

Yu, T. F. L. 1998. "Adaptive Entrepreneurship and the Economic Development of Hong Kong." *World Development* 26 (5): 897–911. doi:10.1016/S0305-750X(98)00013-8.

Do Japanese electronics firms still follow traditional vertical integration strategies? Evidence from the liquid crystal display industry

Derek Lehmberg

Management and Marketing Department, North Dakota State University, Fargo, USA

In the past, Japanese electronics firms have been known for following vertical integration strategies. Such strategies are consistent with Japanese managerial preferences, traditional relationships, and institutions in Japan. However, changes in the technological and competitive environment have resulted in increasing vertical specialization in the electronics industry outside of Japan. This paper examines whether and to what extent Japanese information technology and consumer electronics firms involved in active matrix Liquid Crystal Display production implemented and maintained integration strategies. While focusing on one industry, this paper aims to shed further light on changing attitudes and practices in Japanese management relating to strategy and internationalization.

Introduction

Vertical integration has been a popular strategy with Japanese managers, particularly in the electronics industry where many firms have considered manufacturing process improvement to be an important competitive advantage (Noguchi 2012; Sturgeon 2006). Preferences for vertical integration or quasi integration through *keiretsu* and long-term supply relationships with other Japanese firms have been identified in other industries including the auto industry (e.g. Ahmadjian and Lincoln 2001; McGuire and Dow 2009; Miwa 1994; Tabeta 1998). However, changes in the competitive environment, the introduction of digital technology, and other factors have affected the relative effectiveness and attractiveness of vertical integration, particularly in the area of electronics. This research investigates the involvement of Japanese information technology and electronics manufacturers in the Liquid Crystal Display (LCD) industry, to examine evidence about whether these companies developed and maintained vertical integration strategies or adopted alternative (i.e. non-integration) strategies over a study period beginning with the introduction of active matrix LCD in 1990 and ending in 2009.

This study finds that Japanese electronics firms changed their strategies over the study period. Of the eight firms holding mass production LCD facilities at the beginning of the study, by the end of the study five had exited, and two were following full vertical integration strategies. One of the remaining firms never fully adopted a vertical integration strategy, while one more firm exhibited a complex mix of taper and quasi integration at the end of the period. An additional observation of this study was that, in several circumstances, Japanese firms entered into international cooperative arrangements providing access to low cost quasi integration. These arrangements incorporated technology transfer from the Japanese partner in addition to outsourcing supply to the foreign partner. Taken together, the findings of this study suggest Japanese firms adapted their strategies in the face of economic realities even where the changes went against traditional values and Japanese institutions. Such changes may be indicative of shifting attitudes in Japan relating to international cooperation. This paper contributes to the literature on Japanese management as well as to the broader literature on the evolution of firm scope over different stages of industry evolution.

Literature review

General literature on vertical integration

Firms following vertical integration strategies combine multiple, technologically distinct value chain processes inside the firm (Porter 1980) instead of using alternative market-based transactions to obtain the outcomes of these processes (Harrigan 1984; Williamson 1971, 1985). In addition to full vertical integration, firms can also pursue tapered vertical integration strategies where they buy or sell some of the input or output in the market or quasi vertical integration strategies involving partial ownership of relevant production assets or other cooperative arrangements providing an equivalent to integration (Contractor and Lorange 1988; Harrigan 1985, 1986; Porter 1980; Rothaermel, Hitt, and Jobe 2006).

Amongst the many rationales given for vertical integration are improved coordination, efficiencies from integrating different steps and reduction in transaction costs, greater control of output quality and operational cost, decrease or elimination of reliance on suppliers or buyers with high bargaining power, the ability to create and maintain barriers to entry, and lack of other options when suppliers do not exist (Balakrishnan and Wernerfelt 1986; Fronmueller and Reed 1996; Harrigan 1984, 1986; Porter 1980; Stuckey and White 1993). However, technological improvements have made it possible to achieve some of these outcomes without integration (Osegowitsch and Madhok 2003). Vertical integration has been touted for the potential to develop, improve, and protect proprietary technology and capabilities, which may lead to cost and differentiation based advantages (Argyres 1996; Harrigan 1984; Porter 1980; Quinn and Hilmer 1994). Problems associated with vertical integration include bureaucratic costs, increasing barriers to exit, reduced flexibility, increased risk, and problems stemming from variation in economies of scale in the steps being integrated (D'Aveni and Ravenscraft 1994; Harrigan 1984; Langlois 1992, 2003; Porter 1980). Numerous authors have observed that the reasons given by firms for following integration strategies are not always suited to their actual situations or abilities (Harrigan 1985; Porter 1980; Stuckey and White 1993).

Vertical integration has been identified as an appropriate strategy for some firms depending on their situations regarding industry, technology, and firm specific drivers (Argyres 1996; Barney 1999; Harrigan 1984; Langlois 1992; Porter 1980). Scale and scope economies both play major roles in determining the appropriate or feasible type(s) of vertical integration (Harrigan 1985; Perry 1989; Porter 1980). Suitability of vertical integration strategies also depends on the stage of industry evolution (e.g. Jacobides and Winter 2005; Klepper 1997; Langlois 1992; Macher and Mowery 2004; Sichel 1973; Utterback and Suarez 1993).

Theory suggests that early in the development of an industry, firms may have little choice but to vertically integrate because the small market size blocks the emergence of potential suppliers and the development of intermediate markets (Stigler 1951). Furthermore, pre-emptive vertical integration early in an industry's development has been argued to provide competitive advantages to the pioneering firms that adopt it (Harrigan 1984; Porter 1980). On the other hand, demand uncertainty, which is generally high at earlier stages in industry evolution, is expected to reduce the attractiveness of vertical integration strategies (Harrigan 1984). Overall trends observed by Macher and Mowery (2004), as well as Jacobides (2005) suggest that industries often start off with relatively high levels of integration and proceed towards specialization. Macher and Mowery (2004) explain that company strategy plays a role in changing vertical integration and specialization at the industry level, and while it also reflects existing integration patterns.

As an industry matures, some forces act to increase integration while others decrease it (Jacobides and Winter 2005). Vertical integration can be suitable in mature stable industries where the firm has intellectual property to protect (Harrigan 1984). However, changes to the technologies underlying the firm's key products affect which processes are best internalized or externalized (Afuah 2001). Supply uncertainty increases the motive to integrate (Arrow 1975), although integrating supply does not actually remove the uncertainty but shifts it, raising other issues such as how to set transfer prices in the midst of rapidly changing market environments (Porter 1980; Stuckey and White 1993). In the face of high levels of general environmental uncertainty, high levels of asset specificity lead to increased internalization, while low levels of specificity increase outsourcing (Leiblein and Miller 2003).

Vertical integration has been examined by scholars of strategic management, industrial economics, and transaction cost economics (Klein 1988; Perry 1989; Williamson 1971). Because of this, vertical integration has been framed in many ways, including as a contracting issue, a capability issue, a financial cost-benefit issue, a political issue, an engineering question, and a risk or uncertainty reduction issue. Given the many different potential reasons for vertical integration as well as alternative types (e.g. forms of quasi integration) and levels (full, taper, etc.) along with the existence of multiple theoretical and disciplinary backgrounds, researchers face difficulties in rigorously testing vertical integration (Bresnahan and Levin 2013). Despite decades of attention, research on vertical integration has yet to fully address many questions such as the evolution of firm boundaries over time and the impact of changing boundaries on organizational performance (Jacobides and Billinger 2006).

Observers of practice have noted that vertical integration began to give way to specialization in the 1980s, and this trend has continued (D'Aveni and Ravenscraft 1994). The computer industry has been brought up as a prominent example of de-integration (e.g. Saxenian 1994). Popular sentiment in the United States' business and investment communities view vertical integration as being an ineffectual, obsolete strategy (Osegowitsch and Madhok 2003). However, environmental and institutional changes facilitating the emergence of intermediate markets must take place for an integrated industry to de-integrate (Jacobides 2005). Furthermore, it would be wrong to interpret these changes as always moving towards specialization as the reintegration of industries (or subsections) have also been observed (Jacobides and Winter 2005; Macher and Mowery 2004).

Vertical integration in the Japanese context

Despite arguments that company strategies, such as integration, may be influenced by national culture (Hofstede 2001; Porter, Takeuchi, and Sakakibara 2000), the majority of academic literature on vertical integration does not explicitly consider national context, although some studies implicitly consider it through examining institutional context (Jacobides 2005; Peng 2002). The Japanese managerial literature suggests Japan's national and institutional context play a role in affecting preferences for adopting vertical integration strategies. Japanese managers are observed to hold a preference for vertical integration (Noguchi 2012; Sano 2012; Sturgeon 2007), as summarized by Koichi Ogawa of Tokyo University in a recent article ["Chizumu Kozoteki Mondai: Kurikaesu Tyoraku no Rekishi." (*Nikkei Business* April 2, 2012, 54–57)] '...Japanese manufacturers try to bring operations in-house where possible because they believe that this will generally lead to maximizing the value they add.'

Indeed, there are numerous Japanese factors that appear to systematically promote vertical integration strategies in Japan. These include the motivation to maintain employment of the existing company workforce (e.g. Hareyama 2005; Imai and Komiya 1994), the opportunity for management to reduce or manage uncertainty (Hofstede 2001) by bringing operations in-house, and the potential to tap advantages Japanese firms can build through sharing knowledge (Nonaka and Takeuchi 1995) across the value chain through integration.

Lifetime (or at least long-term) employment is a pillar of Japanese human resource management (e.g. Hareyama 2005; Imai and Komiya 1994; Inagami and Whittaker 2005; Lehmberg 2014). Japanese managers cite the responsibility for maintaining on-going employment as a reason both for continuing in current businesses and entering into new ones. Vertical integration is one form of diversification, and offers the potential for maintaining or increasing the company workforce. Japanese firms have been described as being highly diversified although quantitative studies are rare (Gemba and Kodama 2001; Porter and Sakakibara 2004). Dore and Sako (1989) noted that Japanese managers favoured diversification through organic growth over acquisition because it provided more positions and avoided redundancies. While many have called for Japanese firms to follow more focused strategies – '*Sentaku to shuchu*' or 'choose and focus' is a prescription often heard in Japanese business (Schaede 2008) – actual reduction in overall diversification levels appears to be limited. Fukui and Ushijima (2007) found diversification was actually increasing, although focused only on related business areas, amongst major Japanese firms.

Hofstede (2001) described Japanese culture as being high in uncertainty avoidance. Uncertainty avoidance can play a significant role in managerial decision-making and strategy. In the case of backward integration, where the firm needs to decide whether to make an input itself or not, high levels of uncertainty avoidance appear likely to increase the tendency to vertically integrate for two reasons. First, as the old adage 'if you want something done right, do it yourself' implies, in-house supply increases control over the process (and resulting quality, etc.) and may reduce the level of uncertainty faced as a result. Second, in-house supply reduces uncertainty about external input markets, and therefore market uncertainty surrounding these to a degree. However, as Porter (1985) pointed out, where the company backward integrates into volatile markets, transfer prices become a complex and difficult issue to manage. To some extent, then, uncertainty may be shifted from one part of the organization to another, but managers may still feel that the overall level is lower.

Another driver of integration in the Japanese context is the ability to effectively share knowledge. Japanese firms have been thought to be especially good at developing and sharing knowledge (Nonaka and Takeuchi 1995). This suggests Japanese firms may be relatively more adept at realizing any cost, quality, or other benefits that are available from sharing information across different steps in the value chain. If this is the case, we should expect to observe integration relatively frequently in Japan.

The discussion above considered several reasons why integration may be relatively prominent in the Japanese business community. However, there are also several counterarguments worth mentioning. First, transaction costs appear to be systematically lower in Japan than in the West (Hill 1995; Williamson 1985). Lower transaction costs lead to a decrease in the relative cost of buying rather than making, suggesting lower levels of integration, all else equal. Second, Japanese firms may have lost much of their effectiveness at utilizing internal knowledge sharing (Numagami, Karube, and Kato 2010).

In Japan, vertical integration has been a prominent feature of the electronics and auto industries. The tight coordination facilitated by vertical integration has been considered to be a hallmark of the Japanese electronics industry (Sturgeon 2006). Japanese electronics firms have exhibited the ability to tweak the production processes of finicky analogue electronics technologies such as CRT TV sets because they made the key components as well as the end product (Sturgeon 2006). In fact, all of the major analogue Japanese TV producers, with the exception of Sharp, had vertically integrated CRT production. In the auto industry, quasi integration has been facilitated through vertical *keiretsu* (e.g. Ahmadjian and Lincoln 2001; McGuire and Dow 2009; Miwa 1994; Tabeta 1998).

Digitalization of technology has had far reaching impact in numerous industries including the electronics industry. It has changed both the economic scales of the module fabrication and final goods assembly and the levels of investment required by different stages. It has also affected the potential for realizing benefits through sharing knowledge across the different stages (Baldwin and Clark 2000; "Tokushu Gekiyasu Dejitaru no Kyoi: 5 man-en Terebi wo Ko Tsukuru" (*Nikkei Business*, May 18, 2009: 26–31)). Arguably, these changes have resulted in a trend towards de-integration of products using digital technologies. It is in this environment that electronics manufacturing services have grown to play an important role. However, these changes have not necessarily transformed managerial preferences in Japan (Noguchi 2012; Sturgeon 2006). For example, evidence from the semiconductor industry indicates that previously integrated Japanese firms did not de-integrate despite being at competitive disadvantage to international competitors narrowly specialized in one part of the value chain (Sano 2012). Meanwhile, Sturgeon (2007) observed that Japanese electronics firms are taking incremental steps that partially acknowledge specialization, but have not abandoned vertical integration.

Research questions

Internationally, many industries have shifted from vertical integration to vertical specialization, driven by strategic, technological, and institutional change, and the emergence of efficient specialist competitors. Observers have noted that Japanese business has often been slow to respond to these changes. In the past, Japanese business was described as an anomaly that operates in uniquely Japanese ways and does not always make sense from an economic standpoint (Porter, Takeuchi, and Sakakibara 2000). Japan's institutional environment, which has a strong impact on company strategy and structure, has been slow to respond to environmental changes (Witt 2006). An important question here is: Have Japanese firms started to respond more readily to economic realities, or do they remain highly constrained by tradition and institutions?

This research studies Japanese electronics manufacturers that backward integrated into LCD production, to examine if and how these firms changed their strategies over time. In doing so, it seeks to address several research questions. First, how prominent were vertical integration strategies early in the industry's development? Second, did the study firms change their strategies from the traditional vertical integration to other strategies, and if so, what were the new strategies, and how did these changes occur over time? Third, to what extent do the observations fit with or diverge from past observations of Japanese management? And finally, do the observed changes suggest changes or developments in the broader Japanese business community?

Methodology

This study follows a historical case study methodology (Eisenhardt 1989; Lawrence 1984), using archival data from multiple Japanese sources recognized in the industry. Starting with a database of events and announcements in the industry originally put together for an earlier study (Yin 2014), a historical narrative was built at the industry level. This was important because analysis of changes in the level of vertical integration at the firm level should be performed in the context of the evolution of integration in the industry overall (Jacobides and Winter 2005). Next, firm level historical observations were assembled with firm level data on company resources and investments to develop an understanding of the level or degree of integration and its change. The empirical setting, data gathering, and case research design are discussed further in the sections below.

Empirical setting

This study examines vertical integration in the context of the Japanese LCD industry, over the period from 1990 to 2009. Specifically, it examines the backwards integration of companies making products incorporating displays into LCD fabrication. The focal firms, Fujitsu, Hitachi, Mitsubishi, NEC, Panasonic (formerly called Matsushita), Sanyo, Sharp, Sony, and Toshiba, are consumer electronics companies and computer manufacturers that were also involved in active matrix LCD technology. This group represents the population of such firms rather than a sample.

There are numerous flat panel display (FPD) technologies including several types of liquid crystals, plasma display, organic light emitting diode, field emission display, and others (den Boer 2005). This research focuses on active matrix LCD, specifically amorphous silicon thin film transistor type (a-Si TFT), which is the most common colour FPD used in major FPD applications, such as computer displays and TV sets. The competitive landscape and many aspects of LCD–related technology have changed greatly over the years since the first TFT-LCD production facilities came on line, offering the opportunity to examine changes in company strategies in historical perspective.

Data gathering and sources

This study uses a historical timeline database containing observations related to investments in new plant and equipment, R&D activities, prototype and new product announcements, announcements relating to cooperative arrangements relating to FPDs, and other types of observations, such as evidence of exit. The database was assembled using information gathered from the following Japanese language publications: the Fuji-Chimera series (1998–2007), the Nikkei FPD series (1990–2009), and the Sangyo Times series (1990, 1992–2009). These sources were selected because they were publicly accessible and also because practitioners and academics knowledgeable about the industry indicated they were reputable. Each source has its own focus: Fuji-Chimera examined markets for displays; Nikkei FPD included interviews and presentations by industry managers; and Sangyo Times provided information about current and planned production facilities. The three sources also had overlaps in coverage, which facilitated triangulation. These sources were augmented with additional information from newspaper articles, annual reports, press releases, newspaper and magazine articles, published case studies, and stock analyst reports (Eisenhardt 1989).

Data analysis

Industry level

Japanese firms were the first to commercialize LCD technology (Johnstone 1999; Murtha, Lenway, and Hart 2001; Numagami 1999). With one exception, entrants into the industry already manufactured end products incorporating displays, such as watches, video cameras, word processors, computers, and TV sets. The exception, Hoshiden, primarily produced electrical components and is not included in the study. Over time, the TFT-LCD technology became the most widely used FPD technology and entered into numerous application markets. The makeup of industry players and their strategies also changed. Production technology and its underlying economic attributes played a key role in shaping the industry, and are briefly introduced below. After discussing production technology, industry developments are examined over several stages of time.

Production technology

LCD fabrication includes a capital-intensive step that makes an encapsulated cell and must be performed in a cleanroom environment, using processes relying heavily on production technology originally from the semiconductor industry. After the cell is fabricated, a more labour intensive, low capital-intensive step is required to attach the circuitry, a backlight, and other parts to the cell in order to produce the finished panel.

The production technology used in the capital-intensive fabrication step is categorized by its generation, which indicates the size of glass substrate used (See Table 1). As the production technology matured, the use of larger and larger substrates became possible. With the increase in substrate size, production capacity also grew rapidly, as did the level of investment required. The most recent facilities, Generation 8 and 10, cost billions of US dollars to build.

Table 1. Substrate sizes and facility generations.

Generation	Construction years	Typical substrate dimensions (mm)	Substrate size in square meters
1G	1990–1993	300 × 400	0.12
2G	1993–1996	360 × 465	0.17
3G	1994–1999	550 × 650	0.36
4G	1999–2002	680 × 880	0.60
5G	2002–2003	1100 × 1250	1.38
6G	2002–2006	1500 × 1850	2.78
7G	2005–2008	1870 × 2200	4.11
8G	2005–2008	2200 × 2500	5.50
10G	2008–	2850 × 3050	8.69

Source: Compiled by the author from Deutsche Bank 2003; Fuji-Chimera 2006; Sangyo Times 2009.

Fabricating TFT-LCD panels was initially quite difficult because even minute contamination caused non-functioning pixels and therefore defective displays. Initial production yields were reportedly in the single digits. However, inter and intra firm cooperation in Japan resulted in better techniques and many improvements were built into subsequent generation production equipment. These improvements reduced the difficulty of new firms learning to produce LCD panels.

Evidence from early developments

Several Japanese firms initially started performing research on liquid crystals in the late 1960s. In the 1970s, segment LCDs (an early precursor to the technology examined here), were first commercialized, finding applications in watches and calculators. In the 1970s and 1980s, matrix designs using pixels emerged. Passive matrix (PM) LCD was introduced next. PM-LCD was a low image quality but low cost technology that could be made in relatively large sizes and which was used in early portable computing and word processing applications. Active matrix TFT-LCD, examined in this study, became a strong focus of attention in the industry because of its potential to make energy efficient, high image quality displays. Research and development on TFT-LCD began in the 1980s. Mass production facilities started to come on line in the early 1990s.

The majority of the focal firms initially focused on developing in-house TFT-LCD production capabilities. Of nine focal firms, seven built wholly owned early production TFT-LCD facilities (including pre-Generation 1 and Generation 1), and one other entered into a majority-owned joint venture to build such a plant. Figure 1 exhibits the investment

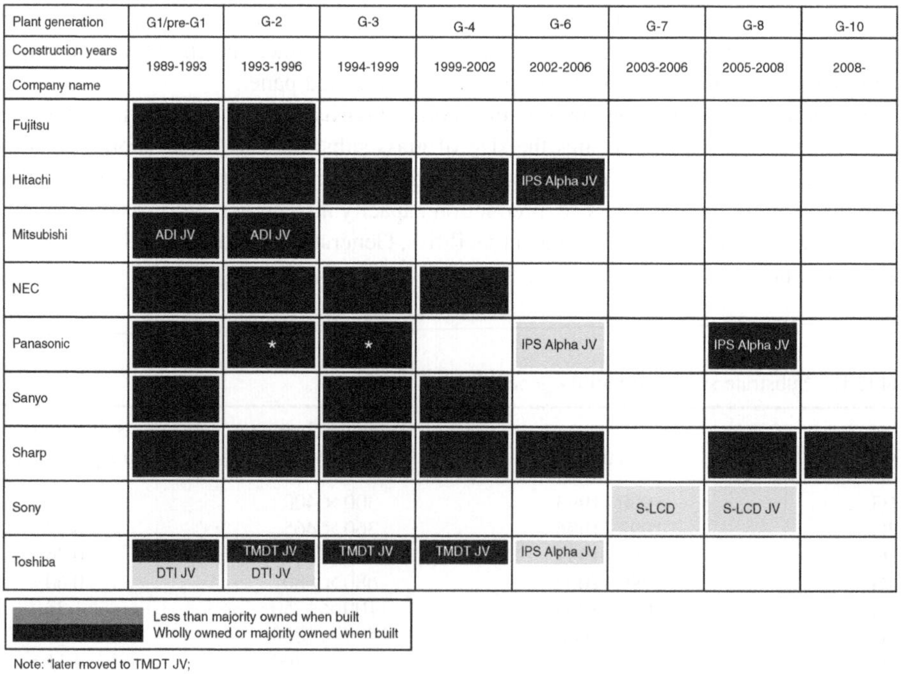

Plant generation	G1/pre-G1	G-2	G-3	G-4	G-6	G-7	G-8	G-10
Construction years / Company name	1989-1993	1993-1996	1994-1999	1999-2002	2002-2006	2003-2006	2005-2008	2008-
Fujitsu	■	■						
Hitachi	■	■	■	■	IPS Alpha JV			
Mitsubishi	ADI JV	ADI JV						
NEC	■	■	■	■				
Panasonic	■	*	*		IPS Alpha JV		IPS Alpha JV	
Sanyo	■		■	■				
Sharp	■	■	■	■	■		■	■
Sony						S-LCD	S-LCD JV	
Toshiba	DTI JV	TMDT JV / DTI JV	TMDT JV	TMDT JV	IPS Alpha JV			

Legend:
- (gray) Less than majority owned when built
- (black) Wholly owned or majority owned when built

Note: *later moved to TMDT JV;

Figure 1. Production facilities by generation, years the generation was built, and firm.
(*Source*: Compiled by author based upon Fuji Chimera (1998–2007), Nikkei BP (1990–2009), and Sangyo Times (1990, 1992–2009)).

by focal firms in the different generation production facilities. The pattern of investment in this early stage constitutes evidence of vertical integration being the predominant strategy amongst the focal firms in early stages of industry development. Information about early intermediate markets for displays is limited; however, it appears these markets were thin because most of the producers needed their production for assembly of finished goods. Competitors had idiosyncratic production capabilities; meaning one firm might be able to make a certain size display at a lower cost than competitors although it was unable to compete on other sizes. Sharp actively developed external markets for LCD panels, initially selling an inexpensive 8.4″ LCD for laptops, in addition to producing LCDs for internal supply.

As noted above, one firm entered into a cooperative arrangement taking a form of vertical quasi integration. This joint venture, Display Technology Incorporated, was formed by Toshiba and IBM, who were already cooperating on LCD R&D (Murtha, Lenway, and Hart 2001; West, Bowen, and Matsui 1997). The motivation behind this particular JV has been documented as being the supply of high quality LCD panels for usage in laptop computers produced by IBM and Toshiba (Sangyo Times 1990). Interestingly, Sony did not invest in LCD mass production at this stage, although it did investigate numerous flat panel technologies.

Growth, standardization, and the emergence of the crystal cycle

Later in the development of the industry, new generations of production equipment incorporated improvements that addressed many previous production difficulties and thereby increased yield. Because of this, the new equipment not only made it easier for existing firms to produce LCDs, but it also lowered the barriers to entry into LCD production.

Industry dynamics began to change as newer, high capacity production facilities came on line, and as some commonly used display types incorporating common size and resolution attributes began to become commoditized. The crystal cycle, a boom and bust cycle similar to that seen in some types of semiconductors, emerged as a result (Mathews 2005). The industry experienced dramatic price swings, and both panel shortages and gluts were observed depending on the stage of the cycle. The crystal cycle affected the integration strategies of Japanese firms and also facilitated the entry by foreign firms by lowering barriers to entry (Mathews 2005).

In 1995, oversupply led to price declines in LCD (Fuji-Chimera 2000), and South Korean firms began to enter the TFT-LCD market (Nikkei BP 1998). In 1996, panel prices increased as demand grew faster than capacity, although later in 1997 oversupply again plagued the industry and got worse in 1998 (Fuji-Chimera 2000; Nikkei BP 1999). It was during this period that Taiwanese firms started to enter (Nikkei BP 1998). This was arguably facilitated by earlier efforts by the Taiwanese government to strengthen research on LCD technology (Sangyo Times 1997).

When demand was tight, vertical integrated firms used most of their panel production to supply in-house demands, resulting in lost market opportunities for non-integrated firms ["2011-nen no Nihon Shijo: Jideji Baburu Hokai" (*Nikkei Business*, January 31, 2011: 25–29)]. However, when the LCD market was in oversupply, Japanese producers lost money on LCDs and reconsidered their investments (Nikkei BP 1999). Japanese firms often looked for ways to reduce exposure to commoditized areas of the display market while refocusing their LCD production activities on high margin segments. During these times, there is evidence of Japanese firms licensing patents, transferring technology, and otherwise facilitating the movement of production knowledge to Korea and Taiwan, although Mathews (2005) notes that Japanese firms did not license to either of the two major Korean firms, Samsung and LG. In the 1997–1998 period, for example, Toshiba, Mitsubishi, and Panasonic each developed relationships with foreign suppliers that included some aspect of technology transfer and/or licensing with contract manufacturing agreements (see Table 2). Entry also appears to have been facilitated by individual engineers who took positions or performed consulting with these overseas companies ("South Korea, Taiwan Firms Raid Japanese Staffs, Buy Technology: Companies Target High-End Research to Meet Demand" (*The Nikkei Weekly*, March 3, 1997: 20); Tabata 2012). Restructuring programmes implemented by Japanese firms may have inadvertently fed the supply of individual talent. Another factor that was reported to have facilitated entry was discounting by the production equipment manufacturers who needed revenue to maintain their business during these slumps (Nikkei BP 2002).

In the midst of these shifting industry dynamics, many of the Japanese firms modified their LCD strategies. Standardization of commonly used panel types and sizes facilitated market procurement of LCDs for use in assembly of finished goods, but market procurement increased the risks that firms would be unable to purchase the volume of panels they needed at prices that made business sense when the market supply became tight. As shown in Table 2, numerous firms pursued quasi integration with new entrants in other countries, providing technological know-how while obtaining access to supply. These firms often used strategies of partial integration where certain types of panels (by size, application, or level of standardization) were outsourced or purchased on the market, while others were made in-house. Joint ventures also played a role in quasi integration strategies. Below, two JVs, IPS-Alpha and S-LCD are discussed.

Table 2. International cooperative arrangements with one Japanese parent which include a combination of technology transfer or licensing and contract manufacturing.

Starting year	Companies involved	Partner country	Sources
1996	Toshiba – Hyundai	South Korea	Sangyo Times 1999.
1997	Mitsubishi (ADI) – CPT	Taiwan	Sangyo Times 1998; Nikkei BP 1998; Fuji-Chimera 2003.
1998	Panasonic – UMC (Unipaq)	Taiwan	Sangyo Times 1999; Fuji-Chimera 2000.
1998	Sharp – Quanta Note: JV in which Sharp takes stake	Taiwan	Fuji-Chimera 2000; Sangyo Times 2001; Techno Associates 2008.
1999	Fujitsu – CMO	Taiwan	Sangyo Times 2000 2002, 2005; Fuji-Chimera 2003
2000	Toshiba – HannStar	Taiwan	Sangyo Times 2000, 2001.
2001	NEC – CMO	Taiwan	Nikkei BP 2002; Sangyo Times 2002.
2002	NEC – SVA	PRC	Sangyo Times 2002 2003.
2002	Fujitsu – AUO Note: AUO takes 20% stake in Fujitsu Display: Technology	Taiwan	Sangyo Times 2003; Fuji-Chimera 2004.
2009	Sharp – CEC Note: JV with Sharp; will transplant existing Sharp line	PRC	Nikkan Kogyo Shimbun 2009.

IPS-Alpha

IPS-Alpha was established in 2005 to produce large, high quality LCDs for TV set applications. Initially, Hitachi controlled the JV with a 50% stake, while Panasonic and Toshiba each held 22.5%, and the Development Bank of Japan had a 5% stake (Hitachi Limited 2004; "Nihon Seisaku Toshi Ginko, Hitachi Toshiba Matsushita no Ekisho Goben Kaisha ni 20 oku en Shusshi." (*Reuters*, December 21, 2004. Retrieved from the *Factiva* Database)). The JV took advantage of Hitachi's high image quality LCD technology called in-plane switching (IPS), which was suitable for TV sets (den Boer 2005). IPS-Alpha provided quasi integration for its partners. As the president of the IPS-Alpha joint venture noted: 'Our shareholders are TV set manufacturers, who we provide vertically integrated supply' (Translated by Author from an interview in Nikkei BP 2007 (Senryaku Hen): 65). Despite its strength in LCD technology, Hitachi had been less successful in consumer TV sets than Panasonic or Toshiba. The relative stakes of the different partners changed at several points over time. In 2008, a series of developments resulted in agreement that Panasonic would acquire the stakes held by Hitachi and Toshiba to make IPS a wholly owned subsidiary (Hitachi Limited 2007, 2008a). Amongst the reasons given for this was Panasonic's intention of 'moving aggressively ahead with the enhancement of a vertically integrated business in the flat-panel TV sector' (Hitachi Limited 2007). Along with this plan was an announcement that IPS-Alpha would build a new facility closer to existing Panasonic plants (Hitachi Limited 2008b). Later, IPS-Alpha was renamed Panasonic LCD Company (Sangyo Times 2013). This move facilitated Panasonic's vertical integration in LCD. Prior to the acquisition, Panasonic had followed a strategy of vertical integration in plasma displays for its TV business.

S-LCD

S-LCD was a joint venture between Sony and South Korea's Samsung. In 2003, the two firms came to an initial agreement to form the JV to produce LCDs for TV sets (Sangyo Times 2004). Sony mainly provided capital and received access to high quality large LCD panels. The JV was set up in an existing Samsung location with a Generation 7 production line, where test production began in 2004 (Sangyo Times 2004). The partners continued with the agreement, adding capacity several times (Sangyo Times 2008). Eventually, Sony sold back its stake in S-LCD to Samsung (Sangyo Times 2013). While it continued, the arrangement constituted a form of quasi integration for Sony.

Industry consolidation

Later, the Japanese LCD industry consolidated as competitors exited the industry, as shown in the firm level observations, summarized in Table 3. Consolidation left only two companies, Sharp and Panasonic, that continued to follow relatively tight vertical integration using current generation production facilities. Both were large players in TV sets. Panasonic had previously been highly integrated in plasma displays and TV sets, but changed its focus to LCD. Sharp had been involved with many different LCD variants and considered LCD to be its main competency. Sony and Toshiba followed strategies of partial and quasi integration, while the remaining firms eventually exited LCD. Below, the firm level observations are discussed in more detail.

Table 3. Summary of firm level observations.

Firm	Early observation	Changes	State at end of study period
Fujitsu	Vertical integration	Entered cooperative arrangements with Taiwanese producers including technology transfer and outsourcing; Later sold LCD business to competitor	Exit – vertical de-integration
Hitachi	Vertical integration	Entered IPS-Alpha JV; later sold stake	Exit – vertical de-integration *Note:* Hitachi retained some small screen LCD production
Mitsubishi	Vertical integration	Entered cooperative arrangements with Taiwanese producers including technology transfer and outsourcing	Exit – vertical de-integration
NEC	Vertical integration	Entered cooperative arrangements with Taiwanese producers including technology transfer and outsourcing	Exit – vertical de-integration *Note:* NEC retained some specialized LCD production
Panasonic	Vertical integration	Switch from vertical integration of Plasma technology to vertical integration of LCD; acquired IPS-Alpha JV	Vertical integration
Sanyo	Vertical integration	Entered into JV with Seiko Epson, then exited LCD by selling stake	Exit – vertical de-integration
Sharp	Vertical integration	Repeatedly invested in cutting edge production facilities; Entered cooperative arrangements with Taiwanese producers including technology transfer and outsourcing	Vertical integration
Sony	Integration not observed	Performed quasi-integration JV with Samsung, but later sold stake. *Note:* during the study period, Sony acquired small screen LCD production capabilities including those formally belonging to International Display Technology JV and Seiko Epson	Did not ever become fully vertically integrated in a-Si LCD *Note:* Sony appears to have pursued vertical integration on other LCD technology such as LTPS and HTPS
Toshiba	Vertical integration + cooperation	Evidence of involvement in numerous cooperative arrangements including domestic IPS-Alpha JV and agreements with Korean and Taiwanese firms	Vertically de-integrated for TV and other common applications, but retains LCD production capability

Firm-level observations

Fujitsu

Fujitsu is an information technology firm. The company invested in plasma display technology in addition to LCD. In 1996 and 1997, Fujitsu announced important technological developments increasing the viewing angle of LCDs (Sangyo Times 1998). It initially invested in LCD production, and there is evidence that suggests it used a large percentage of its output in-house. The company announced it did not plan to develop LCDs for TV sets, but instead to focus on areas it was involved in, including computer, office automation, communication, and factory automation applications (Sangyo Times 1995). As standardized LCDs for computer applications became commoditized and prices fell, Fujitsu shifted to outsourcing for most of its supply, effectively moving from a vertical integration arrangement to quasi integration (Sangyo Times 2005). In 2005, Fujitsu exited LCDs, selling its LCD operations to Sharp (Sangyo Times 2006).

Hitachi

Hitachi is a diversified electronics and electrical equipment firm. It was an early mover into basic LCDs and holds some key patents of IPS LCD technology, a variant of LCD which has high image quality and broad viewing angle. In addition to LCD, Hitachi also developed plasma display technology. Industry observers suggested that Hitachi had some of the best LCD technology, although it had been unable to turn this into a major business success. Hitachi made products using LCDs and also sold displays. At the time Hitachi entered into the IPS-Alpha joint venture to supply TV set manufacturers, it maintained a separate display business for smaller applications; however, it later exited both.

Mitsubishi

Mitsubishi is a diversified electronics and electrical equipment firm. It made information technology and consumer electronics products using FPDs. Mitsubishi developed both LCD and Plasma display technology, exiting plasma very early on. It invested in early stage TFT LCD production, but made only limited follow-on investments. Mitsubishi started cooperating with its Taiwanese partner CPT in 1997, transferring technology to CPT while securing supply from CPT (Nikkei BP 1998). In 2002, Mitsubishi announced it was outsourcing all large volume LCD production to CPT and focusing on specialized LCDs for niche applications (Sangyo Times 2003). Mitsubishi exited LCDs production in 2006 (Sangyo Times 2008).

NEC

NEC is an information technology firm. In the first half of the 1990s, NEC enjoyed a leadership position in Japan in personal computers. NEC developed plasma display technology in addition to LCD. NEC invested in early production facilities for LCD. In 2001, NEC announced it was cooperating with Taiwanese firm CMO on display development and would outsource production of LCDs for laptop computers (Sangyo Times 2002). In 2002, it entered into a joint venture with SVA of China to produce LCDs, some of which were to be supplied to NEC (Sangyo Times 2003). This JV began production in 2005 using a Generation 5 facility (Sangyo Times 2005). Meanwhile, NEC refocused its existing internal production operations on specialized niches such as medicine (Sangyo Times 2005, 2009). After the end of the study, NEC's remaining

Japanese LCD operations were made part of a joint venture with a Chinese partner called Tianma, which also bought the production facility formerly belonging to NEC's JV with SVA (Sangyo Times 2013).

Panasonic

Panasonic is a diversified electronics firm. The company invested into early generations of LCD production, and then placed its operations in a joint venture called Toshiba Matsushita Display Technology, in which its partner, Toshiba, held the controlling stake (Fuji-Chimera 2002). Panasonic invested heavily into plasma technology and maintained vertically integrated Plasma TV set production including displays and the semiconductors used to drive the TV sets, for a long period of time (Akimoto, Endo, and Shibata 2005). It later decided that LCD was a better TV technology, and changed to LCD, acquiring the IPS-Alpha JV (Nikkei BP 2009). While Panasonic changed the display technology it used in TV sets, its vertical integration strategy did not change. This is in keeping with Panasonic's reputation for preferring vertical integration.

Sharp

Sharp is an electronics firm, and is known for commercializing products that incorporate LCDs. Amongst Japanese firms, it is the only one that continued to make investments in cutting-edge LCD production facilities throughout the study period. Former Sharp managers interviewed stated that the company's main strength was its competitive advantage in LCD technology. Sharp used some LCD production to supply internal demand and also sold some output to other firms, although it developed the reputation of supplying its internal demand first (Akiba 2009.). In TV sets, Sharp was more integrated than its competitors, using 100% internally made panels in the late 2000s ["Uredomouredomo Mokaranai Usugata Terebi Yotsu no Gosan no Shinkoku" (*Shukan Daiyamondo*, February 21, 2009: 52–55)]. Sharp's *Kameyama* facility produced TV set LCDs and assembled them into finished TV sets (Sangyo Times 2002). Sharp advertising promoted the high quality of its *Kameyama* models. However, the company may not be as directly integrated as it was in the past because it is trying to sell into markets such as cell phone displays, where it does not have a strong presence in the end product markets. Sharp has worked with several foreign companies to outsource commoditized displays. In the past, Sharp attempted to protect its proprietary LCD knowledge; however, the company also saw the need to be able to source or produce in other countries which have lower input, utility, and transportation costs than Japan (Lehmberg 2011).

Sanyo

Sanyo was an electronics firm that was taken over by Panasonic in 2009. Sanyo had a long history of involvement with LCD technology, and was the first to successfully develop a colour active matrix LCD using a-Si (Sangyo Times 1994). Sanyo's initial TFT-LCD production was used in portable TV sets, 8 mm video decks, projectors, and other audio video applications (Sangyo Times 1990). However, Sanyo later built LCD production capacity in its device business unit, which was not closely integrated with Sanyo's other product lines (Deutsche Bank 2003). While Sanyo produced both LCD TV sets and TV set panels, it did not self-supply. In 2004, Sanyo and Seiko Epson launched a joint venture that included Sanyo's LCD operations (Fuji-Chimera 2004; "Seiko Epuson, Sanyo Denki to

Goben Kaisha Ekisho Jigyo de 10-gatsu Medo" (*Yomiuri Shimbun*, March 25, 2004. Retrieved from the *Factiva* Database)). Sanyo sold its stake in the JV to Epson in 2006, effectively exiting LCD ["Sanyo Denki Ekisho kara Tettai: Goben Kaisha no Zenkabu Baikyaku Keieishigen, Koritsu Hakaru" (*Yomiuri Shimbun*, December 14, 2006. Retrieved from the *Factiva* Database)].

Sony

Sony is a consumer electronics and entertainment company. The company was unusual for this study in that it did not invest in early TFT-LCD production facilities, and it did not engage in vertical integration for a-Si LCD. Sony followed different approaches for small and large panels. Sony did not enter large panel LCD production on its own, but rather became a partner in the S-LCD joint venture with Samsung, which was a major producer. This gave Sony a form of quasi integration. Sony did have some integrated production for specialized LCDs using LTPS or HTPS LCD variants (for example, video camera eyepiece and LCD projector displays), and also integrated production of small to middle sized displays, including those used in smart phones. It is interesting that Sony did not backward integrate in TV set displays given the fact that the Sony Trinitron CRT played a large role in building Sony's brand in the past.

Toshiba

Toshiba is a diversified electronics and electrical equipment firm, which had significant market share in laptop computers and some other kinds of consumer electronics incorporating LCDs. Toshiba developed LCD technology internally and entered into cooperative arrangements with IBM both on LCD R&D and to build a LCD mass-production capacity (Murtha, Lenway, and Hart 2001). Compared with other Japanese firms in the industry, Toshiba entered into a large number of cooperative arrangements with other firms relating to display technologies, including the joint ventures Display Technologies Incorporated with IBM, Toshiba Matsushita Display Technologies (TMDT), a Singapore based JV with Matsushita called AFPD, the IPS-Alpha JV, and SED Inc., a JV with Canon. By the end of 2009, all of these arrangements had been dissolved, with Toshiba acquiring all of TMDT and selling its stakes in the other ventures. Toshiba also cooperated with numerous non-Japanese LCD firms, including at least two that provided Toshiba with a supply of panels (See Table 2). Overall, Toshiba's approach appears to have included many different sources of quasi integration, including Japanese and non-Japanese partners.

Discussion

This study has examined Japanese electronics and IT firms' vertical integration of LCD over time. At the stage where mass production first became possible, most of the firms entered into LCD production. Then, as production technology improved and overall volume increased, the crystal cycle (Mathews 2005) emerged and the industry started to experience large price swings, amidst increasing standardization and commoditization. The study observed that many Japanese firms changed their strategy to include some form of outsourcing in response. Towards the end of the study, a more distinct pattern emerged, with each of the companies following one of the following approaches: full de-integration, partial integration, and maintenance of full vertical integration.

The vertical integration literature emphasizes the importance of firm specific, industry specific, and timing specific, and other situational factors on the effectiveness of vertical integration strategies (e.g. Harrigan 1984). However, extant literature includes several predictions about how firms will change their level of integration over the span of the industry lifecycle (Chandler 1977; Harrigan 1984, 1985; Jacobides 2005; Macher and Mowery 2004; Stigler 1951). While there is some contradiction between these predictions, the majority suggest that industries start off with high levels of vertical integration, which tend to decrease after some point. The findings of this study are in agreement with these predictions.

Early on, LCD production volumes were low and the value of the output was high. Market supply of LCD panels was uncertain and expensive. Relying on outside supply therefore meant potentially losing market opportunities for the end products incorporating LCDs. Meanwhile, firms also appear to have been motivated by the opportunity to pioneer a new industry, which most observers believed would eventually become a large one.

As the production technology improved and the industry structure evolved, LCD became more risky from a financial standpoint. Standardization, commoditization, new entry, and substantial increases in production capacity put severe downward pressure on prices. These changes served as reason for less efficient producers to leave the industry, cooperate with one or more efficient producers, or seek niche markets which could be served by small volume specialized production. Furthermore, full integration strategies became infeasible for many firms because the large output of cost-efficient large-scale production facilities was substantially greater than their in-house demand (Porter 1980).

Product architecture appears to have played a role in facilitating de-integration of LCD (Baldwin and Clark 2000). In a process study of de-integration in the mortgage lending industry, Jacobides (2005) found that simplification of coordination between stages in the value chain (Porter 1985), and information standardization (simplifying communication between different stages in the value chain) were necessary conditions to vertical de-integration. As the industry progressed, many LCD panel specifications, such as resolution, and interfaces with LCD panels were standardized. This meant that assemblers of products using LCDs did not need to have deep knowledge about LCD fabrication or tight integration between panel production and final product assembly. This was a change from the situation with CRT technology, which LCDs replaced in many instances. In the case of CRT-TV for example, vertical integration appears to have played a key role in all of the major Japanese producers' strategies as it allowed the firms to improve the quality of the final product. It is possible that the Japanese firms involved brought the mentality of what had worked in CRT and tried to apply it to LCD. However, as Afuah (2001) argued, as technologies underlying the firm's key products change, so do the set of activities it can efficiently undertake. Altogether, the observed changes in vertical integration by Japanese firms over the study period do not depart from what might be expected according to the general literature on vertical integration (i.e. the literature that does not explicitly consider the Japanese context).

One of the aims of this paper was to examine whether the observations represent a departure from traditional Japanese strategies. Vertical integration strategies have been historically popular in Japan; however, evidence from this study suggests Japanese firms have become open to alternative strategies. Instead of full integration, many of the Japanese firms eventually adopted quasi integration or non-integration strategies. These observations are in agreement with recent articles in the Japanese business press suggesting that attitudes towards vertical integration may be changing. Saiki (2014) stated the prevailing attitude in the electronics industry is that vertical integration is not profitable in TV sets. An article in the Japanese business press titled "Uredomouredomo Mokaranai Usugata Terebi Yotsu no Gosan no Shinkoku" (*Shukan Daiyamondo*, February 21, 2009: 52–55) noted that while vertical integration can be advantageous where a difficult to copy input is the source of meaningful differentiation in the end product, in other cases 'the vertical integration model is no longer advantageous in terms of the end product's quality or differentiation. Rather, its comparatively high costs are a weakness.' Vertical integration strategies have been blamed as a reason why Japanese firms lost their position in both solar collectors and semiconductors ("Chizumu Kozoteki Mondai: Kurikaesu Tyoraku no Rekishi." (*Nikkei Business* April 2, 2012, 54–57); Sano 2012).

Quasi integration arrangements observed in this study often included knowledge transfer to non-Japanese firms in addition to sourcing agreements. Such arrangements reduced any knowledge-based advantage held by the Japanese firms, which contrasts with the commonly held perception of Japanese firms jealously protecting their technology. Why Japanese firms became so willing to give up control over the technology in this particular situation is a matter of conjecture. Perhaps firms believed the benefits of quasi integration were sufficiently large as to counter-balance the action. Another possibility is that the firms realized that they could not protect their knowledge-based advantage. The fact that Samsung and LG were able to enter without licensing would support this argument. Additionally, once the first Japanese firm began to cooperate with an overseas partner, its competitors may have realized that it was only a matter of time until LCD know-how spread.

In the past, Japanese firms have often been characterized as being ethnocentric, favouring doing business with other Japanese firms instead of foreign companies, and staffing foreign operations with higher levels of expatriates than firms from other countries (Beechler et al. 2004; Black and Morrison 2010; Kopp 1994; Trevor 1983; Westney 2001). The developments observed here suggest substantial changes to the mind-set of the Japanese manager, including decreased ethnocentrism and increased openness to exploring new alternatives. The difficult nature of the industry may have facilitated this more open stance.

This study provides additional evidence in agreement with newer research showing the Japanese firms are moving away from a conceptualization of cooperation that is constrained by tradition, and are adopting a willingness to become involved with a more diverse set of partners (Lincoln and Guillot 2011; Okada 2008). Overall, these findings are consistent with an interpretation that Japanese firms are placing reduced emphasis on following institutional norms to become more driven by economic realities. They also provide evidence that Japanese electronic firms are moving away from 'symmetric strategies' (Porter, Takeuchi, and Sakakibara 2000, 84) to adopt more unique, firm specific strategies.

This study has several limitations. The study is based upon publicly available data on the LCD industry. This data has the benefit of being verifiable; however, it is limited. Greater access to the amount of internal consumption of LCD production was not available but would have bolstered the study. Furthermore, because this study was unable to observe internal decision-making processes, it can describe what firms did but not always why. Interviews conducted with industry players and published interviews taken together provide a general sense of rationale taken but do not support a fine-grained analysis.

Implications

Some have argued that Japanese management is changing to become more aligned with economic reality and less influenced by Japan-specific institutions and historic relationships (e.g. Lincoln and Guillot 2011; Schaede 2008). This study uncovered some evidence of Japanese electronics firms that changed and left their traditional comfort zones, by de-integrating previously vertically integrated LCD operations and by developing cooperative arrangements including technology transfer and outsourcing with overseas firms. The findings demonstrate that Japanese firms can and will adopt non-traditional strategies when sufficient economic rationale dictates.

Company strategies are made and implemented in the context of national institutions as well as the economic, competitive, and technological context under which the firm operates. Japanese institutions, in particular those relating to HR practices and the labour market, have proved to be slow to adjust to other changes in the environment, despite calls for change from Japan watchers amongst others. When interpreting the findings of study such as this one, therefore, it is important to bear in mind the sometimes contradictory requirements of economic, institutional, and other requirements placed on the firm in the Japanese context, and the resulting difficult to resolve tensions these incongruities place on some management decisions.

As the LCD industry matured, the crystal cycle emerged, making LCD a more difficult and risky industry to do business in due to high and increasing investment requirements to produce at economic scale combined with large swings in LCD prices (Mathews 2005). In this challenging environment, firms that lost money in the downturns of the crystal cycle may have been willing to consider actions they otherwise would not have, in order to avoid facing yet greater difficulties in the future. Given this, one way to interpret the findings of this study is to consider the severity of the economic consequences of not adopting relatively radical change. From the firm's perspective, the need to avoid these downsides may have been important enough to offset the negatives involved in embracing radical change. If this was the case, management was making a choice between two different, but uncomfortable, outcomes. Therefore, this study does not necessarily constitute evidence of a fundamental swing in managerial attitudes in Japan.

Conclusion

The findings of this research suggest that Japanese firms – which have been described as being reluctant about internationalization (Trevor 1983) – are now more open to international cooperation than in the past. Japanese managers may be adopting a more open stance towards working with new kinds of partners, and making sourcing decisions based largely upon economic repercussions. Despite this, it is worth bearing in mind that Japanese firms continue to face unique challenges when internationalizing, such as difficulties in managing workforces comprising mixed nationalities, and learning how to harness from diversity instead of depending on homogeneity, as is common in Japan. Some of these challenges are ones which many Japanese managers would most likely prefer to avoid, but may learn to embrace if economic reality dictates.

Acknowledgements

The author would like to thank Satomi Funahashi, Kensuke Kishikawa, Rod White, and Paul Beamish for their help and support of this research.

References

Afuah, A. 2001. "Dynamic Boundaries of the Firm: Are Firms Better off Being Vertically Integrated in the Face of a Technological Change?" *The Academy of Management Journal* 44 (6): 1211–1228. doi:10.2307/3069397.

Ahmadjian, C. L., and J. R. Lincoln. 2001. "Keiretsu, Governance, and Learning: Case Studies in Change from the Japanese Automotive Industry." *Organization Science* 12 (6): 683–701. doi:10.1287/orsc.12.6.683.10086.

Akiba, D. 2009. "Saihen: 'Dejitaru no Wana'." *Nikkei Business*, December 14, 2009: 105–107.

Akimoto, D., N. Endo, and M. Shibata. 2005. "Matsushita Denki Fukkatsu he no Shito." *Shukan Daiyamondo*, October 1, 2005: 30–46.

Argyres, N. 1996. "Evidence on the Role of Firm Capabilities in Vertical Integration Decisions." *Strategic Management Journal* 17 (2): 129–150. doi:10.1002/(SICI)1097-0266(199602) 17:2<129:AID-SMJ798>3.0.CO;2-H.

Arrow, K. J. 1975. "Vertical Integration and Communication." *The Bell Journal of Economics* 6 (1): 173–183. doi:10.2307/3003220.

Balakrishnan, S., and B. Wernerfelt. 1986. "Technical Change, Competition and Vertical Integration." *Strategic Management Journal* 7 (4): 347–359. doi:10.1002/smj.4250070405.

Baldwin, C. Y., and K. B. Clark. 2000. *Design Rules: Volume 1, The Power of Modularity*. Cambridge, MA: MIT Press.

Barney, J. B. 1999. "How a Firm's Capabilities Affect Boundary Decisions." *Sloan Management Review* 40 (3): 137–145.

Beechler, S., V. Pucik, J. Stephan, and N. Campbell. 2004. "The Transnational Challenge: Performance and Expatriate Presence in the Overseas Affiliates of Japanese MNCs." In *Advances in International Management Volume 17, Japanese firms in Transition: Responding to the Globalization Challenge*, Joseph C. Cheng and Michael A. Hitt (Series eds), edited by Tom Roehl and Allan Bird, 215–242. Amsterdam: Elsevier.

Black, J. S., and A. J. Morrison. 2010. *Sunset in the Land of the Rising Sun: Why Japanese Multinational Corporations will Struggle in the Global Future*. New York: Palgrave Macmillan.

Bresnahan, T. F., and J. D. Levin. 2013. "Vertical Integration and Market Structure." In *The Handbook of Organizational Economics*, edited by Robert Gibbons and John Roberts, 853–890. Princeton, NJ: Princeton University Press.

Chandler, A. D., Jr. 1977. *The Visible Hand: The Managerial Revolution in American Business*. Cambridge, MA: Harvard University Press.

Contractor, F. J., and P. Lorange. 1988. "Why Should Firms Cooperate? The Strategy and Economics Basis for Cooperative Ventures." In *Cooperative Strategies in International Business: Joint Ventures and Technology Partnerships Between Firms*, edited by F. J. Contractor and P. Lorange. 2nd ed., pp. 3–30. Kidlington, Oxford: Elsevier Science.

D'Aveni, R. A., and D. J. Ravenscraft. 1994. "Economies of Integration versus Bureaucracy Costs: Does Vertical Integration Improve Performance?" *The Academy of Management Journal* 37 (5): 1167–1206. doi:10.2307/256670.

den Boer, W. 2005. *Active Matrix Liquid Crystal Displays: Fundamentals And Applications*. Burlington, MA: Newness.

Deutsche Bank. 2003. *Sanyo Electric*, October 10, 2003. Retrieved from the *InvestText* database.

Dore, R., and M. Sako. 1989. *How The Japanese Learn To Work*. New York: Routledge.

Eisenhardt, K. M. 1989. "Building Theories from Case Study Research." *Academy of Management Review* 14 (4): 532–550. doi:10.5465/AMR.1989.4308385.

Fronmueller, M. P., and R. Reed. 1996. "The Competitive Advantage Potential of Vertical Integration." *Omega* 24 (6): 715–726. doi:10.1016/S0305-0483(96)00011-4.

Fuji-Chimera 1998–2007. 2012. *Ekisho Kanren Shijo no Genjo to Shorai Tenbo*. Tokyo: Fuji-Chimera Research Institute. (Published annually).

Fukui, Y., and T. Ushijima. 2007. "Corporate Diversification, Performance, and Restructuring in the Largest Japanese Manufacturers." *Journal of Japanese and International Economies* 21: 303–323. doi:10.1016/j.jjie.2006.06.002.

Gemba, K., and F. Kodama. 2001. "Diversification Dynamics of the Japanese Industry." *Research Policy* 30 (8): 1165–1184. doi:10.1016/S0048-7333(00)00140-2.

Hareyama, T. 2005. *Nihon Chingin Kanri-shi.* Tokyo: Bunshindo.

Harrigan, K. R. 1984. "Formulating Vertical Integration Strategies." *The Academy of Management Review* 9 (4): 638–652. doi:10.5465/AMR.1984.4277387.

Harrigan, K. R. 1985. "Vertical Integration and Corporate Strategy." *The Academy of Management Journal* 28 (2): 397–425. doi:10.2307/256208.

Harrigan, K. R. 1986. "Matching Vertical Integration Strategies to Competitive Conditions." *Strategic Management Journal* 7 (6): 535–555. doi:10.1002/smj.4250070605.

Hill, C. W. 1995. "National Institutional Structures, Transaction Cost Economizing and Competitive Advantage: The Case of Japan." *Organization Science* 6 (1): 119–131. doi:10.1287/orsc.6.1.119.

Hitachi Corporation. 2004. "Hitachi, Toshiba and Matsushita Conclude Agreement For Establishment of TV LCD Panel Joint Venture, IPS-Alpha Technology." October 29, 2004. http://www.hitachi.com/New/cnews/041029a_041029a.pdf

Hitachi Limited. 2007. "Hitachi, Canon and Matsushita reach basic agreement on LCD panel business." December 25. http://www.hitachi.com/New/cnews/f_071225.pdf

Hitachi Limited. 2008a. "Conclusion of Formal Contract Between Hitachi and Matsushita Related to Comprehensive LCD Panel Business Alliance." February 15, 2008. www.hitachi.com/New/cnews/f_080215a.pdf

Hitachi Limited. 2008b. "IPS-Alpha Technology to build state of the art IPS LCD Panel Plant in Himeji City, Hyogo Prefecture." February 15, 2008. http://www.hitachi.com/New/cnews/080215c.pdf

Hofstede, G. 2001. *Culture's Consequences.* Thousand Oaks, CA: Sage.

Imai, K., and R. Komiya. 1994. "Characteristics of Japanese firms." *Business Enterprise in Japan: View of Leading Japanese Economists*, Japanese version edited by K. Imai and R. Komiya; English translation edited by R. Dore and H. Whittaker., pp. 19–38. Cambridge, MA: MIT Press.

Inagami, T., and D. H. Whittaker. 2005. *The New Community Firm: Employment, Governance and Management Reform in Japan.* Cambridge: Cambridge University Press.

Jacobides, M. G. 2005. "Industry Change through Vertical Disintegration: How and Why Markets Emerged in Mortgage Banking." *The Academy of Management Journal* 48 (3): 465–498. doi:10.5465/AMJ.2005.17407912.

Jacobides, M. G., and S. Billinger. 2006. "Designing the Boundaries of the Firm: From 'Make, Buy, or Ally' to the Dynamic Benefits of Vertical Architecture." *Organization Science* 17 (2): 249–261. doi:10.1287/orsc.1050.0167.

Jacobides, M. G., and S. G. Winter. 2005. "The Co-Evolution of Capabilities and Transaction Costs: Explaining the Institutional Structure of Production." *Strategic Management Journal* 26 (5): 395–413. doi:10.1002/smj.460.

Johnstone, B. 1999. *We Were Burning: Japanese Entrepreneurs and the Forging of the Electronic Age.* New York: Basic Books.

Klein, B. 1988. "Vertical Integration as Organizational Ownership: The Fisher Body-General Motors Relationship Revisited." *Journal of Law, Economics, and Organization* 4 (1): 199–213.

Klepper, S. 1997. "Industry Life Cycles." *Industrial and Corporate Change* 6 (1): 145–182. doi:10.1093/icc/6.1.145.

Kopp, R. 1994. *The Rice-paper Ceiling.* Berkeley, CA: Stone Bridge Press.

Langlois, R. 1992. "Transaction Cost Economics in Real Time." *Industrial and Corporate Change* 1: 99–127. doi:10.1093/icc/1.1.99.

Langlois, R. N. 2003. "The Vanishing Hand: the Changing Dynamics of Industrial Capitalism." *Industrial and Corporate Change* 12 (2): 351–385. doi:10.1093/icc/12.2.351.

Lawrence, B. 1984. "Historical Perspective: Using the Past to Study the Present." *Academy of Management Review* 9 (2): 307–312. doi:10.5465/AMR.1984.4277663.

Lehmberg, D. 2011. "Sharp Corporation: Beyond Japan." Ivey Case Publishing no. 9B11M007.

Lehmberg, D. 2014. "From Advantage to Handicap: Traditional Japanese HRM and the Case for Change." *Organizational Dynamics* 43 (2): 146–153.

Leiblein, M. J., and D. J. Miller. 2003. "An Empirical Examination of Transaction- and Firm-Level Influences on the Vertical Boundaries of the Firm." *Strategic Management Journal* 24 (9): 839–859. doi:10.1002/smj.340.

Lincoln, J. R., and D. Guillot. 2011. "Business Groups, Networks, and Embeddedness: Innovation and Implementation Alliances in Japanese Electronics, 1985–1998." Institute for Research on Labor and Employment. (Working paper). https://escholarship.org/uc/item/35g695gn

Macher, J. T., and D. C. Mowery. 2004. "Vertical Specialization and Industry Structure in High Technology Industries." In *Advances in Strategic Management, Vol. 21: Collaboration and Competition in Business Ecosystems*, edited by Joel A. C. Baum and Anita M. McGahan, 317–355. Amsterdam: Elsevier.

Mathews, J. A. 2005. "Strategy and the Crystal Cycle." *California Management Review* 47 (2): 6–32.

McGuire, J., and S. Dow. 2009. "Japanese Keiretsu: Past, Present and Future." *Asia Pacific Journal of Management* 26 (2): 333–351. doi:10.1007/s10490-008-9104-5.

Miwa, Y. 1994. *Business Enterprise In Japan: View of Leading Japanese Economists*, Japanese version edited by K. Imai and R. Komiya; English translation edited by R. Dore and H. Whittaker., 140–155. Cambridge, MA: MIT Press.

Murtha, T., S. Lenway, and J. Hart. 2001. *Managing New Industry Creation: Global Knowledge Formation and Entrepreneurship in High Technology*. Stanford, CA: Stanford Business Books.

Nikkei BP. 1990–2009 (Published annually). *Flat Panel Display*. Tokyo: Nikkei BP.

Noguchi, Y. 2012. *Nihonshiki Monodukuri no Haisen: Naze Beichu Kigyo ni Katenakunatta no ka*. Tokyo: Toyokeizai Shinpo-Sha.

Nonaka, I., and H. Takeuchi. 1995. *The Knowledge-Creating Company: How Japanese Companies Create the Dynamics of Innovation*. Oxford: Oxford University Press.

Numagami, T. 1999. *Ekisho disupurei no gijutsu kakushin-shi*. Tokyo: Hakuto-Shobo.

Numagami, T., M. Karube, and T. Kato. 2010. "Organizational Deadweight: Learning from Japan." *The Academy of Management Perspectives* 24 (4): 25–37. doi:10.5465/AMP.2010.24.4.3651478.a.

Okada, Y. 2008. "From Vertical to Horizontal Inter-Firm Cooperation: Dynamic Innovation in Japan's Semiconductor Industry." *Asia Pacific Business Review* 14 (3): 379–400. doi:10.1080/13602380802116799.

Osegowitsch, T., and A. Madhok. 2003. "Vertical Integration is Dead, or Is It?" *Business Horizons* 46 (2): 25–34. doi:10.1016/S0007-6813(03)00006-5.

Peng, M. W. 2002. "Towards an Institution-Based View of Business Strategy." *Asia Pacific Journal of Management* 19 (2–3): 251–267. doi:10.1023/A:1016291702714.

Perry, M. K. 1989. "Vertical Integration: Determinants and Effects." In *Handbook of Industrial Organization*, edited by R. Schmalensee and R. D. Willig. 1, 183–255. Amsterdam: Elsevier.

Porter, M. E. 1980. *Competitive Strategy*. New York, NY: Free Press.

Porter, M. E. 1985. *Competitive Advantage*. New York, NY: Free Press.

Porter, M. E., and M. Sakakibara. 2004. "Competition in Japan." *The Journal of Economic Perspectives* 18 (1): 27–50. doi:10.1257/089533004773563421.

Porter, M. E., H. Takeuchi, and M. Sakakibara. 2000. *Can Japan Compete?* Cambridge, MA: Basic Books.

Quinn, J. B., and F. G. Hilmer. 1994. "Strategic Outsourcing." *Sloan Management Review* 35 (4): 43–55.

Rothaermel, F. T., M. A. Hitt, and L. A. Jobe. 2006. "Balancing Vertical Integration and Strategic Outsourcing: Effects on Product Portfolio, Product Success, and Firm Performance." *Strategic Management Journal* 27 (11): 1033–1056. doi:10.1002/smj.559.

Saiki, S. 2014. "Seiko Epuson Seimitsu Kiki Suichoku Togo ni Kodawaru." *Nikkei Business*, May 12, 2014: 48–52.

Sangyo Times. 1990, 1992–2009. *LCD, PDP, EL Meka Keikaku*. Tokyo: Sangyo Times.

Sano, S. 2012. *Handotai Suitai no Genin to Ikinokori no Kagi*. Tokyo: Nikkan Kogyo Shimbunsha.

Saxenian, A. 1994. *Regional Advantage: Culture and Competition in Silicon Valley and Route 128*. Cambridge, MA: Harvard University Press.

Schaede, U. 2008. *Choose and Focus: Japanese Business Strategies for the 21st Century*. Ithaca, NY: Cornell University Press.

"Sharpu Dai-6 Sedai Ekisho-sochi wo Chugoku CEC Panda ni Baiyaku." *Nikkan Klygyo Shimbun*, September 1, 2009.

Sichel, W. 1973. "Vertical Integration as a Dynamic Industry Concept." *Antitrust Bulletin* 18: 463–482.

Stigler, G. J. 1951. "The Division of Labor is Limited by the Extent of the Market." *Journal of Political Economy* 59 (3): 185–193.

Stuckey, J., and D. White. 1993. "When and When not to Vertically Integrate." *McKinsey Quarterly* 3: 3–27.

Sturgeon, T. J. 2006. "Modular Production's Impact on Japan's Electronics Industry." In *Recovering from Success: Innovation and Technology Management in Japan*, edited by D. H. Whittaker and R. E. Cole, 47–69. Oxford: Oxford University Press.

Sturgeon, T. J. 2007. "How Globalization Drives Institutional Diversity." *Journal of East Asian Studies* 7 (1): 1–34.

Tabata, M. 2012. "The Absorption of Japanese Engineers into Taiwan's TFT-LCD Industry: Globalization and Transnational Talent Diffusion." *Asian Survey* 52 (3): 571–594.

Tabeta, N. 1998. "The Kigyo Keiretsu Organization and Opportunism in the Japanese Automobile Manufacturing Industry." *Asia Pacific Journal of Management* 15 (1): 1–18. doi:10.1023/A:1015428707475.

Techno Associates. 2008. *LCD Paneru Meka no Jigyo Senryaku Kenkyu 2008*. Tokyo: Nikkei BP.

Trevor, M. 1983. *Japan's Reluctant Multinationals: Japanese Management at Home and Abroad*. New York, NY: St. Martin's Press.

Utterback, J. M., and F. F. Suarez. 1993. "Innovation, Competition, and Industry Structure." *Research Policy* 22 (1): 1–21. doi:10.1016/0048-7333(93)90030-L.

West, J., H. K. Bowen, and R. Matsui. 1997. "Display Technologies, Inc." Harvard Business School Case: 9-697-117.

Westney, E. 2001. "Japan." In *The Oxford Handbook of International Business*, edited by Allan M. Rugman and Thomas L. Brewer, 623–651. Oxford: Oxford University Press.

Williamson, O. E. 1971. "The Vertical Integration of Production: Market Failure Considerations." *The American Economic Review* 61 (2): 112–123.

Williamson, O. E. 1985. *The Economic Institutions of Capitalism*. New York: Free Press.

Witt, M. A. 2006. *Changing Japanese Capitalism: Societal Coordination and Institutional Adjustment*. Cambridge, MA: Cambridge University Press.

Yin, R. K. 2014. *Case Study Research: Design and Methods*. 5th ed. Thousand Oaks, CA: Sage.

Strategic capabilities and the emergence of the global factory: Omron in China

Robert Fitzgerald and Jiangfeng Lai

Royal Holloway, University of London, London, UK

Omron Shanghai provides a detailed case study of a multinational subsidiary's long-term evolution. The study assesses three streams of international business literature that emphasize the seemingly competing roles of parent firm strategy, national institutions or local management in the development of subsidiaries. It looks at each business function separately to reveal which capabilities were effectively transferred from Japan to China. In tracing Omron Shanghai's development from international joint venture into wholly owned enterprise and then global factory, it is the strategic intent of the parent multinational corporations that emerges as the consistent formative influence on management practices and capabilities.

Introduction

Those theorists credited discovering the multinational corporation (MNC) as a subject in its own right were concerned with two issues: the rationale of any parent firm undertaking the costly and time-consuming process of creating a subsidiary overseas, and the strategic direction and control exercised by the parent MNC, because of its cross-border transfer of 'ownership' advantages in products, technology or management, over its subsidiaries. Undoubtedly, there were strong trends particular to the post-war global economy – such as the dominance of managerially and technologically advanced manufacturing MNCs from the USA, pursuing market-seeking strategies by creating smaller versions of the main company within host nations – that shaped the original ideas about International Business. The first theorists said little about how capabilities could be transferred, and they offered few insights into how internal management structures could ensure the effective use of capabilities in overseas subsidiaries once transferred. Again, for the immediate post-war decades, the historical evidence shows minimal interaction between the headquarters and its subsidiary, despite or because of expatriate managers and technicians.

The conversion of Japanese manufacturers into MNCs, during the course of the 1980s, and notably their arrival in the developed economies of the USA and Western Europe generated fresh insights about the aims of FDI. It additionally, if temporarily, re-confirmed the potency of the parent firm: Japanese manufacturers had evolved capabilities in production, skills, human resources and products within their home economy, and they had strong reason to transfer what was perceived as global 'best practice' to their new subsidiaries. Subsequent studies questioned the extent to which home nation practices could be relocated and the very concept of global best practice. Supported by empirical evidence, they additionally noted examples of host country adaptation. The stagnation of the Japanese economy, after 1990, reinforced doubts about the usefulness as well as the universal applicability of its companies' management and systems.

While the majority of FDI stock can still be found in developed economies, investment flows have switched to emerging and transition economies, since the mid-1990s, and most dramatically in the case of China. Nonetheless, there have been few studies of Japanese subsidiary operations and their capabilities in developing nations in general and in China in particular. Due to differences in levels of economic development between the two countries, and China's policy aim of using inward investment to acquire technological and managerial know-how, Japanese MNCs had both the strategic intent and the opportunity to transfer their practices to their subsidiaries. What is needed as a result is a comprehensive exploration of which systems or capabilities a Japanese firm would choose to transplant to China, and the effects of local, institutional or practical factors on its ability to implement its strategy. A longitudinal approach allows a full assessment of the transfer and management of subsidiary-level capabilities, since the mid-1990s, and an analysis of developments in subsidiaries and their capabilities, since the mid-2000s. We can discover, too, if advances in International Business or IB theory – including the idea of the 'global factory' – can fully help explain the recent strategies of Japanese MNCs in China. At the heart of the debate is the ability of the parent firm or the headquarters to exercise supervision of a subsidiary in a host economy versus the extent that subsidiary is nationally embedded. More recently, the emergence of more globalized, networked and interdependent MNCs – replacing the structure of a core parent firm and dependent subsidiaries – was founded on the enhancement of subsidiary capabilities and the consequent decline of parent control. It is possible, on the other hand, that parent MNCs are founding production headquarters, called global factories, and increasing control of their business through a mix of ownership, control, planning and contracts. Japanese electronic enterprises in China, and Omron in particular, provide clear insights into the competing factors of parent company capabilities and strategic intent, national institutions, subsidiary level agency and globalizing tendencies.

Literature review: FDI theory and the subsidiary
Parent MNC and strategic capabilities

As is often recounted, the theory of FDI or the multinational enterprise or corporation (MNE) began with the insights of Hymer (1960, 1968), and one of his fundamental conclusions was that MNCs had an 'ownership advantage' in innovation, costs, finance or marketing that could offset the 'disadvantage' of operating in foreign markets. As a consequence, they transferred their advantage from a home to a host economy, and did so intra-firm from the parent to the subsidiary. FDI was not simply the movement of capital but the transfer of company resources. It followed that there would be a need for cross-border monitoring and control by the investing firm, or, that is, international management and organization. 'Control is desired in order to fully appropriate the returns of certain skills and abilities' (Hymer 1976, 25). FDI theory from the outset emphasized the role of the parent MNE in setting overseas strategy and, consequently, designing subsidiary practices, even if it presented little in the way of detail. Hymer shows limited interest in looking beyond the initial act of investment towards those questions of why and how strategies and organizational structures change over time, and in analysing which factors determine variations in degrees of headquarters control and international integration.

Vernon elaborated on the work of Hymer through his ideas on the international product life cycle. At the early part of a product's history, overseas demand justifies exports only, but, with growing market awareness and returns to scale, and the accelerating need to gain first mover advantages, the firm undertakes FDI. At a subsequent stage, when rivals put pressure on profits, the parent firm might decide to license cheaper producers or to invest in countries with lower costs. Another scenario is that subsidiaries may acquire the capabilities to export for themselves (Vernon 1966). As with Hymer, Vernon is primarily concerned with the strategies and decisions of the parent company. He provides little insight into the management aspects of MNCs or industry-specific differences, and leaves open issues of business organization, backwards and forwards integration, and cross-border coordination.

Transaction costs

Building on the works of Coase (1937) and Williamson (1975), Buckley and Casson (1976, 1985, 1991, 1998) contend that transaction cost analysis explains the need of MNCs for cross-border internal coordination and control. It outlines why, as a consequence, firms would favour producing in foreign markets as a consequence of FDI over exports or licensing. Since they perceive reliance on outside parties as too uncertain, and they need to protect their proprietorial knowledge in products, systems and markets, MNCs show a preference for the internalization of business activities within managerial hierarchies capable of operating across borders. Limited knowledge of the intentions and actions of others, opportunism, moral hazard, the costs of negotiating and monitoring, the prospects of reputational damage and asset specificity all add to the risks of markets, partnerships or contracting out (Teece 1981, 1985; Hennart 1982, 2000; Anderson and Gatignon 1986; Forsgren 2008).

Buckley and Casson state that Hymer ignores the planning and investment necessary for a parent MNC to build competitive capabilities, and that he is consequently unconcerned with the means of cross-border capability transfer and mechanisms for controlling subsidiaries. Nonetheless, where local firms are entrenched, or potential rivals in a foreign economy possess advantages, an MNC or its subsidiary might seek to reduce costs or risks through strategies of acquisition, merger, joint ventures or, if appropriate, vertical integration. Although it does address the internal dimensions of the firm, transaction cost theory does not extensively explore the relationship between parent MNC and subsidiary, nor does it mention the ways in which the characteristics and capabilities of parent and subsidiary evolve over time and after the initial act of FDI (Hennart 1982, 2000). Furthermore, the emphasis on the strategies and actions of the main company, as a one-way process, means that the subsidiary's role is portrayed as passive. In reality, parent company control can be a contested terrain that creates dysfunctional internal dynamics within an MNC.

Business historians are – by inclination, or by definition – concerned with the long-term development of firms. They have frequently adopted the insights of Penrose (1959) into management resources (as being key to firm growth), and those of Chandler (1962, 1977, 1990) on managerial enterprise (in which a managerial hierarchy is needed to plan and coordinate capabilities in finance, supplies, production, technology and marketing within firms that compete through returns to scale and scope). Williamson's (1975) theories on how transaction costs determine the boundaries, size and activities of a firm formalizes many of the propositions made by both authors. Ideas of Penrose and Chandler can be extended to MNC business, because management personnel and the internal structures of departments and divisions are needed to coordinate finance, supplies, production, technology and marketing between parent firms and their subsidiaries and across borders (Chandler and Daems 1980; Chandler and Mazlish 1997). Their perspective delves into the implications of headquarters strategy and management teams, as against lower level operations, resistance or labour, or, if we move into the arena of IB, the influence of economic and institutional contexts.

Eclectic paradigm

Dunning's highly influential 'eclectic paradigm' and OLI framework are based on the idea that only a broad comprehensive approach can explain the complexities of FDI (Dunning 1980, 1981, 1988, 1993, 1995, 1998, 2000, 2003, and 2006). As is widely known, he uses Hymer's theory to state that an MNC must have ownership (O) advantages – or internal capabilities in technology, management, human resources, finance, production or marketing – and it follows that it must be able to transfer those advantages from its home market to a host economy. In his later writings Dunning and Lundan (2008) specifies three types of O advantage: innovatory capacity, and experience in management and organization (Ownership asset, or Oa); the ability to govern a business organization, and to configure capital, labour and resources effectively and internationally (Ownership transaction, or Ot); and the political, institutional and social context and support that helps MNCs to develop the other two advantages or to substitute for firm-level deficiencies (Ownership institutional, or Oi). Dunning utilizes transaction cost analysis to propose internalization (I) advantages, in which MNCs achieve efficiencies through the coordination of cross-border production, marketing, research and human resources. The stronger the O-advantages, the greater is the incentive to internalize activities, to found cross-border managerial hierarchies, and to reduce the risks of market-based contracts.

Dunning adds the notion of locational (L) advantages to those of ownership and internalization. MNCs can acquire advantages from being based in differing host locations, due to the existence of R&D networks, lower costs, human skills, intermediate inputs, infrastructure, cheaper finance and nearness or better access to markets, or as a result of tariffs and other government policies. For Dunning, O-advantages cannot by themselves explain FDI, since a firm with such advantages can in principle continue with exports and licensing. Only where all three OLI factors apply will a firm engage in FDI. Where locational advantages are absent, an export strategy is more likely. Where both locational and internalization advantages are absent, licensing may be the preferred strategy.

The relative importance of the three factors will vary between industries and over time. Teece (2006) points out how the rise of 'outsourcing' and 'off shoring' from the 1980s onwards demonstrated the growing significance of locational advantages in the strategic calculations of MNCs. Historical evidence shows that the 1980s and more markedly from the 1990s saw MNCs resorting to complex cross-border production networks, and breaking with post-war trends of subsidiaries supplying distinct national or regional markets, while relying predominantly on the support of parent company (Fitzgerald 2014). The greater incidence of cross-border vertical integration suggests, first, the growing relevance of internalization and locational advantages as deciding factors in IB strategy. As, second, a subsidiary achieves scale, or customizes products, services or systems, host locational factors become critical, and levels of control and supervision from the parent MNC would perforce decline. Despite some attempts to integrate the OLI framework with the Environment, Systems and Policy or ESP model (Koopmans and Montias 1971), and with the 'diamond' of national competitive advantage (Porter 1990), the contextual, political or institutional factors determining MNC strategies remain underplayed.

As with its predecessors, the OLI framework has given precedence to the parent MNC and its transferred capabilities. Interpretations have assumed a headquarters-centred rationale for internalization, and stressed the impact of the main company's strategic planning on shaping the competitive advantages of its subsidiaries. Dunning, in his later writings, saw his eclectic paradigm as a highly flexible framework, which is able to explain the existence of complex international business networks founded on high measures of vertically integrated operations and dispersed capabilities (Mathews, 2006a, 2006b; Dunning, 2006). The dynamic interaction of the three OLI advantage factors can provide for hybrid outcomes in every instance of FDI. Potentially, it may create geographically diffuse business networks and capabilities, as against a model of multinational enterprise in which the parent is wholly dominant and capabilities are transferred from parent to subsidiaries in a linear fashion only (Cantwell and Piscitello 2000). Mathews (2002, 2006a, 2006b) has argued that his alternative LLL framework – involving Linkage, Leverage and Learning – is more applicable to the growth strategies of emerging market MNCs. The approach is based on firms enhancing capabilities by forming alliances or acquiring subsidiaries, and forming business networks different to the established hierarchical parent–subsidiary relationship. FDI is not a result of transferring capabilities from a parent company to a subsidiary, but a means of buying or developing capabilities and transferring them back to the investing firm.

International political economy

In contrast to most theorists on the MNE, Kojima and Ozawa look to macro-economic and political factors for answers. Kojima (1973, 1978, 1982, 1985) and Kojima and Ozawa (1984) claim that the first examples of Japanese outward investment in the post-war period aimed to secure the raw materials or components that were required for the home nation's export-orientated industrialization. Then, Japanese manufacturers undertook large-scale FDI in the developed markets of North America and Western Europe, in order to secure the overseas markets their exports had created but, in the 1980s, put under threat from import tariffs and quotas. Ozawa (1989) shows the participation of the Japanese government in assisting firms to acquire and enhance the competitive advantages that enabled them ultimately to make their breakthroughs both as exporters or international investors. Ozawa (1991) continues that the commitment of Japanese firms and most notably so in the developed markets rested on home nation technological capability. Both Kojima and Ozawa record how Japan had to reach a certain stage of economic development before its leading manufacturers could acquire the ownership advantages to engage in FDI. In contrast to the micro-economic perspective, Kojima and Ozawa's ideas are embedded in the intellectual traditions of political economy and comparative advantage.

If we examine carefully the timing and circumstances of Japanese companies transforming themselves into MNCs, it was host country political factors, tariffs, quotas and currency appreciation that persuaded them to abandon international business strategies of exporting. As they set up subsidiaries overseas, Japanese businesses additionally cemented their reputation as world leaders in production management and employment relations, and revealed strong and burgeoning capabilities in R&D. They had acquired and grown these advantages thanks to a particular set of locational, economic and institutional factors in Japan, including government protection of the home market.

Japanese MNCs possessed a strong belief in their management systems, albeit coupled with a willingness to learn from and innovatively adapt global best practices. In general, in Western Europe and North America, they preferred to establish wholly owned, greenfield subsidiaries, over which they could exercise managerial control, minimize any risk to their proprietorial advantages and most easily transfer from the parent business the products and systems they perceived as the source of their success.

The debate about whether Japanese MNCs markedly implemented their systems within a host economy or whether they incrementally accepted the wisdom of hybrid arrangements remains open, however (Elger and Smith 1994). In China, joint ventures were initially the regulatory entry price that MNCs willingly paid. At the outset, Japanese and other foreign companies showed the strategic intent to transfer their ownership advantages. Once China relaxed the rules, as we shall see, Japanese MNCs invariably opted for full ownership and managerial control, and saw this change as the trigger for increasing the flow and extent of capability transfer. In what ways, therefore, did these Japanese MNC subsidiaries in China come to reflect the continuation of Japanese-style management? Or do they highlight a series of adjustments over time to local institutional and market pressures? Or do they, instead, demonstrate a trend towards adopting global best practice that superseded distinctly home and host country influences?

Parent MNE and capability transfer

Westney (1987) categorized the transfer process undertaken by the parent MNE into four types: 'elimination', 'internalization', 'functional equivalents' and 'organization creation'. 'Elimination' describes the selective transfer of elements of the original model according to their fit with the host context and simultaneously eliminating others that are unsuited. 'Internalization' means transferring elements of the original model appropriate to the host context, and simultaneously altering others. 'Functional equivalents' imply that the transferred original model can still work or be effective, even where the host context varies greatly from that of the home nation. 'Organizational creation' means that an MNC helps to change a host context whenever its original transferred model is ill-suited, a process reflecting the transformative impact of FDI. While there is scope for adjustments within the subsidiary, the emphasis is on the parent MNC's strategic intent to transfer and on its capabilities in managing the transfer process. Westney (1993) explicitly stresses the strategic intent and power of the parent MNCs, but allows for the uncertainties of host contexts and the hybridization of transfer outcomes. Given a tendency for firms to adopt or to adapt to national or institutional norms – a form of 'isomorphism' – the MNC can generate essential innovations. Changes to the transferred model can be intended but, due to imperfect information on the host economy, misinterpretations of the original system, and human error, also unintended.

We can ask if international business theories have over-emphasized the motivation or the power of the MNC to determine subsidiary practices. Where MNCs encounter barriers to their control of a subsidiary, or barriers to the transfer of capabilities, they have to deal with the consequences: for management structures and the locale of decision-making, on the one hand, and in the greater diversity of practices and products, on the other. There is, as yet, a comparatively small amount of research on international management, or the relationship between the headquarters and subsidiaries, and, to mention an issue of growing prominence, the relationship between one subsidiary and another.

Taking a strategy-structure perspective, Bartlett and Ghoshal (1986) identify four types of structure designed to fit varying strategies and environmental contexts: the global (meaning centralized control of subsidiaries by the parent company, and adoption of the parent's management practices and standardized products or services), the international (the parent retains and controls core competencies, but the subsidiary adapts and leverages non-core competencies, leading to hybrid subsidiary practices), the multinational or multidomestic (the subsidiary exercises a high degree of autonomy and self-sufficiency, and it uses local practices to produce customized products or services), and the transnational (specialized and interdependent subsidiaries directly participate in integrated worldwide operations, with some near to parent practices and others following local national practices) (Bartlett and Ghoshal 1989; Ghoshal and Nohria 1993). In this taxonomy, the assumption of headquarters strategic control and the one-way transfer of practices remain dominant, as it does in the work of related interpretations (Perlmutter 1969; Stopford and Wells 1972; Ghoshal and Bartlett 1990). For some critics, the schema is too simple, and diverse arrangements may exist in a single MNC. Little is said about what might inhibit practice transfer, such as national institutions, or resistance within the subsidiaries themselves (Evans, Doz, and Laurent 1989; Ruigrok and Van Tulder 1995; Doremus et al. 1998; Birkinshaw 2001).

The MNE and the subsidiary

Those taking a headquarters–subsidiary relationship perspective seek to consider two-way exchanges between subsidiary and parent, the potential for subsidiary-level decision-making, and the influence of the local environment on subsidiary characteristics (Hedlund 1981; Gates and Egelhoff 1986; Ghoshal and Nohria 1989; Arvidsson 1999; Gupta, Govindarajan, and Malhotra 1999; Birkinshaw 2000). A subsidiary perspective would go one stage further, by seeing the headquarters as an external factor, and taking the subsidiary as its starting point. With the evolution of vertically integrated global networks in which subsidiaries can play a central role, and with subsidiaries exporting in the international marketplace, the subsidiary focus has grown in credibility (White and Poynter 1984; D'Cruz 1986; Gupta and Govindarajan 1991; Kilduff 1993; Birkinshaw and Morrison 1995). As the dependence on headquarters resources declines, changes in cross-border governance and local management practices would follow (White and Poynter 1984; D'Cruz 1986; Doz and Prahalad 1993; Beechler and Yang 1994; Dorrenbacher and Geppert 2003; Mudambi and Navarra 2004; Forsgren, Holm, and Johanson 2007; Roth and Nigh 1992).

If the parent MNE and its subsidiaries evolve strategically and organizationally, headquarters–subsidiary relations must inevitably adjust, and this altering relationship in turn affects the strategies, structures and practices of the subsidiary. One potential contributor to this process is the growth in the capabilities of the subsidiary and the agency of local management. From the parent perspective, the headquarters is the formulator of strategy, and it can exercise control over its subsidiaries through formal ownership, on one side, and through its possession and transfer of systems, know-how and personnel, on the other. From a subsidiary perspective, necessary adaptations to local circumstances, the career interests and motivations of subsidiary managers, and resistance to transferred practices can impose limitations and, over time, a lessening of headquarters control. Such subsidiary-level dynamics infer local variations in management practices, and the existence of hybrid systems within an MNC. Attention on the headquarters–subsidiary relationship and the subsidiary itself – adding to analysis of transferred ownership advantages from the parent – broadens our understanding of the MNC. Yet, all three perspectives remain concerned with matters of strategy and organization at the level of the firm. They do not by necessity incorporate political or institutional influences on business practices (Rosenzweig and Nohria 1994).

In their typology of subsidiary-level strategy and structure, White and Poynter (1984) emphasize variations in product strategies, but they are not seeking to address the effects of the host country institutional environment or the actions of local management and labour. Beechler, Bird, and Taylor (1998) conceptualized, first, an exportive model, in which the parent MNC's practices are adopted by the subsidiary as superior with only minor adjustments; second, an adaptive model, in which local practices are dominant; third, a closed hybrid model, in which local influences outside the subsidiary are not significant, but the parent template is adapted to the context; and an open hybrid model in which both parent and local practices exist simultaneously. One major factor in the evolution of a subsidiary will be its capacity for organizational learning. Gupta and Govindarajan (1991) provide a knowledge flow perspective to explain how subsidiaries might rely on parent resources, or alternatively develop their own resources by themselves or in cooperation with the parent. A subsidiary with its own specific capabilities could make a contribution to the success of the whole MNC. There remain, nonetheless, limited insights on the impact of local contexts on subsidiaries or the varied factors driving the need for change or subsidiary-level capabilities.

Japanization literature

The centralization of power within headquarters of Japanese MNCs can be seen as a strategy or a hierarchical management process for the international extension of domestic business models (Westney 1993; Hatch and Yamamura 1996; Seki 1997). For Japanese MNCs, Harzing (2002) notes the nature of parent control and headquarters-driven coordination through the sending of expatriates, bureaucratic rules and standardization, management by results, or acculturation and common values. Groot and Merchant (2000) distinguish between types of control mechanisms to be used in either wholly owned subsidiaries or joint ventures. In the latter, in which there is a greater likelihood of hybrid systems, management strategy has to align partner motivations and organizational strengths, and reflect proportions of equity ownership and board membership. For the participants, contractual safeguards and their monitoring are fundamental.

The literature on Japanization was founded on the notion that strong capabilities were developed in the unique economic and institutional context of the home economy, and motivated Japanese MNCs to transfer their practices abroad. Japanization implied that a global competitive standard had been set and that it was highly transferrable to different national contexts (Turnbull 1986; Stewart 1998; Taylor 1999, 2001; Saka 2003; Florian 2009). The superiority of Japanese lean production was particularly noted (Womack, Jones, and Roos 1990; Florida and Kenney 1991; Oliver and Wilkinson 1992; Alder 1993; Kenney and Florida 1993; Abo 1994). Kenney and Florida (1995) argue that Japanese firms, while keeping the substance of their methods intact, had the capabilities for 'internal adaptation' by which they could create or alter the working environment in a subsidiary as needed. In their interpretation, the strategic intent of the parent company remains paramount, but global best practice can incorporate measures of adaptation. Japanese MNCs preferred greenfield sites, frequently outside areas of traditional industry, and sought to employ a new committed workforce, which could be trained, socialized and controlled through the appointment of expatriates. Critics have questioned the assumption of superior practices and the raising up of a management ideal that was not itself reflective of the realities or the diversity to be found within Japan. They highlight, in addition, the numerous factors that temper the transfer of capabilities to a host country and to foreign subsidiaries (Alder 1999; Florian 2009).

The other important strand of the Japanization literature – on employment systems and human resources – was more concerned with contextual factors and their impact on international system transfer. Yet, while acknowledging the institutional, legal and cultural problems of transferring employment systems, some did see the extensive MNC-ization of systems as feasible (Trevor 1983; Morris 1988; Bratton 1990; Oliver and Wilkinson 1992; Wood 1992). Others questioned whether the international diffusion of Japanese work systems as practised in Japan occurred to a meaningful extent, and presented subsidiary case studies to make their point (Turnbull 1986; Ackroyd et al. 1988; Elger and Smith 1994). The degree to which systems could be transferred from one national context to another was higher in cases of FDI than in instances of indigenous firms outside Japan seeking to emulate global best practice. Notably, Elger and Smith (1994) criticize the idea of contextualization – a simple contrasting of home and host contexts – and argue that the relevant factors are difficult to define and not fixed at any point in time. Competing and contradictory forces – firm level, national and international – continuously shape managerial choices and organizational forms. Some simplistic divergence from or convergence towards some global best practice cannot account for the complex and constantly changing realities.

National institutions

Established international business literature has emphasized the role of the parent MNC in determining subsidiary practices, a result of its ability to transfer capabilities across borders and its strategic intent. 'Institutionalism' – which did not originally show interest in the existence of powerful MNCs and their subsidiaries – is rooted in the idea that national factors determine long-term economic success or business forms. In one strand of this approach, political, administrative, legal and representative institutions explain national economic success by ensuring good governance, inhibiting 'rent seeking', and allowing producers to capture their due rewards. In other words, markets were allowed to operate efficiently (North 1990; Scott 1995). Management theorists extended this perspective by seeing businesses and entrepreneurial initiative as socially embedded and culturally determined, and, in the neo-institutionalist interpretation, national institutions determine the nature of business ownership and organization. Strong national institutions (exerting isomorphic pressures) would lead to comparatively high levels of homogeneity in management, and create large differences in the business systems of different nations. Debates continue to revolve around the idea that nation states or national economies are highly homogenous, and, by extension, that regional, industry and firm-level factors continue are relatively unimportant. The very particular emphasis on national institutions and isomorphic pressures to explain the characteristics of firms robs entrepreneurial or managerial initiative or human agency of any substantive meaning. It is difficult to view the influence of national institutions on firms as one-way and linear, and both are subject to continuous change, contradictory forces and interaction (Meyer and Rowan 1977; Zucker 1977; DiMaggio and Powell 1983; Whitley 1992a, 1992b; Westney 1993; Lane 1994; Hall and Soskice 2001; Tempel and Walgenbach 2003; Smith, McSweeney, and Fitzgerald 2008; Florian 2009).

As in the 'societal effect' approach adopted by Sorge (1991, 2004), the 'national business system' perspective of Whitley (1992a, 1999) places a strong emphasis on national institutions determining business systems, and critics have focused on the approach's assumed levels of national conformity, the lack of human agency, the realities of contested terrains and the absence of forces of change where homogeneity is characteristic (Smith, McSweeney, and Fitzgerald 2008). The variety of capitalism (VOC) approach accepts the importance of or allows greater space for human agency and firm-level action (Hall and Soskice 2001), but nonetheless the flow of determinant influences remains linear, that is from the national institutions downwards to business (Smith, McSweeney, and Fitzgerald 2008).

Institutions and MNCs

Rosenzweig and Singh (1991) note how subsidiaries seek external consistency with their local institutional environment and internal consistency as a consequence of cross-border organization. Part companies instinctively seek to maintain control by applying their own organizational models, but the dual pressures of home and host economy practice lead to variations in outcomes. Kostova (1999) and Kostova and Roth (2002) suggest that the levels of 'institutional distance' between home and host economy shape the differences between parent and subsidiary. They look at transfer processes as well as outcomes, arguing that host institutions interact and shape the nature of capability transfer, and that the process and results of international capability transfer determine the relationship between the headquarters and local management.

Birkinshaw (2000) argues that subsidiaries develop capabilities ultimately suited to their national or institutional contexts. Others stress the restraints institutions impose on the transfer and internationalization of management practices (; Delios and Henisz 2000; Child and Tsai 2005). Peng (2003) states that no firm or MNC subsidiary can be immune from institutional pressures. Peng and Heath (2003) and Peng and Khoury (2009) explore over the short and the long run the influence of institutions on transferred practices. The determining nature of institutions on business organizations and strategies may be especially important in Asian contexts and in cases of state-led development. With respect to China, central and provincial governments are deeply involved in the running of the economy, and political contacts and personal networks are important to all entrepreneurs and key managers (Powell 1996; Hollingsworth and Boyer 1997; Hollingsworth 2000; Taylor 1996). But Geppert and Mayer provide case examples of how the interests and agency of local managers are critical to resisting parent company control and to the emergence of subsidiary level capabilities, as a result avoiding the dangers of institutional determinism (Geppert and Mayer 2005).

Morgan (2001) and Morgan and Whitley (2003) present a typology of transfer outcomes, based on the strength of local institutions versus the ability of an MNC to achieve high degrees of cross-border integration. As a consequence, strong institutions and high integration levels will generate extensive examples of hybridity and variation. Morgan (2001) and Whitley (2001) proposes the concept of 'transnational space', which MNCs can create in their host country operations, and within which they can develop innovative organizational forms. Lane (2000, 2001) argues for 'multiple societal environments' and for the ability of MNCs to structure their activities and goals in different national contexts. The interaction of global best practice and powerful corporate or institutional actors is a cause of varied outcomes in systems.

Overall, institutionalism in its several forms provides an explanation for the hybridization of transferred practices by a parent MNE, but it has to make uneasy accommodations to account for the powerful global forces shaping a national economy, including an investing MNE with substantial managerial, technological and financial resources at its command. While institutionalism can incorporate the evolution of the subsidiary, it has less scope to consider the agency of managers, labour and suppliers. The focus on institutional influences tended originally to see the nation state as intact from global forces and the actions of MNEs. Neo-institutionalism found it difficult to address the fact that MNC subsidiaries would encounter pressure from both their home and host institutions.

Global factory and value-chains

If MNCs evolve away from hierarchical structures towards federative organizations, subsidiaries have greater scope for determining their practices and even influencing MNC strategy (Ghoshal and Bartlett 1990; Andersson, Forsgren, and Holm 2007). Yet, research does not so far confirm how MNCs can act as federations, or the extent to which they seek to do so. Some strands of FDI theory have concerned themselves with the dyadic relationship between headquarters and subsidiary and with issues of global integration versus national responsiveness. Outsourcing, asset seeking FDI strategies and the vertical cross-border integration of finely sliced value production chains undermines the need for MNCs to prioritize the search for host nation responsiveness. Subsidiaries with their own strategic capabilities emerge to supply international markets and replace subsidiaries reliant on parent firm capabilities in order to service a host economy. As a result, the federative MNE is portrayed as being replaced by the global factory (Buckley and Ghauri 2004; Mudambi and Navarra 2004; Yamin and Forsgren 2006; Buckley 2009a, 2009b; Yamin and Sinkovics 2009). The existence of the global factory would entail the emergence of lead factories utilizing best practice capabilities in the best-suited location, and could induce a reduction in the role of the parent company and its output. In practice, however, we might see the reassertion of parental company control. The subsidiary loses control of its own activities – embedded in a national institutional network – to a cross-border network. Inevitably, such outcomes would have implications for subsidiary managers and how they perceive their function (Nolan, Sutherland, and Zhang 2002; Strange and Newton 2006).

The idea of the global factory is seen as rejuvenating international business as a distinctive area of study, and it is fundamentally interested in where business activities should be located and how across borders they should be integrated or controlled. The global factory approach, nevertheless, still has to deal with the issue of production units being embedded in national and institutional contexts and with the potential resistance of local management to external control (Rugman and D'Cruz 2003; Buckley and Ghauri 2004). The global factory comprises a vertical core and a lateral network of suppliers and service providers. While previous parental control was the result of managerial hierarchy versus contracting-out and markets, in which cross-border internalization was the preferred option, the global factory is a combination of hierarchy, contracting-out and markets. Planning by the parent firm replaces ownership as the main means of control over productive resources (Buckley 2009a, 2009b). The global factory uses the organizational abilities of the parent company to coordinate its proprietorial technology, marketing know-how and brands with a network of contracted enterprises. Yet, for some, the global factory design emphasizes operational efficiency and cost cutting over investment in R&D skills, and the enhancement of capabilities. The use of contracted firms relies on the routinization of work rather than on the development of skills (Nolan, Sutherland, and Zhang 2002; Buckley 2010; Leahy and Naghavi 2010).

Research methods and aims

The research sought to discover the processes of capability transfer by a Japanese company into China. It aimed to trace the development of capability transfer over an extended time-period, and to evaluate the influences of parent business strategy, institutions, and market conditions. A further aim was to compare which capabilities were transferred at different rates and at different points. Access to a number of personnel in differing business functions, therefore, was essential, as was access to both Japanese expatriate and local Chinese managers. The selected case had to be large scale in both capital invested and number of employees involved. For these reasons, Omron was selected, and the fieldwork was carried out in 2007–2008 and in 2012. The interviews were carried out at the level of the subsidiary, in order to observe the locale and effects of capability transfer, and to consider the perspectives of directly participating personnel. Interviews adopted a semi-structured interview approach, based around questions related to the research aims and enabling the comparison of answers, while giving interviewees the opportunity to offer further important details and to explain contexts. Information was also collected from company publications, labour manuals and newspapers – in part supplied by the Pudong New Area Association of Enterprises with Foreign Investment – and it was used to supplement and triangulate data collected from interviews.

The research posed a number of connected questions:

- To what extent does the case of the Omron subsidiaries in China demonstrate the formative influences of parent MNC, national institutions or subsidiary personnel on its operations and practices?
- How successfully or fully have Japanese or international business methods been transferred to China, and which business functions and practices reveal over time the greatest transfer propensity?
- Have globalization strategies and trends strengthened or weakened the control of the parent MNC over its subsidiaries?

Omron in China

MNC strategy

Omron is an enterprise with a long history: founded in 1933, as the Tateisi Electric Manufacturing Company, and as a manufacturer of X-ray timers, it grew in size and capabilities during Japan's post-war 'economic miracle'. During 1968, it added its best-known trademark to its corporate name to become Omron Tateisi Electronics Company. In the 1980s, the firm joined the wave of Japanese manufacturers that looked overseas to exploit the advantages they had developed in production, products or price, and it established a regional headquarters in The Netherlands (in 1988), Singapore (1988), and the USA (1989). It re-founded itself as, more simply, the Omron Corporation, in 1990.

Omron has grown its operations in China through four critical phases. The company's founder, Kazuma Tateisi, made his first visit to China, in 1974, and began a process of technical cooperation with a number of state-owned enterprises (SOEs). In the early 1980s, Omron started a second stage by exporting product parts and licensing technology to an SOE called the Huayi Home Appliance Company. From 1991 to 2000, Omron underwent the critical third stage, when it founded an investment vehicle, a trading operation, subsidiary manufacturing enterprises and a joint venture with an SOE. The MNC's investment peaked between 1994 and 1996, with the building of large-scale factories. It created five subsidiaries in total, including, in 1993, its biggest initiative, the Omron (Shanghai) Industrial Automation Company, the joint venture located in Shanghai, and often referred to as Omron Shanghai.

The last, fourth phase began from 2000, when Omron initiated its plan to consolidate and restructure its Chinese factories, with the aim of achieving greater economies of scale and turning them into the MNC's chief production base. The key change occurred in July 2005, done in pursuit of a global strategy, when the company integrated its three Shanghai subsidiaries into Omron (Shanghai) Company Ltd, or, more simply, Omron Shanghai (and later as OMS). The joint venture with the SOE called the China Perfect Machinery Industry Ltd ceased, and Omron (Shanghai) Industrial Automation was fully incorporated into and became the main component of the new merged subsidiary. Omron Shanghai (OMS) was fully owned by the Japanese MNC, and it was assigned the role of global production headquarters for the whole business. Omron Japan, in addition, created Omron China – based in Beijing – to deal with central government, to take charge of R&D activities and to further the development of sales in an expanding domestic market. The MNC revealed a determination to improve the capabilities of its Chinese businesses, in 2004–2005, by expanding its R&D capabilities in Shanghai, founding another research facility in Guangzhou and forging networks with local technological institutions and universities. The company selected Shanghai Jiao Tong University, in particular, as an important partner in product development and recruitment projects. Omron China is a holding company, fully owned by Omron Japan. Both enterprises have formal oversight of OMS, the production headquarters, but OMS coordinates its activities with and reports directly to the parent business.

In its initial FDI in China, from 1991 to 2000, Omron's strategic motive was to avoid Japan's high manufacturing costs; in other words, it wanted to create a low-cost, low-wage production base for worldwide exports. The parent company in Japan designed and developed all products, and sent parts for final assembly in China. Then, to continue the downward pressure on costs, the company began outsourcing to local Chinese suppliers, with the proviso that the parent MNC kept control of and continued to supply key components. A Japanese expatriate executive, OMS's Production Control Manager, recognized the cost and other advantages of locally sourcing parts. Prohibitive import taxes were a deciding factor. Although the subsidiary had to respond to rising wages in China, the localization of production was essential to any plans for a greater share of a rapidly growing but price-sensitive domestic market. Furthermore, local outsourcing would underpin Omron's subsequent decision to turn its Chinese businesses into its 'global production headquarters', because 'the consideration of cost is vital for our competitiveness in both global and local markets' (Interview, July 2007).

According to the Chinese Deputy General Manager, 'Omron Shanghai took over the factories, and also continued to employ the workforce from the old IJV (international joint venture). I was the former factory production manager in the Omron Industrial Automation Company. However, the management system has been restructured and 'Duzi Management style' (it means adopting Japanese-style management) has been implemented. Three factories were integrated in order to achieve maximum production capacity, and to reduce the costs and complications of ownership conflicts' (Interview, July 2007). As well as becoming more directly integrated into international supply and distribution networks, Omron's Chinese factories had to achieve global production standards. A Japanese expatriate responsible for strategic planning explained:

Our company has been introducing the global management idea to our global employees ... Omron in China has been concentrating on producing low cost products for global markets in accordance with Omron's global quality standards, and relies heavily on qualified local managers with knowledge of global management. [W]e see China's factories as the centre of our business network in the future. (Interview, July 2007)

To effect its international strategy, and to implement best practices, OMS had to employ and educate local managers with the requisite technical expertise and strategic understanding; it needed a better trained workforce; and it had to improve its local R&D capability (Interview, Chinese Executive, Deputy General Manager, 2012). One sign of a global production and sales strategy was the company stating that its products were 'made in Omron' rather than 'made in Japan'.

Decision-making and control

In founding a global factory, Omron had to address issues of costs, production standards, and international vertical integration, but linked these goals to matters of ownership and management control. During the fourth phase of its business in China, it had initially proposed continuing its joint venture arrangement, but the partner SOE was short of capital and considering its own independent development strategy. During the 2005 consolidation of subsidiaries, Omron took the opportunity to acquire full ownership control. The change in governance facilitated the restructuring and the integration of the factories. More fundamentally, it made the parent MNC more committed to investing in new plant and manufacturing equipment, and its direct operational control assisted the drive to inculcate in its Chinese factories the international production standards that would be the foundation of its global factory strategy.

On the other hand, OMS remained reliant on the parent MNC's capital and technology, and Japanese expatriates continued to occupy the top managerial positions at the subsidiary, including the roles of president and all the departmental heads, with the notable exception of leadership in the personnel department. There was no reduction in the number of Japanese technical staff, and a support group of technical experts from the parent firm continued to pay frequent visits to Shanghai, in order to monitor and bolster quality control. 'Localization' policy produced visible results only amongst the junior- and middle-level managerial positions. Chinese managers acknowledged that Omron sought to employ and promote qualified local executives, but, as they were too few in number, the subsidiary remained dependent on Japanese expatriates, most obviously for the transfer and inculcation of expertise in the production and R&D departments, and for supervising the total quality control processes (Chinese executive, Logistics Department Manager, August 2007).

Within the OMS subsidiary, managerial authority and decision-making are organized hierarchically, and managers report on performance every day. According to the Chinese Deputy General Manager,

> [A]ll managerial staff are required to be highly committed to their job responsibilities, and the range of those responsibilities is clearly delineated, based on the reporting system. That means there are clear formalized and specified procedures to follow for what you can do and what you must do.

While there was a move to increase the responsibilities of Chinese managers, this occurred within procedures set and monitored by Japanese expatriates. When a manager needs authority to act beyond clearly defined remits, the Japanese General Manager calls a 'decision-making meeting' for all important issues and for resolving differing viewpoints (Interviews, Chinese Deputy General Manager, July 2007, December 2012).

Full ownership of the merged subsidiary created in 2005 enabled Omron Japan to control more fully its investment, and to hasten the transfer and development of managerial and manufacturing expertise. OMS can work out its own budgets and short-term plans, and has a level of operational freedom in local R&D projects, subject to the

MNC's overall strategy and the subsidiary's financial performance. In principle, an ability to diversify and develop products in China can contribute in the long-term to Omron Japan's global strategy (Interviews, Chinese Deputy General Manager, July 2007, December 2012). Strong direction from the parent MNC was potentially a block on the subsidiary responding adequately to local factors, such as government, regulations, human resources, suppliers and domestic markets. Omron Japan mixes 'bottom-up' reporting on the appropriateness of overall strategy, production management and R&D with 'top-down decision-making'.

> Omron Shanghai is a major subsidiary within the global MNC, and implements the parent company's strategy according to plan. Although the decisions from Omron are implemented 'top-down' through the hierarchy, the decision-makers still need feedback, so Omron China, as a regional headquarters, is responsible for reporting and communicating about its operations. A 'bottom-up' reporting system provides reliable information for final decision-making in Omron Japan. (Interview, Chinese Group Manager, Public Relations and Corporate Communication, August 2007)

On the other hand, Japanese expatriate managers at OMS are wholly reliant on their Chinese counterparts for maintaining good relations with local government in Shanghai, and the parent MNC has to depend on guidance from its subsidiary on matters of politics, public relations, law and regulations. One of the responsibilities held by the Chinese Deputy General Manager is to ensure the confidence and assistance of local government and other institutions, and to advise the Japanese General Manager and senior managers in Japan. Omron began its dialogue with Shanghai Pudong's municipal government on the founding of large-scale production, in 1994. When the original promise to build a subway to the suburban area where the factories were located was not forthcoming, Omron was forced to hire a fleet of buses to transport its employees. The company did eventually persuade a new governor to establish the railway line, and the recruitment of better-educated civil servants and the creation of the Shanghai Pudong New Area Investment Promotion Division greatly improved the effectiveness of good relations with local government. Chinese managers have the responsibility of ensuring compliance with laws and regulations, and sound relations with officialdom help to guarantee the stable supply of industrial water, electricity and gas. They carry, too, the duties of communicating with employees, reducing labour disputes, inducting personnel, and helping to inculcate Omron's Japanese corporate culture and philosophy (Interview, Chinese Group Manager, Public Relations and Corporate Communications, August 2007).

Management resources

With regard to managerial staff, OMS prefers to recruit new graduates and to promote internally. The general manager and department managers – with the important exception of the personnel manager – are directly appointed by Omron Japan, and they are responsible for maintaining production quality and introducing advanced manufacturing methods. Most of OMS's managerial and technical staff were inherited from the SOE which had once been its joint venture partner. The subsidiary perceives its personnel as experienced in Japanese working methods, and it sees them as more reliable than people who can be hired externally. The Chinese deputy general manager says that OMS promotes local managers according to their expertise, personality and length of service, and that the long-term objective is to replace as far as possible Japanese expatriates with qualified Chinese.

While OMS does not promise Japanese-style lifetime employment, it does require a commitment from its managerial staff to serve on a long-term basis. Accordingly, the practice of internal promotion has become part of its recruitment policy, and, after the merger in 2005, OMS was able to retain most of the middle-level managerial positions for existing local employees. The Chinese deputy general manager explained: 'The "bottom-up" recommendation process allows current staff to be selected internally [for managerial positions] ... there are personality criteria such as a high level of commitment' (Interview, February 2008). For open labour market selection, new graduates are preferred. Many managerial trainees are selected from Shanghai Jiao Tong University every year before they graduate. Course grades, skills certificates in computing or foreign languages, and pre-job training at Omron or an internship in another Japanese-owned business are determining factors in the first selection process. Chinese managers then organize written tests that explore knowledge and personality profiles, and, once suitability for particular departments is decided, Chinese or Japanese managers conduct personal interviews. The Chinese Deputy R&D Manager also believes that

> Omron Shanghai is more willing [than other firms] to recruit fresh graduates with high commitment and a learning capability, and it ... emphasizes the importance of cooperating with a first-class university on the development of enterprise products and human resources. (Interview, February 2008)

Chinese managers – who occupy the roles of deputy department managers and shop-floor supervisors – remain formally 'temporary employees'. Staff turnover is rising, because of slow or unlikely promotion prospects, and from increasing job opportunities in foreign-owned and local companies.

> Staff mobility and a lack of qualified managerial staff remain obstacles to implementing Omron China's expansion strategy ... Recently, Omron proposed building a global management team and developing global insight training schemes for a group of qualified local managers ... and offering an international standard skill certificate which can benefit local employees' future career development. (Interview, Japanese Production Control Manager, July 2007)

At OMS, internal training programmes are tailored to the manufacturing plan, and include induction for managerial trainees, management knowledge and supervision skills for middle and senior levels, and overseas training programmes for local managers. The Chinese R&D Manager remarks that there is a plentiful supply of well-educated graduates and high-quality recruits in Shanghai, but the 'most important problem is ... for Omron's employees to understand the Japanese management system and corporate culture, not only on paper', with the process beginning as interns before they graduate (Interview, August 2007). Experienced Chinese staff or Japanese expatriates provide technical on-the-job training, in addition to classroom education. Every year, Chinese managers and engineers are selected to visit Japan to acquire up-to-date advanced management and production expertise, and to gain first-hand experience of working in a Japanese factory. The shortest visit is about two to three months, and the longest can last for a year. Extensive training is viewed as an indication of the subsidiary's commitment to long-term contracts (Interview, Chinese Deputy General Manager, July 2007).

Training began, moreover, to reflect changes in needed strategic capabilities. 'Originally, Omron required managerial staff who understood Japanese work methods and the Japanese language, and now Omron proposes the learning of "global management" and English. Local managers should have a global concept, with ideas and innovations in mind' (Interview, Chinese Logistics Department Manager, February 2008). Training programmes aim to develop the managerial staff's professional and communication skills, including the use of international telephone video conferencing and computerized office automation. Omron's global strategy rests, in principal, on its subsidiaries engaging in knowledge sharing and complying with global standards in their practices. OMS also has ISO training programmes intended to replace traditional practices with international standards and what the deputy general manager describes as 'best practices'.

The managerial salary structure contains elements inherited from the old SOE system, including the basic salary, a seniority allowance, a position allowance, a welfare allowance and an annual bonus. Basic salary has been increasing year on year, due to local labour market pressures. Both seniority, that is length of service, and managerial position contribute to the calculation of the basic salary and welfare benefits. After the creation of OMS, performance-related pay was introduced, and, in China, incentive schemes have been increasingly used in manufacturing enterprises. OMS still emphasizes the importance of corporate culture and organizational values in improving performance, since, while its pay is far above the levels generally available in Shanghai, it is not competitive with locally based Western firms in the electronics industry (Chinese Manager, Finance and Accounting, February 2008). There have been complaints that pay does reflect the working hours at Omron, and employees view working in Japanese companies as significantly more stressful than working in an SOE or for a Western MNC.

The Chinese deputy general manager explained:

> A Japanese enterprise pays much greater attention to an employee's commitment. Every managerial staff member must understand this before joining Omron. Although Omron announces the implementation of global management, it has not introduced global levels of pay. This is still a Japanese MNC, and its corporate culture and values still impact on its overseas subsidiaries.

Managerial pay policies are designed locally, and quite separate from the remuneration of Japanese expatriates, although incomes are boosted by accommodation, transport and medical allowances, and there is the prospect of long-term employment (Interview, February 2008). Overall, OMS's human resource development programme addresses two problems: first, the shortage of qualified and experienced local employees, and, second, the reduction of staff turnover.

Labour and skills

There exists a large pool of skilled workers and migrant workers in Shanghai's industrial areas. Most of the permanent shop-floor employees were directly hired from the previous Omron Industrial Automation Co, and they are skilled workers and engineers with many years of experience in electronic manufacturing. The remainder have been selected for their skills, work experience and educational qualifications, such as training certificates, as a result of advertising and individual interviews. Unskilled workers, often migrants from rural areas, are hired on a temporary basis to cope with fluctuating seasonal orders. They are normally engaged in component assembly work, factory cleaning, or warehousing. OMS has contracts with local recruitment agents to hire groups of temporary workers, but prefers, where possible, to employ new graduates from professional skills high schools, because poorly educated migrant workers have what is regarded as inadequate works discipline. The company favours people from the Shanghai area, because it has to offer dormitory accommodation to migrants (Interview, Chinese Deputy Manager, July 2008, December 2012).

There is also an internal promotion policy for shop-floor workers. Usually, skilled workers can be upgraded to a higher level skill group on their supervisors' recommendation, related to years of service and performance. The intention is to limit skilled worker turnover, to minimize training costs and to maintain Omron's corporate culture and values on the shop floor. Induction programmes for all shop-floor workers include an introduction to company regulations, and basic on-the-job training through the observing of experienced workers, and the inculcation of work skills by supervisors. Permanent workers receive internal training related to the specific skills they require, and OMS encourages permanent workers to gain certified qualifications from external training providers. However, job rotation practices, which are commonly adopted in the Japanese parent company's plants, are not found. The Deputy General Manager says:

> Specific skill development is far more important than breadth of skills training in order to ensure global quality standards in our production headquarters [at Omron Shanghai]. Job rotation assumes workers have a long-term future in the company and the high turnover on the shop floor makes different training programmes for particular employees' career development too expensive ... (Interview, Chinese Deputy General Manager, February 2008)

As in the case of managers and technicians, OMS selects highly skilled workers to visit the parent company's Japanese factories every year, and this advanced training is seen as an indication of future promotion. Shop-floor workers complain that their training focuses on operational rules and regulations, but contributes little to skills development. Procedures tend to induce boredom and to demand hard work, with little scope to improve skills. A Japanese expatriate and the Production Control Manager remarks:

> I think the most important aspect of the shop-floor training process is not the difficulty of skills for local employees, but letting them understand the importance of disciplines, rules and regulations. Shop-floor workers, especially temporary workers, have no intention of following the procedures and regulations. For example, they don't think tidiness in the workplace would have a negative impact on their job performance. If I push them too hard, it only makes things worse. They explicitly express their unwillingness to follow what they are told to do, especially temporary workers. I cannot penalize them because they are not permanent employees (Interview, July 2007)

The pay grade of workers is linked to skills, as a device to encourage training, and to enhance performance. There is little difference between the salaries of skilled workers and office clerks, in the hope of limiting turnover amongst skilled workers. To balance the extra costs involved in this policy, OMS hires large numbers of cheap temporary workers. Contracted workers have short-term contracts, normally from one to three years. They are not promised lifetime employment but their welfare allowance and job security is much higher than temporary workers'.

Manufacturing

According to a Chinese supervisor employed in production (Interview, February 2008), OMS continues to receive a high degree of technical support from the parent MNC, which had directly transferred advanced manufacturing technology and work methods. It can manufacture most final products without relying on components from Japan. Accordingly, OMS has adopted JIT (Just in Time Management), in a close approximation of Japanese practices, and it participates in a global inventory network in order to reduce costs and to ease production pressures. Through computerized automation control systems transferred from Japan, the subsidiary has achieved economies of scale and mass production, and has obtained the capability to operate twenty four hours a day.

Formal procedures help to ensure that front-line operators employ the machinery effectively and efficiently. The Zero Defects Policy requires shop-floor workers to exercise discipline and awareness, although, unlike the situation in Japan, it is front-line supervisors that actively maintain this commitment. In addition, the subsidiary follows

Japanese 5S factory management, considered to be the foundation for maintaining an efficient work space and for building mutual understanding about processes: namely *seiri* (sort), *seiton* (systemize or set in order), *seiso* (shine, or clean and maintain), *seiketsu* (standardize, or maintain high standards) and *shitsuke* (self-discipline, or initiative) (Interviews, Chinese Production Supervisor, February 2008, December 2012). After its formation, OMS updated all its production lines with the latest technology in order to emulate performance in Japan. Before any new product is introduced, at least a year's preparation is needed. Chinese engineers are sent to Japan to witness the production process and to gain experience on-site. Omron Japan will send expatriates to give lectures and seminars on any new production technology. These Japanese experts are responsible for installing the production lines, and stay on a long-term basis to ensure correct working methods and machine maintenance.

OMS's Chinese Deputy Manager says:

> Following the formal procedure is not difficult for shop-floor workers, as a result of our basic training courses. However, front-line operations are partly manual and partly automatic, which requires shop-floor workers to have positive work attitudes to improve their performance and skills. Semi-automation requires much more skill than automatic operations. Shop-floor workers have no idea what workers do in a Japanese factory and they rely on gaining insights from supervisors and Japanese expatriates. Personal communications have proved to be an effective way to deal with ambiguous problems and to ensure the diffusion of the transferred work methods. (Interview, February 2008)

OMS has implemented an expatriate-dependent quality control process, and regularly sends personnel from the parent company to the subsidiary. The Japanese Production Control Manager remarks: 'Omron Shanghai emphasizes quality more than cost reduction, and, if raw materials and product parts cannot reach the required standards, it prefers to import more costly parts from Japan'. Local quality control rests on two procedures. One method is to set up quality checkpoints for every production process monitored by quality control groups for all major production lines. These groups report the inspection results horizontally to Omron Japan's quality control department and vertically to the subsidiary's General Manager. To be qualified to undertake inspections, local product quality inspectors receive at least two weeks' training and testing. The second method was to install built-in computerized inspection monitors, as invented by Omron Japan. In time, OMS claimed its quality pass rate was second only to Omron factories in Japan (Interviews, July 2007, December 2012).

Yet, the parent MNC could not fully transplant Japanese total quality control. OMS implemented factory production management and quality control through the heavy use of expatriate supervision and advanced manufacturing equipment rather than through high-quality and multi-skilled shop-floor workers who are committed to output standards and innovation. The factories at OMS, as a designated production headquarters for a global strategy, are rich in advanced manufacturing equipment or hardware, but lack the software of committed, self-motivated workers with the highest skills level. The Japanese Production Control Manager adds:

> In Japan, our total quality control is built into the production process, and shop-floor workers are committed to their jobs but there is a different situation in China's plants. I think we have enough rules and regulations in the front-line operations, but the workers keep ignoring them, because they think they are not necessary. It is difficult to change their attitudes and some shop-floor workers are temporary workers, and we have no system and regulations to punish them if their behaviour doesn't follow the work procedures. (Interview, July 2007)

The Chinese Deputy General Manager said that some shop-floor workers receive merely a brief induction before being put on to the front line. Without proper training, quality education and experience, they cannot be expected to meet the preferred standards, but, in China, there is a trade-off between labour cost and labour quality. OMS has been introducing Japanese production methods, but global 'best practices' have to be adapted (Interview, December 2012).

The development of supplier networks is an important strategic aim, and Omron views competent local suppliers as vital support for scaled production factories and for meeting the demands of global markets. The importing of parts from Japan is expensive and increasingly uncompetitive. Omron continues to show a bias for those Japanese suppliers that had set up facilities in China to meet orders from MNCs, yet they are unable to meet all of OMS's orders. The subsidiary has as a result forged links with local Chinese suppliers, providing technical support in order to improve the quality and to secure the quantity of components. The strategy, on other hand, is long-term. The Japanese expatriate responsible for strategic planning notes that OMS is able to make most of its components within its own factories, and that, critically, it imports key or high technology parts from Japan (Interview, July 2007).

R&D and marketing

Omron Japan is responsible for product design and research development. It has retained its core R&D capabilities in its home economy, and decides which technologies will be transferred according to its global manufacturing plan. Nonetheless, Omron in Shanghai founded an R&D centre in 2000, and it trains technicians and engineers in cooperation with Jiao Tong University. Since 2005, the MNC's declared global strategy is to share R&D knowledge amongst its home and overseas businesses, and, to that end, it has been willing to concede the traditional autonomy of the parent company. Nonetheless, the Chinese Human Resources and Administration Manager, at the Omron China holding company, makes the point that '90 per cent of Omron Shanghai's products have been designed, developed and tested in Japan. Omron Japan has a cutting-edge research laboratory for basic science technology development, with a substantial budget, and train a significant group of qualified scientists'. Therefore, OMS's R&D centre mainly undertakes the adaptation of products for different markets, and does not engage in fundamental research. It is closely tied to marketing considerations, and trains local engineers and technical staff in cooperation with Jiao Tong University. Omron's global strategy is to share different R&D knowledge amongst its overseas subsidiaries, and it is willing to give away some autonomy, seeing young graduates from China's best universities as a huge talent pool. It sees the young graduates from China's best universities as a large human resource pool (Interviews, February 2008, December 2012).

R&D funding mainly depends on OMS's financial performance, with Japan providing technical support rather than finance. It adapts core technology, and helps to design some small household products. The growing demand for quality products in China has encouraged the expansion of local R&D (Interview, Deputy R&D Manager, February 2008). In overseeing the absorption and adaptation of technology and products from Japan, the R&D centre has to coordinate closely with the production and marketing departments, which advise on the step-by-step adjustment of designs or improvements in product quality. Once production has begun, the R&D centre has to monitor production and quality standards in line with the global standards. Omron had originally assembled products in China for re-export, and it had established Omron China in order to build a domestic sales network that could better meet growing levels of demand. According to the Japanese Production Quality Manager, Omron Japan sought to replicate and develop global marketing standards in China, and the subsidiary organizes training courses in combination with the parent MNC. Omron Japan leaves the management of distribution, sales and advertising to local personnel, with their better understanding of the Chinese market, and encourages them to share their experience and knowledge with Japan and all overseas subsidiaries (Interview, July 2007).

Implications

We set out some implications by answering a set of key questions.

To what extent does the case of the Omron subsidiaries in China demonstrate the formative influences of parent MNC, national institutions, or subsidiary personnel on its operations and practices?

In other words, if we follow three important streams of FDI/IB literature – parent company strategy, institutionalism and subsidiary agency – can we adequately explain the evolving case of OMS? The evidence reveals that, if we are to understand its development, since 1993, there have been a number of determining factors. At the outset, two factors set the context in which the subsidiary operated. The institutional framework, namely central government insistence that investing foreign firms establish joint ventures with SOEs, directly shaped ownership and management structures. Huayi Home Appliance Company had representation on the board, and it had the right to appoint members of the senior management team. It was, furthermore, its HR system that was transferred to OMS, although it was the Japanese MNC that took on issues of training and skills and implemented needed changes. For obvious reasons of pragmatism, Chinese managers were responsible for all employment matters and for contacts and negotiations with Shanghai's civic authorities.

On the other hand, one reason for Communist China encouraging FDI and the joint venture condition was to access the managerial and technological capabilities of foreign companies. Marked differences in the economic development of home and host economies were at the root of the leverage Omron exercised, as the parent MNC, in order to control the day-to-day activities and ultimately the long-term evolution of the subsidiary. Contrary to some theories, the strictures of joint venture did not restrain the commitment of Omron Japan to dispatching key personnel to influence and control much of the subsidiary. Indeed, the MNC's capabilities in transferring, maintaining and improving technology, production, product quality and work skills became increasingly entrenched through its use of expatriates and the involvement of the parent MNC. Japanese managers took on the tasks of subsidiary chairman and heads of all departments, with the sole exception of human resources. From the outset, management decisions were made in conjunction with Omron Japan, not only through the subsidiary headquarters but also with Shanghai staff in production and other functions talking directly to other relevant operational staff in Kyoto.

Against the influences of institutional regulation and the SOE partner, it was the transfer of sought capabilities, the control the parent MNC operated through its capabilities and the expatriate team needed to supervise transferred systems that determined the agenda for OMS. The creation of a wholly owned subsidiary gave the parent the possibility of strengthening its control. The transformation of the ownership structure coincided nonetheless with the strategic decision to convert OMS into a global factory. For this objective, in principle, the capabilities of the subsidiary and the agency of its managers would have an enhanced role, and OMS would become more networked with other Omron subsidiaries and less dependent on its interactions with Japan. The Omron case, at this juncture of its history, highlights how the parent firm acts as a dynamic rather than a fixed element on the evolution of the subsidiary. Omron aspired to be a global business rather than as a Japanese-dominated business with overseas satellites. The parent company remained the driving force behind the adding of global product and production standards to Japanese systems, and, while the agency of the Chinese managers was an important part of the process, their commitment was to effective implementation of imported international practices. Admittedly, the ability of the labour force to reach these goals remained an objective as opposed to a task achieved, but OMS did become at any early point capable of making products for world markets. Both Japanese and Chinese managers and supervisors were needed in the upgrading of work skills, factory discipline, and output quality.

How successfully or fully have Japanese or international business methods been transferred to China, and which business functions and practices reveal over time the greatest transfer propensity?

The complex influences and interactions of parent company, national institutions and local management meant that some measure of adaptation and practice hybridity at OMS was inevitable. We should not anticipate uniform practices within either single national economies or a single MNC. From the beginning, Omron Japan made clear its strategic intent to transfer its products and production processes, and the joint venture arrangement, a condition set by the Chinese government, and other institutional contexts were supportive of its intent. Omron's managerial and technological lead and its belief in the effectiveness of its capabilities led to a high transfer propensity. The term 'transfer capability' refers to the ability of a firm to conduct transfer due to its size, power resources, technology and international experience, all of which Omron possessed. The term 'transfer propensity' refers more directly to the strategic intent of a firm, or its commitment to installing its capabilities within overseas subsidiaries. Moreover, for the period of the joint venture, and additionally since the formation of a wholly owned enterprise, Chinese managers expressed their wish to implement Japanese or global best practice. There is small evidence of 'partial transfer' in the sense of a parent MNC selectively adapting practices to make them a 'best fit' to local conditions, since there was confidence that the core of the parent systems could be transferred.

Undoubtedly, and for several reasons, some adaptation was necessitated in practice at the level of subsidiary operations. During the period of the joint venture, production and quality processes relied more heavily on managerial supervision than in the case at the parent firm, since there remained difficulties over skill levels, quality expectations and work attitudes amongst the labour force, themselves linked to the nature and stability of employment in China. Yet, under the wholly owned subsidiary, none of these issues were considered problematic enough to jeopardize greater investment and the expansion of output. With the benefit of greater ownership, Omron Japan showed greater strategic intent to improve the capabilities of its subsidiary, while simultaneously increasing cross-border control and interdependence. The expansion of in R&D in China was part of its new policy towards its subsidiary, although these new arrangements concentrated on product customization, while core product and production knowledge was maintained at home. There was no contradiction between the aims of parent control, greater local capabilities and a global strategy.

Japan-grown and later international systems in production were transferred to the subsidiary, and Chinese managers took an active role in instilling these practices. Key and advanced components were imported from the parent firm, and Omron Japan encouraged its suppliers to invest in China. But local sourcing was integral to the long-term reduction in costs, in line with the pursuit of export markets and subsequently the global factory strategy. The reality of 'partial' JIT management was a consequence of an unstable local supplier network and lower component quality, and quality control rested on the enforcement of procedures by front-line supervisors rather than the work teams or individual workers. There was never any intent to transfer human resource systems, although a parent-led but customized system of training was introduced. Multi-skilling was not sought, due to the short-term employment horizons and labour-intensive assembly operations typical at the subsidiary. Performance related pay was used – a common hybrid innovation – to secure employee motivation.

Omron demonstrates the complexity of measuring degrees of centralization–decentralization and levels of practice hybridity for an MNC or even a subsidiary as a whole. The interacting influences of MNC strategy, institutions and local managers have affected each business function differently. The parent firm maintained a strong control over production, products and R&D, and accepted greater delegation for human resources, host country marketing and external affairs. The functions of production, product development and technology at the subsidiary reflected patterns of MNC strategy and intent, whereas those functions related to employment and pay were more markedly reflective of institutionalized and contextual patterns in China. Differences between functions were based on perceived necessary responses to international versus local conditions, or to the demands of required cross-border integration (led by the MNC) versus domestic assimilation (shaped by institutions). 'Harder' or more tangible capabilities were easier to transfer internationally than 'softer' or less tangible capabilities in human resource practice, leaving aside some convergence in skills towards a Japanese or international standards through training programmes.

Have globalization strategies and trends strengthened or weakened the control of the parent MNC over its subsidiaries?

As a transitional economy, undergoing degrees of 'de-institutionalization', China offers greater scope for MNC parent strategies, widening scope in the selection of competing international practices, and more space for subsidiary management agency, or at least China has done so in specific manufacturing industries, such as electronics. The search for increased local management capabilities and agency does not perforce mean greater independence from parent company ownership, control or direction. The continued and pivotal role of the parent suggests a persistent dominance effect by those MNCs and nation states in charge of key economic resources and capabilities.

One aim of Omron in establishing a wholly owned subsidiary, in 2005, was, as we have seen, to transfer and develop the international best practices needed for a global factory. In theory, OMS would become integrated with the MNC's global network, and move beyond mainly reporting to and coordinating with the parent firm. Omron Japan confirmed that Shanghai would form its main international production base. The subsidiary had begun as an international joint venture and as a brownfield operation reliant on the transplanting of Japanese technology and methods through parent company control and expatriate personnel. The mechanisms were available for the transfer of additional production processes and R&D activities, and for the inculcation of international standards.

If we look for insights from managerial strategy literature, the Resource Based View would suggest that the parent MNC has a powerful means of controlling a subsidiary through its ownership of core capabilities. Can we take the parallel interpretation that advanced or rising capabilities within a subsidiary act as a counter to parental control? Omron's has been a strategy of efficiency seeking, in location and labour costs, and of off-shoring production in China. OMS on its founding prioritized export markets, but its conversion to a global factory with a central place in a cross-border value chain occurred in parallel to acquiring greater responsiveness to China's expanding domestic market. Although the aspiration to be a global factory did see attempts to inculcate international standards and practices, the control as well as the ownership of the parent MNC over its subsidiary did not decline but in fact increased.

Conclusion

The strategic motivation for the founding of Shanghai Omron was efficiency-seeking and the meeting of export demand. Omron was obliged by the institutional requirements of the time to adopt a joint venture with an SOE. The parent MNC revealed a strong strategic intent to transfer practices to its subsidiary, with the pragmatic exception of human resource policies which was based on Chinese SOE traditions and left to Chinese managers and from which Japanese expatriates exempted themselves. Institutional isomorphic pressures (if mainly in human resources) existed alongside the MNC's need for cross-border symmetry (most obviously in production methods and quality standards). Given the joint venture arrangements, Omron was cautious about the transfer of its core technology and technological knowledge, but effectives in transferring its production and product quality even if inevitable variations in processes and outcomes were detectable.

When Omron Shanghai was converted into a wholly owned enterprise, it accelerated the transfer of capabilities, including R&D, and indicated the ingrained caution commonly associated with Japanese businesses about the loss of proprietorial knowledge to strategic partners. The formation of a wholly owned subsidiary coincided with Omron's adoption of its global factory policy, with China as the low-cost production centre manufacturing for world markets, and the policy was based on the inculcation of international as opposed to strictly Japanese 'best practice'. To expand production capacity, and to optimize product quality, the MNC sought to enhance the role of local management and subsidiary capability, while integrating the Chinese operation more fully with its international networks and ensuring tight parent company involvement. In dealing with changes in the nature of global competition and MNC business structures from the 1990s onwards, Omron was able to maintain its competitive position by merging international, home grown and host country subsidiary practices and to pursue a global factory strategy while increasing the role of the parent firm within the MNC. While Omron Japan retained leading capabilities that enabled it to achieve its strategic objectives, it showed itself adaptable enough to learn from and to absorb international best practices.

What does the case of Omron in China reveal about the characteristics of international business or the specific issues caused by FDI? How, therefore, did Omron deal with the changing requirements of cross-border transactions and organization, or with differing macro-economic or institutional environments? The idea of the global factory – seen as renewing IB as a distinctive area of study – saw the dyadic parent–subsidiary relationship as superseded by a more complex set of questions about where business activities should be located, integrated and controlled in order to meet a global demand. Yet, alongside the lateral network of suppliers and service providers at Omron, the vertical core includes the headquarters (which owns or controls key capabilities) and the main production unit (in which key capabilities are located). Differences in the economic development of Japan and China are connected to differences in the capabilities of the Omron parent firm and OMS, and to the overall acceptance of local management to the adoption of Japanese or international standards and practices and to parent firm control. In converting its subsidiary into its main production unit, Omron Japan had to continue the process of capability transfer, and reinforced its ownership and control. It has not adopted a strategy of coordinating its proprietorial technology and products amongst a network of contracted producers. As a result, its approach to being a global factory has not seen a cutting of investment in R&D and skills, but, since ownership and control of the subsidiary has been maintained, the opposite. The major feature in the evolution of OMS, its management practices, and capabilities – as an international joint venture, as a wholly owned enterprise, or as a global factory – has been the strategic intent and influence of the parent business, when compared against national institutions or local management agency. The case of Omron China fits with the growing sway of MNCs over global production, technology, investment and trade. It highlights, in addition, questions about how governments retain the commitment of MNCs to the transfer and enhancement of strategic resources and capabilities, while the control MNCs exercise over subsidiaries, associated with that commitment, may place constraints on the economic benefits to the host economy.

Disclosure statement

No potential conflict of interest was reported by the authors.

References

Abo, T. 1994. *Hybrid Factory: The Japanese Production System in the United States*. New York: Oxford University Press.

Ackroyd, S. S., G.G. Burrell, M.M. Hughes, A.A. Whitaker, and S. Ackroyd. 1988. "The Japanisation of British Industry?" *Industrial Relations Journal* 19 (1): 11–23.

Alder, P. S. 1993. "The Learning Bureaucracy: New United Motors Manufacturing, Inc." In *Research in Organizational Behavior*, edited by B. M. Straw and L. L. Cummings. vol. 15, 111–194. Greenwich, CT: JAI Press.

Alder, P. S. 1999. "Hybridization: Human Resource Management at Two Toyota Transplants." In *Remade in America: Transplanting and Transforming Japanese Management Systems*, edited by J. K. Liker, W. M. Fruin, and P. S. Alder, 75–116. New York: Oxford University Press.

Anderson, E., and H. Gatignon. 1986. "Modes of Foreign Entry: A Transaction Cost Analysis and Propositions." *Journal of International Business Studies* 17 (3): 1–26. doi:10.1057/palgrave. jibs.8490432.

Andersson, U., M. Forsgren, and U. Holm. 2007. "Balancing Subsidiary Influence in the Federative MNC: A Business Network View." *Journal of International Business Studies* 38 (4): 802–818.

Arvidsson, N. 1999. "The Ignorant MNE: The Role of Perception Gaps in Knowledge Management." PhD diss., Stockholm School of Economics.

Bartlett, C. A., and S. Ghoshal. 1986. "Tap Your Subsidiaries for Global Reach." *Harvard Business Review* 64: 87–94.

Bartlett, C. A., and S. Ghoshal. 1989. *Managing Across Borders: The Transnational Solution*. London: Hutchinson Business.

Beechler, S., A. Bird, and S. Taylor, eds. 1998. *Japanese MNCs Abroad: Individual and Organizational Learning*. New York: Oxford University Press.

Beechler, S., and J. Z. Yang. 1994. "The Transfer of Japanese-Style Management to American Subsidiaries: Constraints, and Competencies." *Journal of International Business Studies* 25 (3): 467–491. doi:10.1057/palgrave.jibs.8490208.

Birkinshaw, J. 2000. *Entrepreneurship in the Global Firm*. Thousand Oaks: Sage.

Birkinshaw, J. 2001. "Strategy and Management in MNE Subsidiaries." In *The Oxford Handbook of International Business*, edited by A. M. Rugman and T. Brewer, 380–401. Oxford: Oxford University Press.

Birkinshaw, J., and A. Morrison. 1995. "Configurations of Strategy and Structure in Subsidiaries of Multinational Corporations." *Journal of International Business Studies* 26 (4): 729–753. doi:10. 1057/palgrave.jibs.8490818.

Bratton, J. 1990. *Japanisation at Work*. Basingstoke: Macmillan.

Buckley, P. 2009a. "The Impact of the Global Factory on Economic Development." *Journal of World Business* 44 (2): 131–143. doi:10.1016/j.jwb.2008.05.003.

Buckley, P. J. 2009b. "The Role of Headquarters in the Global Factory." In *Headquarters Role in the Contemporary MNE*, edited by V. Holm and V. Andersson. Cheltenham: Edward Elgar.

Buckley, P. 2010. "The Theory of International Business Pre-Hymer." *Journal of World Business* 46 (1): 61–73.

Buckley, P. J., and M. C. Casson. 1976. *The Future of the Multinational Enterprise*. London: Macmillan.

Buckley, P. J., and M. C. Casson. 1985. *The Economic Theory of the Multinational Enterprise*. London: Macmillan.

Buckley, P. J., and M. C. Casson. 1991. *The Future of the Multinational Enterprise*. London: Macmillan.

Buckley, P. J., and M. C. Casson. 1998. "Models of the Multinational Enterprise." *Journal of International Business Studies* 29 (1): 21–44. doi:10.1057/palgrave.jibs.8490023.

Buckley, P. J., and P. N. Ghauri. 2004. "Globalisation, Economic Geography and the Strategy of Multinational Enterprises." *Journal of International Business Studies* 35 (2): 81–98. doi:10. 1057/palgrave.jibs.8400076.

Cantwell, J., and L. Piscitello. 2000. "The Location of MNC's Technological Activities in Europe: Agglomerative Tendencies and Other Territorial Externalities." ERSA conference papers.

Chandler, A. D. 1962. *Strategy and Structure: Chapters in the History of American Industrial Enterprise*. Cambridge, MA: MIT Press.

Chandler, A. D. 1977. *The Visible Hand: The Managerial Revolution in American Business*. Cambridge, MA: Harvard University Press.

Chandler, A. D. 1990. *Scale and Scope: The Dynamics of Industrial Enterprise*. Cambridge, MA: Harvard University Press.

Chandler, A. D., and H. Daems, eds. 1980. *Managerial Hierarchies: Comparative Perspectives on the Rise of the Modern Industrial Enterprise*. Cambridge, MA: Harvard University Press.

Chandler, A. D., and B. Mazlish, eds. 1997. *Leviathans: Multinational Corporations and the New Global History*. Cambridge: Cambridge University Press.

Child, J., and T. Tsai. 2005. "The Dynamic between Firms' Environmental Strategies and Institutional Constraints in Emerging Economies: Evidence from China and Taiwan." *Journal of Management Studies* 42 (1): 95–125. doi:10.1111/j.1467-6486.2005.00490.x.

Coase, R. H. 1937. "The Nature of the Firm." *Economica*, NS 4 (16): 386–405. doi:10.1111/j.1468-0335.1937.tb00002.x.

D'Cruz, J. R. 1986. "Strategic Management of Subsidiaries." In *Managing the MNC Subsidiary*, edited by H. Etemad and L. S. Dulude. London: Croom Helm.

Delios, A., and W. J. Henisz. 2000. "Japanese Firms' Investment Strategies in Emerging Economies." *Academy of Management Journal* 43 (3): 305–323. doi:10.2307/1556397.

DiMaggio, P. J., and W. W. Powell. 1983. "The Iron Cage Revisited: Institutional Isomorphism and Collective Rationality in Organizational Fields." *American Sociological Review* 48 (2): 147–160. doi:10.2307/2095101.

Doremus, P. N., W. W. Keller, L. W. Pauly, and S. Reich. 1998. *The Myth of the Global Corporation*. Princteon, NJ: Princeton University Press.

Dorrenbacher, C., and M. Geppert. 2003. *Politics and Power in the Multinational Corporation: The Role of Institutions, Interests and Identities*. Cambridge: Cambride University Press.

Doz, Y., and C. K. Prahalad. 1993. "Managing DMNCs: A Search for a New Paradigm." In *Organizational Theory and the Multinational Corporation*, edited by S. Ghoshal and D. E. Westney. New York: St Martins Press.

Dunning, J. H. 1980. "Toward an Eclectic Theory of International Production: Some Empirical Tests." *Journal of International Business Studies* 11 (1): 9–31. doi:10.1057/palgrave.jibs. 8490593.

Dunning, J. H. 1981. *International Production and Multinational Enterprises*. London: George Allen & Unwin.

Dunning, J. H. 1988. "The Eclectic Paradigm of International Production: A Restatement and Some Possible Extensions." *Journal of International Business Studies* 19 (1): 1–31. doi:10.1057/palgrave.jibs.8490372.

Dunning, J. H. 1993. *The Globalization of Business: The Challenge of the 1990s*. London: Routledge.

Dunning, J. H. 1995. "Reappraising the Eclectic Paradigm in an Age of Alliance Capitalism." *Journal of International Business Studies* 26 (3): 461–491. doi:10.1057/palgrave.jibs.8490183.

Dunning, J. H. 1998. "Location and the Multinational Enterprise: A Neglected Factor?" *Journal of International Business Studies* 29 (1): 45–66. doi:10.1057/palgrave.jibs.8490024.

Dunning, J. H. 2000. "The Eclectic Paradigm as an Envelope for Economic and Business Theories of MNE Activity." *International Business Review* 9 (2): 163–190. doi:10.1016/S0969-5931(99)00035-9.

Dunning, J. H. 2003. "The Eclectic (OLI) Paradigm of International Production: Past, Present and the Future." In *International Business and the Eclectic Paradigm: Developing the OLI Framework*, edited by J. Cantwell and R. Narula, 25–46. New York: Routledge.

Dunning, J. H. 2006. "Comment on Dragon Multinationals: New Players in 21st Century Globalization." *Asia Pacific Journal of Management* 23 (2): 139–141. doi:10.1007/s10490-006-7161-1.

Dunning, J. H., and S. Lundan. 2008. *Multinational Enterprises and the Global Economy*. Aldershot: Edward Elgar.

Elger, T., and C. Smith. 1994. *Global Japanisation? The Transnational Transformation of the Labour Process*. London: Routledge.

Evans, P. A. L., Y. Doz, and A. Laurent. 1989. *Human Resource Management in International Firms: Change, Globalization and Innovation*. New York: Martin's Press.

Fitzgerald, R. 2014. *Rise of the Global Company: The MNC Entreprise and the Making of the Modern World*. Cambridge: Cambridge University Press.

Florian, A. 2009. *Hybridization of MNE Subsidiaries: The Automotive Sector in India*. London: Palgrave Macmillan.

Florida, R., and M. Kenney. 1991. "Organisation vs. Culture: Japanese Automotive Transplants in the US." *Industrial Relations Journal* 22 (3): 181–196. doi:10.1111/j.1468-2338.1991.tb00636. x.

Forsgren, M. 2008. *Theories of the MNC Firm: A Multidimensional Creature in the Global Economy*. Basingstoke: Edward Elgar.

Forsgren, M., U. Holm, and J. Johanson. 2007. *Managing the Embedded MNC: A Business Network View*. Montpellier: Edward Elgar.

Gates, S., and W. Egelhoff. 1986. "Centralization in Headquarters–Subsidiary Relationships." *Journal of International Business* 17 (2): 71–92. doi:10.1057/palgrave.jibs.8490425.

Geppert, M., and M. Mayer. 2005. *Global, National and Local Practices in Multinational Companies*. Basingstoke: Palgrave.

Ghoshal, S., and C. A. Bartlett. 1990. "The Multinational Corporation as an Interorganizational Network." *Academy of Management Review* 15 (4): 603–625.

Ghoshal, S, and N. Nohria. 1989. "Internal Differentiation within Multinational Corporations." *Strategic Management Journal* 10 (4): 323–337. doi:10.1002/smj.4250100403.

Ghoshal, S., and N. Nohria. 1993. "Horses for Courses: Organizational Forms for Multinational Corporations." *Sloan Management Review* Winter: 23–35.

Groot, L., and K. Merchant. 2000. "Control of International Joint Ventures." *Accounting, Organizations and Society* 25 (6): 579–607. doi:10.1016/S0361-3682(99)00057-4.

Gupta, A. K., and V. Govindarajan. 1991. "Knowledge Flows and the Structure of Control within Multinational Corporations." *Academy of Management Journal* 16 (4): 768–792.

Gupta, V., K. Govindarajan, and A. Malhotra. 1999. "Feedback-Seeking Behavior within Multinational Corporations." *Strategic Management Journal* 20 (3): 205–222. doi:10.1002/(SICI)1097-0266(199903)20:3<205:AID-SMJ17>3.0.CO;2-H.

Hall, P. A., and S. Soskice, eds. 2001. *Varieties of Capitalism: The Institutional Foundations of Comparative Advantage*. Oxford: Oxford University Press.

Harzing, A. W. 2002. "Acquisitions versus Greenfield Investments: International Strategy and Management of Entry Modes." *Strategic Management Journal* 23 (3): 211–227. doi:10.1002/smj.218.

Hatch, W., and K. Yamamura. 1996. *Asia in Japan's Embrace: Building a Regional Production Alliance*. Cambridge: Cambridge University Press.

Hedlund, G. 1981. "Autonomy of Subsidiaries and Formalization of Headquarters-Subsidiary Relations in Swedish MNCs." In *The Management of Headquarters: Subsidiary Relationships in Multinational Corporations*, edited by L. Otterbeck, 25–78. Gower: Aldershot.

Hennart, J. 1982. *A Theory of Multinational Enterprise*. Ann Arbor: University of Michigan Press.

Hennart, J. 2000. "Transaction Costs Theory and the Multinational Enterprise." In *The Nature of the Transnational Firm*, edited by C. Pitelis and R. Sugden. 2nd ed. London: Routledge.

Hollingsworth, J. R. 2000. "Doing Institutional Analysis: Implications for the Study of Innovations." *Review of International Political Economy* 7 (4): 595–644. doi:10.1080/096922900750034563.

Hollingsworth, J. R., and R. Boyer, eds. 1997. *Contemporary Capitalism: The Embeddedness of Institutions*. Cambridge: Cambridge University Press.

Hymer, S. 1960. "The International Operations of National Firms: A Study of Direct Foreign Investment." PhD thesis, MIT.

Hymer, S. 1968. "La Grande Firme MNCe." *Revue Economique* 19: 949–973.

Hymer, S. 1976. *The International Operations of National Firms*. Lexington, MA: Lexington Books.

Kenney, M., and R. Florida. 1993. *Beyond Mass Production: The Japanese System and Its Transfer to the US*. New York: Oxford University Press.

Kenney, M., and R. Florida. 1995. "The Transfer of Japanese Management Styles in Two US Transplant Industries: Autos and Electronics." *Journal of Management Studies* 32 (6): 789–802. doi:10.1111/j.1467-6486.1995.tb00152.x.

Kilduff, M. 1993. "The Reproduction of Inertia in Multinational Corporations." In *Organization Theory and the Multinational Corporation*, edited by S. Ghoshal and E. Westney. New York: St Martin's Press.

Kojima, K. 1973. "A Macroeconomic Approach to Foreign Direct Investment." *Hitosubashi Journal of Economics* 14: 1–21.

Kojima, K. 1978. *Direct Foreign Investment: A Japanese Model of MNC Business Operations*. London: Croom Helm.

Kojima, K. 1982. "Macroeconomics versus International Business Approaches to Foreign Direct Investment." *Hitosubashi Journal of Economics* 25: 1–19.

Kojima, K. 1985. "Japanese and American Direct Investment in Asia: A Comparative Analysis." *Hitotsubashi Journal of Economics* 26: 1–35.

Kojima, K., and T. Ozawa. 1984. *Japan's General Trading Companies: Merchants of Economic Development*. Paris: OECD.

Koopmans, T. C., and T. Montias. 1971. "On the Description and Comparison of Economic Systems." In *Comparison of Economic Systems: Theoretical and Methodological Approaches*, edited by A. Eckstein. Berkeley: University of California Press.

Kostova, T. 1999. "Transnational Transfer of Strategic Organizational Practices: A Contextual Perspective." *Academy of Management Review* 24: 308–324.

Kostova, T., and K. Roth. 2002. "Adoption of an Organizational Practice by Subsidiaries of Multinational Corporations: Institutional and Relational Effects." *Academy of Management Journal* 45 (1): 215–233. doi:10.2307/3069293.

Lane, C. 1994. "Industrial Order and the Transformation of Industrial Relations: Britain, Germany and France." In *New Frontiers in European Industrial Relations*, edited by R. Hyman and A. Ferner, 167–195. Oxford: Blackwell.

Lane, C. 2000. "Understanding the Globalization Strategies of German and British MNC Companies: Is a 'Societal Effects' Approach Still Useful?" In *Embedding Organizations: Societal Analysis of Actors, Organizations and Socio-economic Context*, edited by M. Maurice and A. Sorge, 189–208. Amsterdam: John Benjamins.

Lane, C. 2001. "The Emergence of German Transnational Companies: A Theoretical Analysis and Empirical Study of the Globalization Process." In *The MNC Firm. Organizing Across Institutional and National Divides*, edited by G. Morgan, P. H. Kristensen, and R. Whitley, 69–96. Oxford: Oxford University Press.

Leahy, A., and G. Naghavi. 2010. "Intellectual Property Rights and Entry into a Foreign Market: FDI versus Joint Ventures." *Review of International Economics* 18 (4): 633–649. doi:10.1111/j.1467-9396.2010.00901.x.

Mathews, J. A. 2002. *Dragon MNCs: Towards a New Model of Global Growth*. New York: Oxford University Press.

Mathews, J. A. 2006a. "Dragon Multinationals: New Players in 21st Century Globalization." *Asia Pacific Journal of Management* 23 (1): 5–27. doi:10.1007/s10490-006-6113-0.

Mathews, J. A. 2006b. "Response to Professors Dunning and Narula." *Asia Pacific Journal of Management* 23 (2): 153–155. doi:10.1007/s10490-006-7163-z.

Meyer, J. W., and B. Rowan. 1977. "Institutionalized Organizations: Formal Structure as Myth and Ceremony." *American Journal of Sociology* 83 (2): 340–363. doi:10.1086/226550.

Morgan, G. 2001. "The MNC Firm: Organizing Across Institutional and National Divides." In *The MNC Firm: Organizing Across Institutional and National Divides*, edited by G. Morgan, P. H. Kristensen, and R. Whitley, 1–24. Oxford: Oxford University Press.

Morgan, G., and R. Whitley. 2003. "Introduction." *Journal of Management Studies* 40 (3): 609–616. doi:10.1111/1467-6486.00353.

Morris, J. 1988. "The Who, Why and Where of Japanese Manufacturing Investment in the UK." *Industrial Relations Journal* 19 (1): 31–40. doi:10.1111/j.1468-2338.1988.tb00012.x.

Mudambi, R., and P. Navarra. 2004. "Is Knowledge Power? Knowledge Flows, Subsidiary Power and Rent-Seeking within MNCs." *Journal of International Business Studies* 35 (5): 385–406. doi:10.1057/palgrave.jibs.8400093.

Nolan, P., D. Sutherland, and J. Zhang. 2002. "The Challenge of the Global Business Revolution." *Contributions to Political Economy* 21 (1): 91–110. doi:10.1093/cpe/21.1.91.

North, D. C. 1990. *Institutions, Institutional Change, and Economic Performance*. Cambridge, MA: Harvard University Press.

Oliver, N., and B. Wilkinson. 1992. *The Japanisation of British Industry: Developments in the 1990s*. Oxford: Blackwell.

Ozawa, T. 1989. *Recycling Japan's Surpluses for Developing Countries*. Paris: OECD.

Ozawa, T. 1991. "Japan in a New Phase of MNCism and Industrial Upgrading: Functional Integration of Trade, Growth and FDI." *Journal of World Trade* 25 (1): 43–60.

Peng, M. W. 2003. "Institutional Transitions and Strategic Choices." *Academy of Management Review* 28 (2): 275–296.

Peng, M. W., and P. Heath. 2003. "The Growth of the Firm in Planned Economies in Transition: Institutions, Organizations, and Strategic Choices." *Academy of Management Review* 21 (2): 492–528.

Peng, M. W., and T. A. Khoury. 2009. "Unbundling the Institution-Based View of International Business Strategy." In *Oxford Handbook of International Business*, edited by A. Rugman and T. Brewer. Oxford: Oxford University Press.

Penrose, E. 1959. *The Theory of the Growth of the Firm*. Oxford: Oxford University Press.

Perlmutter, H. V. 1969. "The Tortuous Evolution of the Multinational Company." *Columbia Journal of World Business* 4 (1): 9–18.

Porter, M. E. 1990. *The Competitive Advantage of Nations*. New York: Simon and Schuster.

Powell, W. W. 1996. "Inter-Organizational Collaboration in the Biotechnology Industry." *Journal of Institutional and Theoretical Economics* 120 (1): 197–215.

Rosenzweig, P. M., and N. Nohria. 1994. "Influences on Human Resource Management Practices in Multinational Corporations." *Journal of International Business Studies* 25 (2): 229–251. doi:10.1057/palgrave.jibs.8490199.

Rosenzweig, P. M., and J. Singh. 1991. "Organizational Environment and the Multinational Enterprise." *Academy of Management Review* 16: 340–361.

Roth, K., and D. Nigh. 1992. "The Effectiveness of Headquarters-Subsidiary Relationships: The Role of Coordination, Control, and CONFLICT." *Journal of Business Research* 25 (4): 277–301. doi:10.1016/0148-2963(92)90025-7.

Rugman, A. M., and J. R. D'Cruz. 2003. *Multinationals as Flagship Firms: Regional Business Networks: Regional Business Networks*. Oxford: Oxford University Press.

Ruigrok, W., and R. Van Tulder. 1995. *The Logic of International Restructuring*. London: Routledge.

Saka, A. 2003. *Cross-national Appropriation of Work Systems: Japanese Firms in the UK*. Cheltenham: Edward Elgar.

Scott, W. R. 1995. *Institutions and Organizations*. Thousand Oaks, CA: Sage.

Seki, M. 1997. *Kudoka o koete: gijutsu to chiiki no saikochiku* (Overcoming Hollowing Out: The Reorganization of Technique and Regions). Tokyo: Nihon Keizai Shinbunsha.

Smith, C., B. McSweeney, and R. Fitzgerald, eds. 2008. *Remaking Management: Between Global and Local*. Cambridge: Cambridge University Press.

Sorge, A. 1991. "Strategic Fit and the Societal Effect: Interpreting Cross-national Comparisons of Technology, Organization and Human Resources." *Organization Studies* 12 (2): 161–190. doi:10.1177/017084069101200201.

Sorge, A. 2004. "Cross-national Differences in Human Resources and Organization." In *International Human Resource Management*, edited by A. W. Harzing and J. Van Ruysseveldt, 117–140. London: Sage.

Stewart, P. 1998. "Out of Chaos Comes Order: From Japanization to Lean Production." *Employee Relations* 20 (3): 213–223. doi:10.1108/01425459810228252.

Stopford, J. M., and L. T. Wells. 1972. *Managing the Multinational Enterprise: Organization of the Firm and Ownership of the Subsidiaries*. New York: Basic Books.

Strange, R., and J. Newton. 2006. "Stephen Hymer and the Externalization of Production." *International Business Review* 15 (2): 180–193. doi:10.1016/j.ibusrev.2005.07.007.

Taylor, R. 1996. *Greater China and Japan: Prospects for an Economic Partnership in East Asia*. London: Routledge.

Taylor, B. 1999. "Japanese Management Style in China? Production Practices in Japanese Manufacturing Plants." *New Technology, Work and Employment Journal* 14 (2): 129–142.

Taylor, B. 2001. "The Management of Labour in Japanese Manufacturing Plants in China." *International Journal of Human Resource Management* 12 (4): 601–620. doi:10.1080/09585190122913.

Teece, D. J. 1981. "The Market for Know-how and the Efficient International Transfer of Technology." *Annals of the Academy of Political and Social Science* 458 (1): 81–96. doi:10.1177/000271628145800107.

Teece, D. J. 1985. "Multinational Enterprises, Internal Governance, and Industrial Organization." *The American Economic Review* 75 (2): 233–238.

Teece, D. J. 2006. "Reflections on the Hymer Thesis and the Multinational Enterprise." *International Business Review* 15 (2): 124–139. doi:10.1016/j.ibusrev.2005.11.003.

Tempel, A., and P. Walgenbach. 2003. "Global Standardization of Organizational Forms and Management Practices?: Combining American and European Institutionalism." Paper presented at the 3rd Conference of the European Academy of Management, Milan.

Trevor, M. 1983. *Japan's Reluctant MNCs*. New York: St. Martin's Press.

Turnbull, P. 1986. "The 'Japanisation' of Production and Industrial Relations at Lucas Electrical." *Industrial Relations Journal* 17 (3): 193–206. doi:10.1111/j.1468-2338.1986.tb00537.x.

Vernon, R. 1966. "International Investment and International Trade in the Product Cycle." *Quarterly Journal of Economics* 80 (2): 190–207. doi:10.2307/1880689.

Westney, D. E. 1987. *Imitation and Innovation*. Cambridge, MA: Harvard University Press.

Westney, D. E. 1993. "Institutionalization Theory and the Multinational Corporation." In *Organization Theory and the Multinational Corporation*, edited by S. Ghoshal and D. E. Westney, 237–255. New York: St. Martin's Press.

White, R. E., and T. A. Poynter. 1984. "Strategies for Foreign-Owned Subsidiaries in Canada." *Business Quarterly* 49 (2): 59–69.

Whitley, R. 1992a. *Business Systems in East Asia: Firms, Markets and Societies*. London: Sage.

Whitley, R. 1992b. "Society, Firms and Markets: The Social Structuring of Business System." In *European Business System: Firms and Markets in their National Context*, edited by R. Whitley, 5–45. London: Sage.

Whitley, R. 1999. *Divergent Capitalisms: The Social Structuring and Change of Business Systems*. Oxford: Oxford University Press.

Whitley, R. 2001. "How and Why Are International Firms Different? The Consequences of Cross-border Managerial Coordination for Firm Characteristics and Behavior." In *The MNC Firm:*

Organizing Across Institutional and National Divides, edited by G. Morgan, P. H. Kristensen, and R. Whitley. Oxford: Oxford University Press.

Williamson, O. 1975. *Markets and Hierarchies: Analysis and Antitrust Implications: A Study in the Economics of Internal Organization*. New York: Free Press.

Womack, J. P., and D. T. Jones. 1996. *Lean Thinking*. New York: Simon and Schuster.

Womack, J. P., D. T. Jones, and D. Roos. 1990. *The Machine that Changed the World*. New York: Macmillan.

Wood, S. J. 1992. "Japanization and/or Toyotaism?" *Work, Employment and Society* 5 (4): 567–600. doi:10.1177/0950017091005004006.

Yamin, M., and M. Forsgren. 2006. "Hymer's Analysis of the Multinational Organization: Power Retention and the Demise of the Federative MNE." *International Business Review* 15 (2): 166–179. doi:10.1016/j.ibusrev.2005.07.006.

Yamin, M., and R. R. Sinkovics. 2009. "Infrastructure or Foreign Direct Investment?" *Journal of World Business* 44 (2): 144–157. doi:10.1016/j.jwb.2008.05.004.

Yan, A., and B. Gray. 1996. "Linking Management Control and Interpartner Relationships with Performance in US-China Joint Ventures." In *Management Issues in China: International Enterprises*, edited by J. Child and Y. Lu. London: Routledge.

Zucker, L. G. 1977. "The Role of Institutionalization in Cultural Persistence." *American Sociological Review* 42 (5): 726–743. doi:10.2307/2094862.

Boundary-crossing and the localization of capabilities in a Japanese multinational firm

Jacky F.L. Hong[a] and Robin Stanley Snell[b]

[a]Faculty of Business Administration, University of Macau, Av. Padre Tomas Pereira, S.J. Taipa, Macau S.A.R., P.R. China; [b]Department of Management, Lingnan University, Hong Kong, P.R. China

We conducted a case study to explore the challenges encountered by a foreign subsidiary of a Japanese multinational firm when localizing its organizational capabilities in China. Drawing on the concepts of boundaries and boundary-crossing, we identify pragmatic and cultural knowledge boundaries, which denied opportunities for the host-country employees to contribute their local expertise to augment the firm's core capabilities within the domains of research and development and operational protocols. However, within those domains that were regarded as complementary to or peripheral to the firm's core capabilities, host-country employees were granted more scope to cross the associated pragmatic boundaries.

Introduction

Japanese multinational corporations (MNCs) continue to engage in foreign direct investment through offshoring and outsourcing to low-cost countries, in order to enhance cost effectiveness and improve operational flexibility (Buckley 2009). Their attempts to shift the locus of knowledge work away from the home country to developing countries epitomize a general trend among MNCs (Gammeltoft, Barnard, and Madhok 2010; Jensen and Pedersen 2011). However, once regarded as formidable challengers to the dominance of western MNCs, Japanese MNCs have declined in stature over the past two decades (Buckley 2009; Horn and Cross 2009). We shall analyse the source of their difficulties in transferring their core organizational capabilities abroad (Leonard-Barton 1992) and identify opportunities for them to augment and enhance their capabilities with locally captured knowledge (Beechler and Bird 1999; Hong, Easterby-Smith, and Snell 2006a).

While the international competitiveness of Japanese MNCs has been adversely affected by the prolonged economic slowdown faced in the home environment, their long-term decline is also attributable to their adoption of an ethnocentric approach to globalization (Black and Morrison 2012; Collinson and Rugman 2008), which has impaired their adaptation to changing foreign environments (Bartlett and Yoshihara 1992; Collinson and Rugman 2008; Itagaki 2009; Marukawa 2009; Numagami, Karube, and Kato 2010). In particular, Japanese MNCs' almost exclusive reliance on the prior knowledge and experience of home country personnel (Black and Morrison 2012), i.e., knowledge inertia (Collinson and Wilson 2006), has led to the marginalization of host-country employees from knowledge sharing and knowledge creation routines (Byun and Ybema 2005; Hong and Snell 2008; Hong, Snell, and Easterby-Smith 2006b). This has limited the MNCs' ability to transfer firm-specific learning capabilities abroad (Beechler and Bird 1999; Busser 2008; Itagaki 2009; Lam 2003; Marukawa 2009).

Our literature review section, which follows next, begins with definitions and explanations of knowledge boundaries and of boundary-crossing (Carlile 2002, 2004). Then, drawing on these concepts, we shall argue that Japanese MNCs' adoption of a universalist perspective on the localization of capabilities has created knowledge boundaries between Japanese expatriates and host-country personnel, impeding the flow of knowledge (Bechky 2003; Carlile 2002, 2004; Sturdy et al. 2009a) and limiting opportunities for host-country employees to join in the building of local capabilities. Following the literature review section, we shall describe the methodology that we adopted for a qualitative case study of one China-based subsidiary of a Japanese MNC. In reporting our case study findings, we shall bring out illustrations of knowledge boundaries, while also indicating the conditions under which such boundaries can be more easily crossed. In our concluding section, we shall identify theoretical and practical implications for cross-cultural knowledge work at foreign subsidiaries of Japanese MNCs, along with issues for further research.

Literature review

Knowledge boundaries

The concept of a knowledge boundary refers to a set of qualitative distinctions between the specific frames of reference that are assumed, adopted and applied by members of different specialist and/or cultural groups (Carlile 2002, 2004). When two or more such groups work together, knowledge boundaries can present challenges to the sharing of insights and expertise, the development of mutual understanding, and the creation and synthesis of new organizational knowledge (Edmondson 2003; Scarbrough et al. 2004; Sturdy et al. 2009b).

Prior research has identified several types of knowledge boundary. Syntactic boundaries reflect differential usage of specialist or idiosyncratic jargon, whereas semantic boundaries refer to different sets of implicit cognitive assumptions (Carlile 2002, 2004). Problems arising from such boundaries can be substantially reduced by providing sufficient training (Sturdy et al. 2009a) and by arranging adequate communication channels (Orlikowski 2002). Our main focus in this paper is on pragmatic and cultural boundaries, explained next.

Pragmatic boundaries

Pragmatic boundaries reflect differences and contrasts between groups in terms of preferred ways of solving practical problems and perceptions of how particular actions or arrangements impact or are impacted by special interests that are 'at stake' (Carlile 2002, 445). In MNCs, such boundaries can be reinforced by a mutual sense of political struggle, with interactions between different groups 'characterized by tensions, conflicts and considerable power differentials' (Ailon and Kunda 2009, 708).

In particular, home country-based managers, expatriates and visiting experts in MNCs that are headquartered in developed countries are likely to assume that their expertise is *de facto* superior in pragmatic terms to that of host-country employees from developing countries (Alcadipani et al. 2012; Frenkel 2008; Mir and Mir 2009), who face an uphill struggle in seeking to justify their local knowledge and locally preferred practices (Tippmann, Scott, and Mangematin 2012). The former may dismiss objections, and alternative perspectives and ideas voiced by the latter as unsophisticated or opportunistic (Jack and Westwood 2006), thereby carrying the risk of cognitive inertia (Collinson and Wilson 2006) by ignoring rich, unique and potentially valid local insights (Yanow 2004), which might otherwise form the basis of knowledge flow in the 'reverse' direction (Bhagat et al. 2002; Roney 1997).

Cultural boundaries

Cultural boundaries encompass both cognitive and affective divisions between groups from different cultural backgrounds (Sturdy et al. 2009b, 33). Cognitively oriented cultural boundaries are associated with difficulties in coming to appreciate and accept 'alien' ideas and their underlying 'logic of appropriateness' (Bourdieu 1977; Carlile 2002; Czarniawska and Sevón 1996). The legitimacy of particular work arrangements or practices is established between two groups if 'there is little question in the minds of (both sets of) actors that it serves as the natural way to effect some kind of collective action' (Hannan and Carroll 1992, 34). However, if there are cognitively oriented cultural boundaries between the groups, practices that have originated in the context of cultural assumptions shared by one group may fail to gain legitimacy within the other group's cultural context (Frenkel 2008).

Affectively oriented cultural boundaries reflect mutual attraction among members of the same culture, who can develop a common sense of belongingness, joint enterprise and in-group identity, and a corresponding lack of identification with non-members (Sturdy et al. 2009a; Wenger 1998). Members of different national cultures who come into contact with each other may thus face both interpretive barriers (Dougherty 1992) and social identity barriers (Handley et al. 2006). These cognitive and affective divisions are inter-related, and can form a boundary 'knot' that constitutes 'the demarcation of the social structure' (Santos and Eisenhardt 2005, 491), distinguishing insiders from outsiders (Sturdy et al. 2009b). This divide may undermine each group's ability to absorb the other's ideas, and discourage open discussion and intergroup collaboration (Bechky 2003; Child and Rodrigues 1996).

Crossing knowledge boundaries

Boundary-crossing can involve the use of 'boundary objects' to bridge and reconcile the frames of reference of different groups (Bechky 2003). Boundary objects serve as shared reference points that can capture attention, focus discussion and facilitate exchange of expertise and resolution of conflicting interests (Carlile 2002, 2004). In manufacturing contexts, boundary objects that can help cross syntactic and semantic boundaries concerning operational effectiveness typically include physical artefacts, such as prototypes, defective items and malfunctioning machines; data repositories, such as various sets of test results; proformas for sharing data; and representational devices, such as lexicons, policy statements, codes of practice, standard procedures, maps and graphical displays. However, tangible boundary objects of this kind may be insufficient to facilitate the crossing of cultural and pragmatic boundaries, where differences between conflicting groups reflect deeper and less tangible issues that cannot be settled with reference to 'hard' evidence only.

A prior study found that a Japanese MNC encountered pragmatic and cultural boundaries when operating a subsidiary in the Pearl River Delta (Hong, Snell, and Mak 2015). Furthermore, Fruin (1997) notes:

> When capabilities are site- and relation-specific, as in Knowledge Works, the transfer is likely to be especially problematic, resulting in wasted efforts and opportunities. (154)

Crossing pragmatic and cultural boundaries requires expatriates to serve as boundary spanners, first by recognizing the existence of such boundaries, and then by affording legitimacy to host-country employees' concerns, insights, and reasoning (Taylor 1999) in order to capitalize on the latters' localized and socially embedded knowledge (Blackler 1995; Hsiao, Tsai, and Lee 2006). Serving as boundary spanners (Schotter and Beamish 2011) requires expatriates to open their ears and minds, not just their mouths and rulebooks. As explained below, this involves a paradigm shift from a universalist to a particularistic perspective on knowledge transfer.

Shifting from a universalist to a particularistic perspective

Applied within Japanese MNCs, the universalist perspective assumes that the Japanese model adopted on home soil comprises worldwide best practices that are independent of Japanese cultural legacies and institutional systems (Adler and Cole 1993). Management groups with this perspective are likely also to assume that they hold a global mandate of knowledge transfer and integration (Kostova 1999), and have the right unilaterally to impose their practices onto foreign subsidiaries (Gómez 2004). Accordingly, they will seek to distil their firm's core capabilities into a set of coherent and comprehensible processes and practices, and attempt to replicate them overseas, irrespective of local circumstances (Zhang and Cantwell 2011). Such attempts at knowledge diffusion are likely to emphasize a 'systematic global strategy' (Abo 1994, 180), and rely on ownership control (Taylor 1999), expatriation (Wong and Hendry 1997) and corporate training of local employees (Ma 1998) in order to 'survive the transfer to a foreign environment' (Abo 1995, 81).

In contrast, the particularistic perspective encourages Japanese expatriates to cross pragmatic and cultural boundaries, by relinquishing myopic mindsets that assume their geopolitical superiority (Frenkel 2008), and by acknowledging that the core capabilities developed by their firm on home soil are culturally and institutionally embedded (Byun and Ybema 2005; Collinson and Wilson 2006; Dirks 1995; Lam 1997, 2003; Roney 1997).

Particularistically minded expatriates may recognize the need to serve as 'cultural diplomats' (Loveridge 2005), and apply the maxim that 'cultural understanding facilitates learning' (Lau and Bruton 2008, 36), in seeking to adapt exemplary Japanese production and management practices to local cultural and pragmatic imperatives (Itagaki 2002). They may acknowledge that cooperative production and collective learning arrangements in Japan, under which core workers undergo extensive job rotation and on-the-job training to foster participation in knowledge sharing and build workforce solidarity (Koike 1994), reflect unique institutional and cultural circumstances (Dirks 1995). Thus, may appreciate that although Japan-based frontline employees are conditioned spontaneously and voluntarily to participate in collective learning activities (Adler and Cole 1993), such spontaneity is unlikely to happen in China-based subsidiaries, because of the different cultural and institutional context, which requires arrangements that may be very different from those at home (Gamble, Morris, and Wilkinson 2003; Hong, Easterby-Smith, and Snell 2006a). Although accustomed to dealing with vigorous upward initiatives when on home soil, they may recognize the need to be patient and flexible in providing close supervision and role modelling to host-country subordinates (Hong, Snell, and Easterby-Smith 2006b; Itagaki 2009).

In summary, because the cross-border transfer of capabilities in Japanese MNCs requires substantial adaptation, alteration and supplementation of core knowledge and practices (Gamble 2010; Itagaki 2002; Lam 1997), it is desirable that Japanese expatriates should manifest open-minded, particularistic attitudes and deploy soft managerial skills in order to facilitate the crossing of pragmatic and cultural boundaries.

Methodology

Research design and research questions

We adopted a single case study research design (Eisenhardt 1989; Stake 2005), because of its inductive power to cast light on otherwise implicit, overlooked and misapprehended patterns and dynamics of human interaction. Drawing on theoretical sampling (Eisenhardt and Graebner 2007), we targeted an MNC manufacturer as the inwardly investing company, with Japan as its home country, reflecting that organizations of this type remain highly regarded for knowledge creation, but have encountered challenges in ensuring global quality standards. We also targeted a long-established China-based subsidiary as the focal site of study because China has become a major offshoring centre, yet has presented major cross-cultural challenges to MNCs in their attempts to manage knowledge there (Child and Markóczy 1993; Hong, Easterby-Smith, and Snell 2006a; Hong, Snell, and Easterby-Smith 2009; Lau and Bruton 2008). We addressed two research questions, given below:

> RQ1: How, and under what circumstances, does a Japanese MNC cross pragmatic boundaries to localize capabilities in a long-established China-based subsidiary?
> RQ2: How, and under what circumstances, does a Japanese MNC cross cultural boundaries to localize capabilities in a long-established China-based subsidiary?

In addressing the research questions, we sought to discover how effectively the boundary-crossing challenges arising in collaborative knowledge work (Bechky 2003) between the Japanese expatriates, home-based managers and visiting experts on the one hand and the home country employees on the other were being addressed. We were especially interested in how issues that involved cultural boundaries between contrasting preferences and assumptions about the nature of salient organizational 'realities' (d'Iribarne 2009) were being managed, and in how issues that involved pragmatic boundaries between contrasting practical imperatives and vested interests (Carlile 2002; Hong and Snell 2008; Orlikowski 2002; Wenger 1998) were being managed. We also looked for evidence of local re-contextualization (Brannen 2004), involving constructive and open-minded dialogue between members of the two different cultural groups to make sense of day-to-day experience, regardless of power relations and vested interests, as a sign that cultural and pragmatic boundaries had been crossed.

The site for the case study

We secured access to Toshiba TEC Information Systems (S.Z.) Co., Ltd (TESS), formally known as Toshiba Copy Machine (Shenzhen), Co., Ltd (TCOS), specializing in the production and assembly of a range of multifunctional copy machines for both worldwide export and local (Chinese) markets. The predecessor of this subsidiary was set up in Shenzhen, in the southern part of China, in 1993, under a joint venture arrangement with a partner, also headquartered in Japan, which had an established subsidiary in Hong Kong. Three years later, TCOS was constituted in its present form, with the parent Toshiba Group as the majority shareholder. TCOS was renamed as TESS on 1 April 2007 to better reflect its expanding scope of manufacturing activities. At the time of study, production at the site was mainly for export (75%), but the local management anticipated that locally focused research and development (R&D) activities would be initiated at some point in the future (Table 1).

Data collection

Qualitative interviews were used as the major means of data collection and were supplemented with some non-participant observation sessions, which afforded opportunities for triangulation (Bechky 2006). Between 2007 and 2012, the first author conducted 37 one-to-one, semi-structured interviews with a total of 35 organizational members (12 Japanese expatriates and 23 Chinese employees), supplemented by non-participant observation sessions. Interviews with Chinese interviewees were conducted in Chinese Mandarin or Chinese Cantonese. Interviews with Japanese interviewees were conducted in Chinese Mandarin through a company translator. All interviews were tape-recorded and were subsequently translated and transcribed directly into English on a near-verbatim basis. Table 2 summarizes the profile of each of the interviewees, including their respective code names, to which we shall refer when quoting passages from interview transcripts in the findings section.

Interviews with the two respondents bearing the title of President began by asking about the history of the company, before addressing strategic directions, business plans and major challenges for the next few years. Interviews with the other respondents began by asking about the nature of their work, and thereafter were guided by an indicative list of open-ended questions about organizational learning themes, such as learning relationships with cultural counterparts, joint problem solving, and quality and efficiency enhancement. All respondents were encouraged to provide concrete workplace examples based on personal experiences and direct observations.

The first author also conducted non-participant observation of four meetings at TESS, all of which were conducted in Chinese Mandarin. The first meeting was interdepartmental and routine in nature, and had been convened in order to marshal and disseminate

Table 1.   Company background.

Full name	TESS [Toshiba TEC Information Systems (S.Z.) Co., Ltd]
Factory location	Shenzhen, China
Year established in China	1993
Total investment	US$20,158,000
Source of capital	Toshiba Group (96.1%)
	Others (3.9%)
Major product lines	16–85 cpm monochrome copiers; 11–35 cpm full colour copiers, point of sale terminals, copiers options and accessories, electronic cash registers, electronic whiteboards
Main brands	*Yangtze River, Rhone, Hudson, Rio Grande, Denali, K2, Alabama, Loire, EX-Mash, EX-Broad Peak*
Major markets	Overseas (75%)
	Local Chinese (25%)
Major achievements	Market leader in China from 2000 to 2011
	ISO14001 certifications
No. of employees in the factory as on 1 October 2011	3906 (Japanese – 45, Chinese – 3861)

Table 2. Profile of interviewees.

Code	Position	Department (division)	Nationality
TESS1	President	–	Japanese
TESS2	Senior Manager	Quality Assurance	Japanese
TESS3	Manager	Quality Assurance	Chinese
TESS4	Manager	Quality Assurance	Chinese
TESS5	Supervisor (Complaints)	Quality Assurance	Chinese
TESSS6(1)	Senior manager	Quality Assurance	Chinese
TESS7	Senior manager	Engineering	Chinese
TESS8	Chief specialist	Engineering	Japanese
TESS9(1)	Senior manager	Procurement centre	Japanese
TESS9(2)	Senior manager	Procurement centre	Japanese
TESS10	Assistant senior manager	Procurement centre	Japanese
TESS11	Senior manager	Production engineering	Japanese
TESS12	Senior manager	Production	Japanese
TESS13	Assistant section manager	Production	Chinese
TESS14	Dep. Specialist (BP model)	Production	Chinese
TESS15	Supervisor	Production	Chinese
TESS16	Team Leader (BP model)	Production	Chinese
TESS17	Manager	Production and materials control	Chinese
TESS18	Senior manager	Production management control	Japanese
TESS19	Assistant section manager	Production management control	Chinese
TESS20	Senior manager	Value Engineering Promotion	Japanese
TESS21	Assistant manager	Value Engineering Promotion	Chinese
TESS22	Assistant manager	Value Engineering Promotion	Chinese
TESS6(2)	Senior manager	ISO and Environmental Management	Chinese
TESS23	Assistant manager	ISO and Environmental Management	Chinese
TESS24	Manager	Administration	Chinese
TESS25	Supervisor	Administration	Chinese
TESS26	Supervisor	Administration	Chinese
TESS27	Supervisor	Administration	Chinese
TESS28	Staff	Administration	Chinese
TESS29	President	(Parts division)	Japanese
TESS30	General manager	(Parts division)	Japanese
TESS31	Assistant senior manager	Manufacturing (Parts division)	Japanese
TESS32	Manager	Mechanical production (Parts division)	Chinese
TESS33	Manager	PCB mounting (Parts division)	Chinese
TESS34	Manager	Production planning (Parts division)	Chinese
TESS35	Manager	Quality assurance (Parts division)	Chinese

Note: Brackets in the code column indicate those employees, who were interviewed twice.

information about changes in the design of particular components. The second and third meetings involved particular teams, were chaired by the respective team leaders and took the form of instructional sessions concerning quality assurance and various company principles. The fourth meeting was relatively less formal and more interactive than the other three. It was attended by team leaders and front-line workers from various functions, along with representatives from some supplier firms, and the focus was on collaborative problem solving. Each observed meeting lasted between 40 and 90 min.

The meetings were not tape-recorded. Instead, the observer took field notes in English under the following headings: individual participants and job titles; apparent purposes of the meeting; issues and questions raised by the participants; points of agreement and how these were reached or facilitated (such as by use of boundary objects); knowledge shared among the participants; non-verbal behaviours (posture, tone of voice, gestures, facial expression); and key phrases used. The observer added further notes and reflections in the 24 h immediately following the each of the meetings.

Data analysis

We adopted interpretive sense-making as an approach to analysing the interview and observational data, paying close attention to the different ways in which the Japanese and Chinese respondents 'ascribe(d) meaning to their own behaviour' (Welch et al. 2011, 747). We developed general narratives from their specific descriptions of intercultural encounters and from their observations of the context (Gertsen and Søderberg 2011). The data analysis began with initial data coding and data sorting, followed by 'a complete rendering of the story within the text' (Eisenhardt and Graebner 2007). In tandem with the interviews and observations, the authors met several times to exchange and challenge interpretations, review the data and identify theoretical implications. Each author analysed the same batch of interviews/observations separately before meeting to compare notes, discuss the emerging theory and reach agreement through discussion.

The coding of interview transcripts and observation notes began by using pre-existing schemata, such as the concepts of local knowledge (Yanow 2004), boundary-crossing (Carlile 2002, 2004) and intercultural collaboration (Gertsen and Søderberg 2011). We also analysed, compared and contrasted the perceptions, feelings, assumptions and attributions held by members of the expatriate managers and host-country employees (Moore 2012). Our data analysis procedure was iterative (Miles and Huberman 1994), and as we developed a deeper understanding of Chinese and Japanese respondents viewed and interacted with each other, we discovered the limits of our initial categorizations. At this point, our approach to analysis evolved into a more inductive one, through which we developed new categories and theory to capture the novel aspects of our data, on the basis of constant comparisons between emerging theory and the data (Strauss and Corbin 1990), until we reached the point of 'theoretical saturation' (Strauss 1987).

Findings

As explained in the following subsections, our main findings were as follows. The Japanese had facilitated the crossing of semantic and syntactic boundaries, through training and coaching, in order to localize basic manufacturing capabilities. However, they had withheld opportunities from host-country employees to cross a pragmatic boundary regarding the firm's core competence in the domain of R&D, despite criticisms that this restriction was resulting directly in reduced time-to-market efficiency, and indirectly in local isolation from the market and from end-user experience. Moreover, the Japanese had failed to cross a cultural boundary regarding strict adherence to operational protocols; host-country employees working in production tended to regard the protocols as a foreign imposition that reduced motivation for constructive improvisation at the grassroots level. Nonetheless, host-country employees had been invited and encouraged to cross pragmatic boundaries to localize capabilities relating to the sourcing of local suppliers and to environmental protection.

Crossing semantic and syntactic boundaries to localize basic manufacturing capabilities

It appeared that TESS was building manufacturing capabilities at the local site by importing concepts and role modelling practices based on the home country experience.

It appeared that semantic and syntactic boundaries were being readily crossed through effective training and communication. Chinese employees tended to regard the Japanese as expert coaches and instructors, and working relationships between them were generally cordial. For example:

> TESS18: I'll try to teach them by actually solving the problems together. Through a process of cooperation, they can have an actual experience of the problem solving process.

> TESS22: The Japanese specialists are articulate and pay attention to the details. They are good role models for us .... Moreover, they are really very professional and can't be faulted on their knowledge. They'll stay behind after office hours and complete all the work. Their spirit of professionalism really deserves our respect and emulation.

> TESS5: They (Japanese) won't hide any technical knowledge from anybody. This will be shared openly during the meetings ....

Failure to cross a pragmatic boundary regarding core competence in R&D

TESS was Toshiba's worldwide centre for manufacturing low-end photocopier machines and other office equipment, yet every model produced was developed exclusively by design engineers, who were located at the HQ in Japan. These Japan-based specialists issued the designs of the new models, received end-user feedback on the performance of newly designed models and authorized modifications to their own original designs. The parent company kept the entire R&D function at the HQ, at least for the time being, and was wary of taking any steps towards delegating any R&D responsibilities to the local plant. Expatriates and host-country employees expressed different perspectives on this issue:

> TESS12: At this moment, we are still considering how to transfer the R&D to the Chinese market and engage in local product development. But it is under the planning stage ... The biggest problem I can imagine is the unemployment problem. If we shift all the R&D activities to China, Japanese workers will have nothing to do.

> TESS21: We have no idea about the newly developed products before the blueprints are delivered here .... Especially with some core technologies, the HQ won't disclose information to us since it involves company secrets.

Host-country employees complained that retaining the R&D function at the HQ was adversely affecting time to market efficiency and was denying the local subsidiary access to market information and the end-user experience. We explain these problems next.

Reduced time-to-market efficiency

Host country employees identified four factors associated with centralizing the R&D function in Japan, which appeared to be impairing time-to-market efficiency. These were: over-reliance on the design blueprints as boundary objects, unrealistic design assumptions, rigidity of the design configurations and multiple rounds of pre-launch component testing.

Over-reliance on the design blueprints

Host-country employees regarded these as an insufficient means for conveying the 'thought world' (Dougherty 1992) of the designers. They typically found it difficult to infer the designers'' intentions regarding the function of particular component parts. A host-country senior manager explained:

> TESS7: It's almost impossible to completely follow the design in the blueprints to assemble the copy machines. We just have to rely on our basic knowledge and our hands-on understanding about the nature of copy machines to determine the technical relevance of the parts in the machine.

Furthermore, the design drafts themselves were not necessarily adequate representations of fully functional products:

> TESS22: There have been occasions when the finished machines fulfill all the specifications in the design drafts, yet we've discovered that certain functional problems persist. People in the customer service department think that this is unacceptable since it will cause customer dissatisfaction, yet we may not know which specific parts would lead to customer discontent.

Unrealistic design assumptions

Host-country employees perceived that the designs issued by the HQ were primarily 'concept-driven' and failed to take account of 'lived realities' (Yanow 2004, 10), such as capability limitations across the local supplier network and the distinctive composition of locally sourced materials. Typical complaints by host country managers were:

> TESS14: Perhaps those designs only look good on paper. But some technical problems only come to light when we're assembling the parts together. The designers are only specialized in design and they won't bother to try it out in actual practice. That is why they don't anticipate those operational problems.

> TESS32: They don't understand our actual situation. Our machines, technology and factory environment may create certain constraints but they don't understand. They think they are 100% correct all the time but this is not the case.

Rigidity

It was inherently difficult to make changes to the design blueprints. Multiple interdependencies among the component parts allowed only minor modifications. In the event that local suppliers were unable to meet the specifications of particular components, the HQ management sent specialist production engineers from Japan as troubleshooters to help them. HQ-based managers regarded changing the designs as a last resort.

> TESS19: There are about 3000 spare parts in a copy machine and we need to source them from different channels. So if we've made any changes for a single supplier, it would affect the rest. That is why it's almost impossible to change … and the suppliers all know this fact.

> TESS35: We're treated as an assembly plant. According to the mentality of the headquarters, we should do whatever we are told to do. We'd better not change anything. This is the factory mode.

Multiple rounds of pre-launch component testing

Meeting rigid specifications, which local suppliers found very difficult to meet, necessitated multiple rounds of remotely controlled testing, adjustment, re-testing and approvals. The pre-launch testing and design adjustment period for a new model could take as long as 18 months, until all the problems in meeting specifications and achieving functionality targets had all been resolved and mass production could begin. Host-country employees expressed frustration about the delays.

> TESS21: If we could complete the whole cycle in three to six months, there would be significant benefits. So we are now considering how to reduce the production lead time and have the ultimate decision making transferred to our side.

Isolation from the market and from end-user experience

End-user feedback during the first 3 years after the initial release of newly designed models was channelled directly to the HQ, by-passing TESS. This was an indirect consequence of continuing to locate the entire R&D function in Japan. Host-country employees complained that they lacked access to end-user feedback about particular models until a mature stage in the product life cycle where no further design adjustments were required. Thus:

> TESS22: Although the R&D department at HQ will keep on providing us information about our competitors, to give us a better idea about our products' position in the market, currently we are not sufficiently exposed to market information.

Failure to cross a cultural boundary regarding strict adherence to operational protocols

Japanese expatriates at the TESS plant were working closely with host-country managers and supervisors in the production and quality assurance departments to develop operational protocols for assembly, quality checking, problem reporting and problem solving relating to each new model. Once these protocols had been established, the Japanese required employees to follow them in a comprehensive and rigorous manner. A Japanese manager explained:

> TESS12: These behaviors involve the standard operating procedures, such as how to use the screwdrivers and turn the screws in particular ways .... If we can standardize these operative requirements on the production site, it'll be easier for the managers to properly plan and manage their behavior .... We can improve the quality standards by managing the employees' behavior.

Host-country managers and supervisors characterized what they referred to as the 'Japanese Way' as the practice of developing operational protocols for virtually everything, combined with disciplined, fine-grained adherence. For example:

> TESS7: One good thing about Japanese management is that they are very systematic. Everything has a very clear requirement. So if everyone follows the rule, there won't be any oversight.

> TESS34: I believe that what Japanese companies want is a collective way of operating, like a machine. Following the predetermined modes of operation, we should undertake the same steps, so there is a high requirement for synchronous coordination. They (the Japanese) value not individuality but rather good teamwork to accomplish the tasks.

It appeared, however, that some host-country employees were unconvinced about the need for rigorous adherence to the protocols. Accounts from Chinese and Japanese respondents alike indicated that Chinese employees often skipped procedural steps because they considered them to be unnecessarily risk averse and/or over-elaborated. Thus:

> TESS7: Japanese management also has a weakness. For example, we know that there's a short cut from here to there, but the Japanese won't do it this way. Instead they'll first try to exclude all other possibilities and then derive the final path. We Chinese want to do things directly and seldom consider other external factors first. We may be influenced by our culture.

Faced with deviations from the stipulated protocols, the Japanese responded by arranging more intensive surveillance and by establishing individual accountability:

> TESS2: Our QA department performs a PQC inspection once a week, which is about the management and control of each worker's assembly process. We'll examine if each worker has followed the operational manual to carry out their work and checking activity.

> TESS31: Committing a first-time mistake will be corrected by education, the second time they will receive a reminder, and the third time they will be issued with an internal warning.

Reduced constructive improvisation at the grassroots

The main consequence of the strict enforcement of the Japanese Way on the production line was that the host-country employees working there did not regard this as 'Our Way'. Although there was some flexibility to accommodate grassroots suggestions during the initial development of an operational protocol, once established, it could only be changed if there was factual evidence to support the change. Host-country employees indicated that obtaining such evidence was beyond their reach and that the need to adhere to the Japanese Way as the default position diminished the motivation for grassroots improvisation.

> TESS16: I usually wouldn't propose any suggestions, since they're just my personal opinions, so the company wouldn't accept them. Even though I've had some ideas, I didn't propose them.

> TESS3: When we receive the instructions, we must follow them and put them into operation before raising any objections .... We can't participate in changing the overall principles since there's insufficient evidence for us to propose our opinions.

Crossing a pragmatic boundary to localize some sourcing capabilities

Although the HQ had laid down standardized testing and evaluation procedures for establishing the suitability or otherwise of potential suppliers, and assumed responsibility for approving the final selections arising from these procedures, the task of shortlisting local suppliers had been delegated to host-country employees at TESS. Interviews indicated that host-country employees were contributing expertise to the scouting process.

> TESS20: Although the processes for the evaluation, confirmation and selection of suppliers have been transferred from Japan, the local engineers could understand them after a short while. So far there is not any problem. They have a relatively good understanding about the processes.

Some areas of weakness persisted within the supplier network, and new designs often called for new types of component. Host-country employees therefore remained on the lookout for new suppliers:

> TESS21: During the setting-up process we'll have to look for new suppliers. Sometimes we may have to rely on referrals by our relatives, friends or even competitors ... we need to ask their supplier networks .... Finding appropriate external suppliers with the cheapest price and highest quality is our aim.

The designs from the HQ did not specify what materials should be used for particular components. This was a matter left to the local subsidiary for negotiating with the suppliers:

> TESS30: We're trying to improve the raw materials composition for each model's printed circuit board. We need to investigate the appropriate chemical composition, such as silver, zinc, copper and tin, which are different for each model. We need to consider three issues: safety, quality and complexity of operation ... Generally speaking, we'll follow these three principles to come up with improvements.

Crossing a pragmatic boundary to localize environmental protection capabilities

Although the HQ had originally introduced the basic ideas and concepts of environmental protection to TESS, the fine details of implementation had been completely delegated to a team of host-country employees serving as environmental specialists. A host-country manager explained that the team designed and implemented local projects to meet targets set by the HQ:

TESS6(2): It's a matter of the HQ giving us challenges and seeing if we can meet them .... They mainly focus on guiding principles and the attainment of objectives. But their actual help is very limited since they don't know much about our actual situation and they wouldn't want to work out some environmental ideas together with us.

Team members reported several local innovations that had arisen as a result of their environmental protection projects. For example:

TESS23: Industrial alcohol is mainly used to clean the components. We conducted a study and found out that using a cloth rod rather than a piece of cloth can help significantly reduce the usage of industrial alcohol.

TESS35: We have to do tin soldering on the plate, which leaves some residue in the equipment. We suggested recycling the residue which had previously been discarded as waste. This has saved 200,000 RMB a month since the first half of last year.

Discussion and implications

Our case study illustrates some boundary-crossing challenges for Japanese MNCs in relation to localizing their capabilities overseas. It appeared that the Japanese sought to retain tight control over the firm's core competencies in two domains: R&D and operational protocols (See Table 3). To main control over R&D, the Japanese enforced a pragmatic boundary by keeping the entire function in Japan. To maintain control over operational protocols, the Japanese applied close supervision to ensure that employee behaviour on the production line conformed to standards perceived as 'Japanese'. Within these two core domains, the local subsidiary and its host-country employees were denied opportunities to adapt and modify home country routines to match local circumstances and preferences.

Regarding R&D, pragmatic knowledge boundaries continued to concentrate responsibility for the creation of the original design prototypes in the hands of the Japanese designers at the HQ, along with sole authority to approve any subsequent modifications to them. This arrangement persisted, despite Fruin's (1997) prior discovery, in a study at TESS's elder sister subsidiary in Japan, that it was advantageous to locate the design function next door to the manufacturing operations, so as to expedite rapid iteration between design choices and manufacturability experiments.

Once the R&D work had been undertaken at HQ, it was 'frozen' into the blueprints and left limited scope for subsequent modifications. There were long delays in bringing newly designed models to the market, as host-country employees and local suppliers puzzled out the principles behind each new design, struggled to achieve conformance with

Table 3. Pragmatic and cultural boundaries and the localization of firm capabilities.

Types of capabilities	Boundaries (boundary-crossing is shown in brackets)	
	Pragmatic	Cultural
Core capabilities	HQ's concern to avoid 'hollowing out' in the domain of R&D	Expatriates' aversion to risk taking and their myopic mindset in the domain of manufacturing protocol
Complementary and peripheral capabilities	(HQ's delegation allows TESS to prove its effectiveness in the domains of component materials sourcing and environmental protection)	

the associated specifications, and strove to solve manufacturability problems and achieve efficient assembly methods. Given that there were so many dysfunctional consequences of retaining the R&D function at the HQ, we came to ask ourselves the question, why had the most senior Japanese procrastinated for so long about locating the design function adjacent to the manufacturing operations in China? It appears that this inertia reflected parochial rather than universalistic concerns among the most senior Japanese, i.e., the desire to avoid 'hollowing out' (Kidd and Richter 2001) the employment prospects of their compatriots.

Regarding operational protocols, we could identify at least one cultural boundary, relating to the strong felt need for uncertainty avoidance in Japanese culture (Hofstede 1991), which was reflected in the requirement for host-country employees to adhere to a strict sequence of steps, developed locally, but under close supervision by Japanese expatriates. It is possible also that the insistence by the Japanese on their strict protocols also reflected universalistic assumptions about geopolitical superiority (Frenkel 2008). There were signs of resistance to the protocols by some front-line host-country employees, who perceived them as unnecessarily fussy and risk-averse, with many redundant steps. Although the management appeared to have won a war of control over host-country employees' behaviour, there may have been some cost in terms of reduced goodwill and motivation to participate in continuous improvement campaigns.

The Japanese appeared, by contrast, to allow substantially more scope for host-country employees to cross pragmatic boundaries in domains that they (the Japanese) regarded as relatively peripheral to or complementary to the firm's core capabilities, such as component sourcing and environmental protection (See the bottom row of Table 3). These non-core domains appeared to be free of cultural legacies and pragmatic possessiveness, leaving scope for particularism. Within them, the HQ and the expatriates, although preoccupied with the need to meet outcome targets, allowed host-country employees to develop their own means for meeting these targets. Thus, they were relatively more open to the possibility that the local subsidiary and host-country employees might complement Japanese core competencies with their local repertoire of latent, host country's knowledge and organizational routines (Collinson and Wilson 2006).

Conclusion

Applying a knowledge boundary and boundary-crossing perspective (Bechky 2003; Carlile 2002, 2004) to this case study has enabled us to make two main contributions to research on the globalization of Japanese MNCs. First, we have examined the micro-issues of power relations and politics (Geppert and Dörrenbächer 2014) between a Japanese HQ and a foreign subsidiary, which can potentially impede transfer of organizational capabilities to the host country (Busser 2008). Second, we have illustrated how reluctance by the Japanese to allow host-country employees to cross pragmatic and cultural knowledge boundaries may have slowed down the process of localization of organizational capabilities, thereby adversely impacting organizational adaptation and improvisation.

For the host-country employees, only those activities that were perceived to be outside the HQ's areas of core competence allowed particularism to creep in, affording empowerment to engage in double-loop learning. These areas included environmental protection and scouting for potential suppliers of components. The host-country employees' contributions to environmental protection suggest that sharing knowledge and best practices across cultures for the purpose of double-loop learning is a dynamic and dialectical process (Shenkar, Luo, and Yeheskel 2008). Because environmental protection was not regarded as a core competence of the MNC, it appeared that cultural and pragmatic boundaries exerted less interference with processes of mutual accommodation (Balogun, Jarzabkowski, and Vaara 2011) within that domain.

We conjecture that in order to facilitate joint enterprise in knowledge domains where there is assumed asymmetry between the home and host countries in terms of core competencies (Frenkel 2008; Mir and Mir 2009), it is necessary for members of the home culture to create a learning space in which they can suspend their universalistic assumptions about home superiority and find ways to help home country members characterize and express their different ideas, observations and perspectives (Moore 2012). It is only through collective self-reflection and articulation that conflicts and frustrations associated with cross-cultural learning encounters (Hong, Snell, and Easterby-Smith 2006b) can be revealed to both parties and potentially resolved. It appears, however, that core competencies in Japanese MNCs may be inextricably connected to cultural legacies and may be prone to become core rigidities rather than remaining as core competencies. This may be a key underlying reason Japanese MNCs have failed to adapt within changing environments.

Our study has two main limitations. Ideally, studies of boundaries in organizations (Bechky 2003; Carlile 2002; Sturdy et al. 2009a) should incorporate both ethnographic interviews and participant observation in order to obtain 'thick descriptions' for understanding the nuances of boundary-crossing challenges. However, due to resource constraints and access limitations, the bulk of the case study data were collected via in-depth interviews, and opportunities for direct observation of work routines were relatively few and far between. Furthermore, recent socio-economic trends and geopolitical events involving Japan and China, and the associated changes in the institutional environment, may have had an impact on power relations between the HQ and its Chinese subsidiaries, and on cross-cultural perceptions between expatriates and host-country employees. Although we have excluded these more macro factors from our analysis and discussion, their impact on and implications for localization strategies constitute an important area for future research.

Acknowledgement
This work was supported by the General Research Fund of the Research Grants Council of Hong Kong [grant number LU341813].

Disclosure statement
No potential conflict of interest was reported by the authors.

References

Abo, T. 1994. "Sanyo's Overseas Production Activities: Seven Large Plants in the US, Mexico, the UK, Germany, Spain and China." In *The Global Competitiveness of the Asian Firm*, edited by H. Schutte, 179–200. London: St Martin's Press.

Abo, T. 1995. "A Comparison of Japanese Hybrid Factories in US, Europe and Asia." *Management International Review* 35 (1) Special Issue: 79–93.

Adler, P., and R. Cole. 1993. "Designed for Learning: A Tale of Two Auto Plants." *Sloan Management Review* 34 (3): 85–94.

Ailon, G., and G. Kunda. 2009. "'The One-Company Approach': Transnationalism in an Israeli–Palestinian subsidiary of a multinational corporation." *Organization Studies* 30 (7): 693–712. doi:10.1177/0170840609104808.

Alcadipani, R., F. Khan, E. Gantman, and S. Nkomo. 2012. "Southern Voices in Management and Organization Knowledge." *Organization* 19 (2): 131–143. doi:10.1177/1350508411431910.

Balogun, J., P. Jarzabkowski, and E. Vaara. 2011. "Selling, Resistance and Reconciliation: A Critical Discursive Approach to Subsidiary Role Evolution in MNEs." *Journal of International Business Studies* 42 (6): 765–786. doi:10.1057/jibs.2011.13.

Bartlett, C., and H. Yoshihara. 1992. "New Challenges for Japanese Multinationals: Is Organization Adaptation Their Achilles Heel?" In *Globalizing Management: Creating and Learning the Competitive Organization*, edited by V. Pucik, N. Tichy, and C. Barnett, 276–299. New York: John Wiley & Sons.

Bechky, B. 2003. "Sharing Meaning across Occupational Communities: The Transformation of Understanding on a Production Floor." *Organization Science* 14 (3): 312–330. doi:10.1287/orsc.14.3.312.15162.

Bechky, B. 2006. "Talking about Machines, Thick Description, and Knowledge Work." *Organization Studies* 27 (12): 1757–1768. doi:10.1177/0170840606071894.

Beechler, S., and A. Bird. 1999. *Japanese Multinationals Abroad: Individual and Organizational Learning*. New York: Oxford University Press.

Bhagat, R., B. Kedia, P. Harveston, and H. Triandis. 2002. "Cultural Variations in the Cross-Border Transfer of Organizational Knowledge: An Integrative Framework." *Academy of Management Review* 27: 204–221.

Black, J., and A. Morrison. 2012. "The Japanese Global Leadership Challenge: What It Means for the Rest of the World." *Asia Pacific Business Review* 18 (4): 551–566. doi:10.1080/13602381.2012.690300.

Blackler, F. 1995. "Knowledge, Knowledge Work and Organizations: An Overview and Interpretation." *Organization Studies* 16 (6): 1021–1046. doi:10.1177/017084069501600605.

Bourdieu, P. 1977. *Outline of a Theory of Practice*. Cambridge: Cambridge University Press.

Brannen, M. Y. 2004. "When Mickey Loses Face: Recontextualization, Semantic Fit, and the Semiotics of Foreignness." *Academy of Management Review* 29: 593–616.

Buckley, P. 2009. "The Rise of the Japanese Multinational Enterprise: Then and Now." *Asia Pacific Business Review* 15 (3): 309–321. doi:10.1080/13602380802667247.

Busser, R. 2008. "'Detroit of the East'? Industrial Upgrading, Japanese Car Producers and the Development of the Automotive Industry in Thailand." In *Multinationals, Technology and Localization in Automotive firms in Asia*, edited by R. Rajah, Y. Sadoi, and R. Busser, 29–45. New York: Routledge.

Byun, H., and S. Ybema. 2005. "Japanese Business in the Dutch Polder: The Experience of Cultural Differences in Asymmetric Power Relations." *Asia Pacific Business Review* 11 (4): 535–552. doi:10.1080/13602380500135836.

Carlile, P. 2002. "A Pragmatic View of Knowledge and Boundaries: Boundary Objects in New Product Development." *Organization Science* 13 (4): 442–455. doi:10.1287/orsc.13.4.442.2953.

Carlile, P. 2004. "Transferring, Translating, and Transforming: An Integrative Framework for Managing Knowledge across Boundaries." *Organization Science* 15 (5): 555–568. doi:10.1287/orsc.1040.0094.

Child, J., and L. Markóczy. 1993. "Host-Country Managerial Behaviour and Learning in Chinese and Hungarian Joint Ventures." *Journal of Management Studies* 30 (4): 611–631. doi:10.1111/j.1467-6486.1993.tb00318.x.

Child, J., and S. Rodrigues. 1996. "The Role of Social Identity in the International Transfer of Knowledge through Joint Ventures." In *The Politics of Management Knowledge*, edited by S. Clegg and G. Palmer, 46–68. London: Sage.

Collinson, S., and A. Rugman. 2008. "The Regional Nature of Japanese Multinational Business." *Journal of International Business Studies* 39 (2): 215–230. doi:10.1057/palgrave.jibs.8400347.

Collinson, S., and D. Wilson. 2006. "Inertia in Japanese Organizations: Knowledge Management Routines and Failure to Innovate." *Organization Studies* 27 (9): 1359–1387. doi:10.1177/0170840606067248.

Czarniawska, B., and G. Sevón, eds. 1996. *Translating Organizational Change*. Berlin: de Gruyter.

d'Iribarne, P. 2009. "National Cultures and Organisations in Search of a Theory: An Interpretative Approach." *International Journal of Cross-Cultural Management* 9 (3): 309–321. doi:10.1177/1470595809346601.

Dirks, D. 1995. "The Quest for Organizational Competence: Japanese Management Abroad." *Management International Review* 35: 75–90.

Dougherty, D. 1992. "Interpretive Barriers to Successful Product Innovation in Large Firms." *Organization Science* 3 (2): 179–202. doi:10.1287/orsc.3.2.179.

Edmondson, A. 2003. "Framing for Learning: Lessons in Successful Technology Implementation." *California Management Review* 45 (2): 34–54. doi:10.2307/41166164.

Eisenhardt, K. 1989. "Building Theories from Case Study Research." *Academy of Management Review* 14: 532–550.

Eisenhardt, K. M., and M. E. Graebner. 2007. "Theory Building from Cases: Opportunities and Challenges." *Academy of Management Journal* 50 (1): 25–32. doi:10.5465/AMJ.2007.24160888.

Frenkel, M. 2008. "The Multinational Corporation as a Third Space: Rethinking International Management Discourse on Knowledge Transfer Through Homi Bhabha." *Academy of Management Review* 33 (4): 924–942. doi:10.5465/AMR.2008.34422002.

Fruin, W. M. 1997. *Knowledge Works: Managing Intellectual Capital at Toshiba*. New York: Oxford University Press.

Gamble, J. 2010. "Transferring Organizational Practices and the Dynamics of Hybridization: Japanese Retail Multinationals in China." *Journal of Management Studies* 47 (4): 705–732. doi:10.1111/j.1467-6486.2009.00876.x.

Gamble, J., J. Morris, and B. Wilkinson. 2003. "Japanese and Korean Multinationals: The Replication and Integration of their National Business Systems in China." *Asian Business and Management* 2 (3): 347–369. doi:10.1057/palgrave.abm.9200059.

Gammeltoft, P., H. Barnard, and A. Madhok. 2010. "Emerging Multinationals, Emerging Theory: Macro- and Micro-Level Perspectives." *Journal of International Management* 16 (2): 95–101. doi:10.1016/j.intman.2010.03.001.

Geppert, M., and C. Dörrenbächer. 2014. "Politics and Power within Multinational Corporations: Mainstream Studies, Emerging Critical Approaches and Suggestions for Future Research." *International Journal of Management Reviews* 16 (2): 226–244. doi:10.1111/ijmr.12018.

Gertsen, M., and A. Søderberg. 2011. "Intercultural Collaboration Stories: On Narrative Inquiry and Analysis as Tools for Research in International Business." *Journal of International Business Studies* 42 (6): 787–804. doi:10.1057/jibs.2011.15.

Gómez, C. 2004. "The Influence of Environmental, Organizational, Organizational, and HRM Factors on Employee Behaviors in Subsidiaries: A Mexican Case Study of Organizational Learning." *Journal of World Business* 39: 1–11.

Handley, K., A. Sturdy, R. Fincham, and T. Clark. 2006. "Within and Beyond Communities of Practice: Making Sense of Learning through Participation, Identity and Practice." *Journal of Management Studies* 43 (3): 641–653. doi:10.1111/j.1467-6486.2006.00605.x.

Hannan, M., and G. Carroll. 1992. *Dynamics of Organizational Populations: Density, Competition, and Legitimation*. New York: Oxford University Press.

Hofstede, G. 1991. *Cultures and Organizations: Software of the Mind*. London: McGraw-Hill.

Hong, J., M. Easterby-Smith, and R. Snell. 2006a. "Transferring Organizational Learning Systems to Japanese Subsidiaries in China." *Journal of Management Studies* 43 (5): 1027–1058. doi:10.1111/j.1467-6486.2006.00628.x.

Hong, J., R. Snell, and M. Easterby-Smith. 2006b. "Cross-cultural Influences on Organizational Learning in MNCs: The Case of Japanese Companies in China." *Journal of International Management* 12 (4): 408–429. doi:10.1016/j.intman.2006.09.005.

Hong, J., and R. Snell. 2008. "Power Inequality in Cross-cultural Learning: The Case of Japanese Transplants in China." *Asia Pacific Business Review* 14 (2): 253–273. doi:10.1080/13602380701314750.

Hong, J., R. Snell, and M. Easterby-Smith. 2009. "Knowledge Flow and Boundary Crossing at the Periphery of a MNC." *International Business Review* 18 (6): 539–554. doi:10.1016/j.ibusrev.2009.08.001.

Hong, J., R. Snell, and C. Mak. 2015. "Contextualizing Nonaka's Theory of Knowledge in China: When Samurai Meets Bruce Lee." In *Handbook of Research on Knowledge Management: Adaptation and Context*, edited by A. Örtenblad, 343–365. Cheltenham: Edward Elgar.

Horn, S., and A. Cross. 2009. "Japanese Management at a Crossroads? The Changing Role of China in the Transformation of Corporate Japan." *Asia Pacific Business Review* 15 (3): 285–308. doi:10.1080/13602380802667221.

Hsiao, R. L., S. D. H. Tsai, and C. F. Lee. 2006. "The Problems of Embeddedness: Knowledge Transfer, Coordination and Re-Use in Information Systems." *Organization Studies* 27 (9): 1289–1317. doi:10.1177/0170840606064108.

Itagaki, H. 2002. "Japanese Multinational Enterprises: The Paradox of High Efficiency and Low Profitability." *Asian Business and Management* 1 (1): 101–124. doi:10.1057/palgrave.abm.9200001.

Itagaki, H. 2009. "Competitiveness, Localization and Japanese Companies in China: Realities and Alternate Approaches." *Asia Pacific Business Review* 15 (3): 451–462. doi:10.1080/13602380802667502.

Jack, G., and R. Westwood. 2006. "Postcolonialism and the Politics of Qualitative Research in International Business." *Management International Review* 46 (4): 481–501. doi:10.1007/s11575-006-0102-x.

Jensen, P., and T. Pedersen. 2011. "The Economic Geography of Offshoring: The Fit Between Activities and Local Context." *Journal of Management Studies* 48: 352–372.

Kidd, J., and F. Richter. 2001. "The Hollowing Out of the Workforce: What Potential for Organisational Learning?" *Human Systems Management* 20: 7–18.

Koike, K. 1994. "Learning and Incentive Systems in Japanese Industry." In *The Japanese Firm: Sources of Competitive Strength*, edited by M. Aoki and R. Dore, 42–65. Oxford: Clarendon Press.

Kostova, T. 1999. "Transnational Transfer of Strategic Organizational Practices: A Contextual Perspective." *Academy of Management Review* 24: 308–325.

Lam, A. 1997. "Embedded Firms, Embedded Knowledge: Problems of Collaboration and Knowledge Transfer in Global Cooperative Ventures." *Organization Studies* 18 (6): 973–996. doi:10.1177/017084069701800604.

Lam, A. 2003. "Organizational Learning in Multinationals: R&D Networks of Japanese and US MNEs in the UK." *Journal of Management Studies* 40 (3): 673–703. doi:10.1111/1467-6486.00356.

Lau, C. M., and G. Bruton. 2008. "FDI in China: What We Know and What We Need to Study Next." *Academy of Management Perspectives* 22 (4): 30–44. doi:10.5465/AMP.2008.35590352.

Leonard-Barton, D. 1992. "Core Capabilities and Core Rigidities: A Paradox in Managing New Product Development." *Strategic Management Journal* 13 (S1): 111–125. doi:10.1002/smj.4250131009.

Loveridge, R. 2005. "Embedding the Multinational: Bridging Internal and External Networks in Transitional Institutional Contexts." *Asian Business and Management* 4 (4): 389–409. doi:10.1057/palgrave.abm.9200143.

Ma, Z. 1998. "What to Learn from the Japanese? The Process of Japanese Style Management Transfer to China." In *Management in China: The Experience of Foreign Businesses*, edited by R. Strange, 118–130. London: Frank Cass.

Marukawa, T. 2009. "Why Japanese Multinationals Failed in the Chinese Mobile Phone Market: A Comparative Study of New Product Development in Japan and China." *Asia Pacific Business Review* 15 (3): 411–431. doi:10.1080/13602380802667387.

Miles, M. B., and A. M. Huberman. 1994. *Qualitative Data analysis: An Expanded Source Book.* Thousand Oaks, CA: Sage Publications.

Mir, R., and A. Mir. 2009. "From the Colony to the Corporation: Studying Knowledge Transfer Across International Boundaries." *Group and Organization Management* 34 (1): 90–113. doi:10.1177/1059601108329714.

Moore, F. 2012. "Identity, Knowledge and Strategy in the UK Subsidiary of an Anglo-German Automobile Manufacturer." *International Business Review* 21 (2): 281–292. doi:10.1016/j.ibusrev.2011.03.003.

Numagami, T., M. Karube, and T. Kato. 2010. "Organizational Deadweight: Learning from Japan." *Academy of Management Perspectives* 24 (4): 25–37.

Orlikowski, W. 2002. "Knowing in Practice: Enacting a Collective Capability in Distributed Organizing." *Organization Science* 13 (3): 249–273. doi:10.1287/orsc.13.3.249.2776.

Roney, J. 1997. "Cultural Implications of Implementing TQM in Poland." *Journal of World Business* 32 (2): 152–168. doi:10.1016/S1090-9516(97)90005-5.

Santos, F. M., and K. Eisenhardt. 2005. "Organizational Boundaries and Theories of Organization." *Organization Science* 16 (5): 491–508. doi:10.1287/orsc.1050.0152.

Scarbrough, H., J. Swan, S. Laurent, M. Bresnen, L. Edeman, and S. Newell. 2004. "Project-Based Learning and the Role of Learning Boundaries." *Organization Studies* 25 (9): 1579–1600. doi:10.1177/0170840604048001.

Shenkar, O., Y. Luo, and O. Yeheskel. 2008. "From 'Distance' to 'Friction': Substituting Metaphors and Redirecting Intercultural Research." *Academy of Management Review* 33 (4): 905–923. doi:10.5465/AMR.2008.34421999.

Schotter, A., and P. Beamish. 2011. "Performance Effects of MNC Headquarters-Subsidiary Conflict and the Role of Boundary Spanners: The Case of Headquarter Initiative Rejection." *Journal of International Management* 17 (3): 243–259. doi:10.1016/j.intman.2011.05.006.

Stake, R. E. 2005. "Qualitative Case Studies." In *Sage Handbook of Qualitative Research*, edited by N. K. Denzin and Y. S. Lincoln. 3rd ed., 433–466. Thousand Oaks, CA: Sage Publications.

Strauss, A. 1987. *Qualitative Analysis for Social Scientists*. Cambridge, UK: Cambridge University Press.

Strauss, A., and J. Corbin. 1990. *Basics of Qualitative Research: Grounded Theory Procedures and Techniques*. Newbury Park, CA: Sage.

Sturdy, A., T. Clark, R. Fincham, and K. Handley. 2009a. "Between Innovation and Legitimation – Boundaries and Knowledge Flow in Management Consultancy." *Organization* 16 (5): 627–653. doi:10.1177/1350508409338435.

Sturdy, A., K. Handley, T. Clark, and R. Fincham. 2009b. *Management Consultancy: Boundaries and Knowledge in Action*. Oxford: Oxford University Press.

Taylor, B. 1999. "Patterns of Control Within Japanese Manufacturing Plants in China: Doubts About Japanization in Asia." *Journal of Management Studies* 36 (6): 853–873. doi:10.1111/1467-6486.00161.

Tippmann, E., P. Scott, and V. Mangematin. 2012. "Problem Solving in MNCs: How Local and Global Solutions are (and are Not) Created." *Journal of International Business Studies* 43 (8): 746–771. doi:10.1057/jibs.2012.25.

Welch, C., R. Piekkari, E. Plakoyiannaki, and E. Paavilainen-Mäntymänki. 2011. "Theorising from Case Studies: Towards a Pluralist Future for International Business Research." *Journal of International Business Studies* 42 (5): 740–762. doi:10.1057/jibs.2010.55.

Wenger, E. 1998. *Communities of Practice: Learning, Meaning and Identity*. Cambridge: Cambridge University Press.

Wong, M., and C. Hendry. 1997. "A Study of the Employment System of Japanese Multinational Retailers in Hong Kong." *The International Journal of Human Resources Management* 8 (5): 629–643. doi:10.1080/095851997341423.

Yanow, D. 2004. "Translating Local Knowledge at Organizational Peripheries." *British Journal of Management* 15 (S1): 9–25. doi:10.1111/j.1467-8551.2004.t01-1-00403.x.

Zhang, Y., and J. Cantwell. 2011. "Exploration and Exploitation: The Different Impacts of Two Types of Japanese Business Group Network on Firm Innovation and Global Learning." *Asian Business and Management* 10 (2): 151–181. doi:10.1057/abm.2011.7.

Do Japanese MNCs use expatriates to contain risk in Asian host countries?

Jean-Pascal Bassino[a], Marion Dovis[b] and Pierre van der Eng[c]

[a]Department of Social Sciences, École Normale Supérieure de Lyon, Lyons, France; [b]Aix-Marseille School of Economics, Aix-Marselle University, Aix-en-Provence, France; [c]Research School of Management, ANU College of Business and Economics, Australian National University, Canberra, Australia

We investigate the impact of host-country risk on the expatriation strategies of multinational firms, using data on Japanese subsidiary firms in manufacturing industries in 13 host countries in Asia. We find that country risk is negatively correlated with the degree of expatriation and that, rather than host-country risk, firm-specific factors (particularly capital intensity, ownership share of parent firms in subsidiaries and the age of the venture) explain most of the variation in the degree to which subsidiaries rely on Japanese expatriates. Contrary to previous studies, the capital intensity of production is a key explanatory firm-specific variable that correlates positively with the degree of expatriation. Japanese multinational companies do not rely on expatria127=tes to off-set host-country risk, but to mitigate risk to parent investment in subsidiaries.

Introduction

The expatriation or localization of management of foreign subsidiaries of multinational companies (MNCs) has been the subject of ongoing research in international business since at least the mid-1970s. Such research is pertinent, as firms need to determine what expatriate staffing levels are appropriate for their subsidies, given the cost of selecting, training and maintaining expatriate managers, as well as the cost of expatriate failure. Available studies have probed the issue in various ways, but are yet to yield consensus about the factors that determine the choice by MNCs to dispatch expatriate managers to subsidiary firms or depend on locally recruited senior staff.

In essence, the choice between expatriation and localization is considered in two ways. The 'coordination and control' approach considers that internationalization of a company's activities involves transplanting some core capabilities and practices from the parent firm to subsidiaries (e.g. Boyacigiller 1990; Watson O'Donnell 2000). If these capabilities require close scrutiny by the parent, internationalization may imply the relocation of experienced managers from the parent for the purpose of overseeing the transplantation and ongoing implementation of the core capabilities in the foreign subsidiary. An advantage is that expatriates are familiar with the organization and strategy of the MNC, and steeped in the MNC's corporate culture. They may be better able to keep the objectives of the foreign subsidiary aligned with those of the parent, allowing the parent to avoid any dangers of opportunistic behaviour by a local joint-venture (JV) partner.

Other studies regard the engagement of expatriate managers as a transitory but necessary phase in the development of a foreign subsidiary. Subsidiaries depend in their initial stages on the transmission of core capabilities and practices from their parents, and expatriate managers perform an important facilitating role in that process (e.g. Downes and Thomas 2000; Kawai and Strange 2014). This 'transitory phase' approach argues that expatriates (and their families) tend to be costly to maintain, while the cost of expatriate failure can be considerable. As a subsidiary gains experience in the business environment of a host country, the parent is likely to localize subsidiary management. Advantages of localizing management include in-depth knowledge of the business conditions in the host country that local managers tend to have, and the fact that they are less costly. In due time, MNCs may allow foreign subsidiaries to increase their engagement of locals in senior management positions, particularly after local managers have gained experience and familiarity with the international organization and strategy, as well as the corporate culture of the parent. Given cost aspects, localization of management in foreign subsidiaries may be more financially advantageous than maintaining a contingent of expatriates.

Despite a significant accumulation of studies analysing the degree of expatriation in subsidiary firms, there is no consensus on the fundamental factors that explain the choice between expatiation and localization of management of foreign subsidiaries. Different methodologies (e.g. case studies, surveys and variance analysis) and data-sets have yielded different outcomes, or outcomes that are difficult to generalize.

This paper focuses on an important common element in both strands of the literature, which is that MNCs commit valuable resources to their foreign subsidiaries and expose these to host-country risk. The resources take the form of proprietary capabilities and practices, human resources, as well as financial resources in the form of investment in the production technologies used by subsidiaries and debt guarantees. Few relevant studies account for the commitment of financial resources. As far as they do, they improperly account for the true value of committed capital, as the next section explains. Another drawback of existing studies is that they control for risks in the host country by using a composite of very broad general indicators of differences in the business environments of home and host countries, or country risk indicators that may be relevant to portfolio investors, but not necessarily to MNCs that can 'unpack' country risk and respond to the different host-country risk elements they perceive relevant to protecting the resources they commit to their foreign subsidiaries.

It can be hypothesized that MNCs with considerable investments in foreign subsidiaries seek to minimize the risk to that investment by maximizing the returns on the core capabilities engaged in subsidiaries, and possibly by aligning the objectives of the subsidiary with those of the parent firm. A relatively high number of home-country expatriates in key management positions may be a means to that end. Hence, variation of the degree of expatriation needs to strike a balance between explanatory factors that are specific to the subsidiary firm and the host country. This paper analyses this issue on the basis of a large database containing firm-level data for Japanese subsidiary firms in other Asian countries and territories. These host countries were chosen in order to minimize the possible impact of cross-cultural differences between the host countries on expatriation. The study also focuses on manufacturing firms in order to minimize the possible consequences of the fact that Japanese subsidiary firms are active across host countries in different combinations of industries.

Literature review

The study of the expatriation strategies of MNCs is dominated by issues of international human resource management, particularly recruitment practices, and the risk/cost to the firm of expatriates failing (e.g. Selmer 1995; Baruch and Altman 2002). Early studies seeking to explain the choice between expatriation and localization were considerably hampered by the availability of data. For instance, Boyacigiller (1990) and Downes and Thomas (2000) base their arguments on expatriation in the subsidiaries of just one firm. More recent research relies on case studies or country studies. The number of cases in a study is often limited, which makes it difficult to generalize the findings.

During the last 15 years, several studies have started to use large firm-level data-sets, combining country-level data for home and host countries to explain variations in the degree of expatriation of subsidiary companies (e.g. Gaur, Delios, and Singh 2007). This would be appropriate if the combination of home-country firms across all host countries is broadly similar and, therefore, comparable. But this is never the case, as firms from the same home country are attracted to a host country for a range of different reasons. In other words, the 'average home-country firm' does not exist. It, therefore, remains unclear whether the specifics of parent and subsidiary firms, rather than the specifics of home and host countries, explain the degree of expatriation in subsidiaries of MNCs across host countries.

Several empirical studies analyse expatriation by Japanese firms (e.g. Konopaske, Werner, and Neupert 2002; Gong 2003; Paik and Sohn 2004; Belderbos and Heijltjes 2005; Tan and Mahoney 2006; Gaur, Delios, and Singh 2007; Wilkinson et al. 2008; Fang et al. 2010; Widmier, Brouthers, and Beamish 2008; Peng and Beamish 2014; Ando and Paik 2013). A few take account of parent investments in subsidiary firms, but fail to account for the true value of committed capital by correcting for inflation since the year of establishment, which consequently leads them to conclude that capital investment is not a significant explanatory variable (e.g. Widmier, Brouthers, and Beamish 2008, 1616; Fang et al. 2010, 43), or that capital was marginally significant as an explanatory variable and negatively correlated with the degree of expatriation (Gaur, Delios, and Singh 2007, 625 and 627). In addition, these studies do not account for the fact that competing firms in different industries are able to apply a range of different technologies to produce similar goods, ranging, e.g. from labour-intensive to capital-intensive technologies. Relative factor prices in host countries are likely to be an important determinant of the choice of technology along the production frontier, but individual firms also have other reasons to select a specific technology, which, therefore, require an eclectic approach to explaining the choice of technology, as Chen (1983) explains. An element in this 'choice of technology' literature is the fact that a firm's choice for a higher capital intensity of production (as indicated by the ratio of capital and employment) necessarily requires a greater commitment of financial resources.

A further drawback of relevant multi-country studies is that they control for risks in the host country on the basis of broad composite indicators of differences in the business environments of host countries that are assumed to be proxies of risk. These are generally composite country risk indicators obtained from readily available sources such as *Euromoney, Institutional Investor* or *Political Risk Yearbook* and designed for analysis of portfolio investments (e.g. Click 2005). Using such indicators ignores the subjectivity underlying them, due to the choice and weighting of the underlying variables and can, therefore, be misleading, as Oetzel, Bettis, and Zenner (2001) argue. More recently, studies have started to use similar indicators of 'institutional distance' between home and host countries, which suffer from similar drawbacks related to variable selection and weighting, as Zaheer, Spring-Schomaker, and Nachum (2012) argue.

More importantly, these indicators are at best suited to analysing the decisions of portfolio investors who have few opportunities to hedge perceived country risks, and a broad-based indicator may suffice for them. But in the case of foreign direct investment

(FDI), MNCs are in a position to 'unpack' country risk and respond to the different risk elements they perceive relevant to their foreign subsidiaries in order to protect the resources they commit to foreign subsidiaries. They can strategically shape subsidiary ventures, e.g. through the choice of JV partners, the share of their commitment in the subsidiary, the choice of technology, expatriation, embedding a subsidiary in the business environment of the host country and so on. Hence, using composite indicators of country risk or institutional distance between home and host countries may not adequately contribute to the analysis of expatriation by MNCs engaged in FDI.

Japanese MNCs rely to a higher degree on expatriates in key management positions of their foreign subsidiaries, compared to MNCs from other countries (Keeley 2001, 115– 120; Yoshihara 2005, 244–246; Jaussaud and Schaaper 2007, 236–238). For example, in 1998, 72% of Japanese subsidiary manufacturing firms in Asia had a Japanese national as top executive, significantly higher than US and European firms (METI 2003, 160–161). This phenomenon has been related to the particular human resource management practices of Japanese firms (e.g. Beechler and Zhuang 1994). It has also been related to the idea that Japanese firms replicated *keiretsu* structures in other countries, requiring intensive intra-firm communications with headquarters in Japan and inter-firm communications with *keiretsu*-associated Japanese subsidiaries in host countries and, therefore, Japanese expatriates in senior positions (e.g. Yoshihara 2005, 247–249; Yoshihara 2008, 7–9). Shiraki (2007, 9–10) found the need for subsidiaries to coordinate with headquarters in Japan as well as the need for the 'penetration of the management principles/methods' of headquarters in Japan to be the main reasons. Legewie (2002) argues that a prevailing innate 'insider-outsider mentality' prevents Japanese firms from localizing the management of their subsidiaries, while many Japanese firms in China are resource rather than market seeking and do not require the local feedback that senior local managers can generate.

Even though Japanese subsidiary firms depend to a large extent on expatriates in senior positions, the variation in the degree to which the foreign subsidiaries of Japanese MNCs employ home-country expatriates has not yet been fully explained. Several empirical studies have addressed this issue, but they arguably contain methodological limitations. For example, Belderbos and Heijltjes (2005) seek to explain the appointment of expatriate and local managers as managing directors (CEOs) of 844 subsidiary firms of Japanese electronics-producing companies in eight Asian countries in 1995. They find that the strategic dependence of a parent firm on the affiliate increased the propensity to appoint expatriates. However, (a) the study only analyses CEO appointments, which fails to account for the possibility that managing directors have been token appointments, as Yoshihara (2008, 6–7) explains, and that the appointment of Japanese expatriates in other senior management positions serves the purpose of maintaining control.[1] (b) It takes the ratio of affiliate employees and employees of the parent firm as an indication of the size of the subsidiary firm, which does not take account of the capital intensity of production and thus the potential risk to the investment made by parent firms and their lenders.

Gaur, Delios, and Singh (2007) seek to explain the appointment of expatriate and local managers as general managers (i.e. CEOs) on the basis of the 'institutional distance' of the host country with Japan. They analyse the impact of that appointment on firm performance for almost 13,000 subsidiaries of Japanese firms in 48 countries in 2002 and find that a higher 'institutional distance' encourages firms to rely more on expatriates. This study (a) does not take account of the appointment of Japanese expatriates in other senior positions than a CEO, possibly in order to offset the consequences of the appointment of a local CEO. (b) It creates composite country-level indicators of 'regulative' and 'normative' distance between Japan and the host country, but does not explain in detail what factors are included and how they are weighted. As explained above, the problem is that firms making FDI-related decisions may utilize different combinations of ways to mitigate the potential negative consequences of distance. (c) It uses sales per employee as indicator of productivity. This is at best a proxy indicator of performance. Some firms have high sales/worker ratios because they depend to a high degree on purchased inputs, add little value themselves to the value of sales and require a high turnover to generate sufficient net returns. This indicator also takes no account of the differences in capital intensity of production across different industries and, therefore, the differences in risk that parent firms experience as a consequence of the differences in the relative size of their investment.

Tan and Mahoney (2006) seek to explain variations in the ratio of expatriate managers and total employment in 284 subsidiaries of Japanese firms in the USA in 2000. They use a range of explanatory variables, several of which were industry-specific rather than firm-specific. While this study focuses on all expatriate employment in subsidiaries and not just on the nationality of the CEO, it fails to account for the role of investment by parent firms in the subsidiaries. The control variable for firm size is employment and the JV indicator is a simple dummy variable, rather than the share of the parent firm in a JV.

Wilkinson et al. (2008) seek to explain variations in the ratio of expatriate managers and total employment in 5296 subsidiaries of Japanese firms around the world in 2001, by focusing on 'cultural distance' between Japan and host countries. They find that 'cultural distance' enhances the rate of expatriation. Leaving difficulties of measuring and interpreting 'cultural distance' aside, their choice of control variables may skew the results of this study. While the study does not account for capital investment, several of the firm-level controls are actually more statistically significant than the indicators of 'cultural distance', which actually have low predictive power.

Ando and Paik (2013) offer a more involved explanation of variations in the ratio of expatriate managers and total employment in 2980 subsidiaries of Japanese firms in 2008. Their approach includes parent firm characteristics, such as their international experience, and they use the more relevant World Bank *Governance* indicators to define 'institutional distance'. They find a significant negative correlation between expatriation and 'institutional distance', but do not account for the size of subsidiaries, nor parent investment.

Lastly, Peng and Beamish (2014) seek to explain variations in the ratio of expatriate managers and total employment in 11,754 subsidiaries of Japanese firms during 1996–2005, by focusing on the size of subsidiaries and by also including parent firm characteristics in the analysis. However, they define subsidiary size simply as the number of employees, do not control for the size of parent firm capital investment – except the percentage equity ownership by parent firms – and approximate host-country risk with credit ratings from *Institutional Investor*. For reasons explained above, such limitations may affect their findings.

Theory and hypotheses

This brief discussion of the literature indicates that several issues require further research. One is that available studies tend to use only total employment as an indication of size of subsidiary firms. This fails to account for the fact that in several industries firms can choose from a range of production technologies in a continuum from labour intensive to capital intensive. For that reason, a clear distinction has to be made between firms according to the capital intensity of production, as Jaussaud, Schaaper, and Zhang (2001) suggest. It can be assumed that capital-intensive production requires a subsidiary company to rely on proprietary technology and the transfer of capabilities and practices from the parent MNC in order to be able to make optimum productive use of the technology. Another way to consider this is that capital-intensive production requires certainty that a subsidiary firm will be able to generate net income that allows it to service capital invested in its plant, whether in the form of parent-guaranteed debt or equity. It would not matter in this case whether the investment is large or small. The relevant issue is that invested capital needs to be serviced. Dependence on experienced expatriates may offer some guarantee to that effect.

Hypothesis 1:   There is a positive relationship between the capital intensity of a foreign subsidiary firm and the share of home-country expatriates in total employment of that firm.

Where parent firms engage local JV partners in their foreign subsidiaries, the local partners may have expectations about the employment of locals in senior management positions. Either to acknowledge the valuable contribution of local partners to the JV, or possibly for the purpose of mollifying local partners, parent firms may, therefore, agree to the engagement of local managers in senior positions. But where the role of local partners in a JV is small, foreign parent firms may not be inclined to consider engaging such local managers.

Hypothesis 2:   There is a positive relationship between the ownership share of foreign parent firms in a foreign JV and the share of home-country expatriates in total employment of that venture.

Many foreign subsidiaries may start as modest operations and then grow as they create and grasp opportunities, reinvesting profits to finance expansion. At the same time, senior expatriate managers of subsidiary firms may gain sufficient experience with the local business environment to understand the potential risks to the firm. A parent firm may then decide to utilize this experience in the form of supervision of the subsidiary from the home country, thus allowing local managers to subsume senior roles in the subsidiary firm. In addition, local junior managers may gain experience in the firm and trust from senior managers, before being promoted to senior positions. This is in essence the 'transitory phase' argument, as explained above.

Hypothesis 3:   There is a negative relationship between the age of the foreign subsidiary firm and the share of home-country expatriates in total employment of that subsidiary.

An extension of both the 'coordination and control' and 'transitory phase' arguments is that engagement of expatriates in senior positions in a subsidiary firm is a response to elements of uncertainty in the business environment. These require the involvement of experienced managers who understand the operations of both parent firm and subsidiary and their markets, and who are able to draw on that experience to mitigate risk to the subsidiary firm. Their role may diminish and they may make way for local managers when the firm has developed ways to anticipate and accommodate risk. For example, Wilkinson et al. (2008, 99–101) find that host-country risk was indeed positively correlated with the expatriation ratio. However, their choice of country credit ratings from *Institutional Investor* may be an imperfect indicator of country risk for the purpose of analysing MNC commitments to the FDI.

Hypothesis 4:   There is a negative relationship between the perceived risk in a host country and the share of home-country expatriates in total employment in a foreign subsidiary firm.

Formal testing of these hypotheses requires firm-level data that allow a comparison of like-with-like. For example, the capital intensity of production (Hypothesis 1) may be related to the level of technical sophistication in the industry of the firm. Hence, steel-producing firms generally use widely established technologies and tend to increase their competitiveness by capturing scale economies, while semiconductor-producing firms operate at a technological frontier and maintain their competitiveness by pushing it further out. In both cases, operations may be capital intensive, but the required level of technical sophistication could be significantly higher in the second case, requiring expatriate managers for 'coordination and control', if not the protection of intellectual property. Hence, formal testing in principle needs to account for the industries in which subsidiary firms operate.

Methodology

Quantitative firm-level data used in this paper were obtained from the annual Tōyō Keizai database containing data on Japanese subsidiary firms for each year 1999–2004.[2] We compiled a subset with panel data for 13 Asian countries: South Korea, China, Hong Kong, Taiwan, Vietnam, The Philippines, Thailand, Malaysia, Singapore, Indonesia, India, Pakistan and Sri Lanka. These countries were selected in order to accommodate the impact of different levels of risk perceived by subsidiary firms and their parents on investment decisions in the analysis.[3] In order to avoid possible outliers, we cleaned the data-set. The initial number of observations was 29,977. We excluded all Japanese subsidiary firms without data on total and/or expatriate employment, as well as firms with zero or one employee, which generally were representative offices of Japanese manufacturing firms without manufacturing plants. We also eliminated subsidiaries without information on paid-up capital, and we left out firms that were included in the database for less than three consecutive years. Lastly, we rejected observations where capital or employment grew by more than 300% or decreased by more than 50% from one year to the next. The cleaned data-set comprised 26,048 observations. The following variables from the data-set were used: age, or the number of years since the establishment of the subsidiary firm; number of Japanese expatriate employees; total number of employees; number of Japanese JV partners; paid-up capital, converted to US$ in constant 2000 prices[4]; share of Japanese parent firms in paid-up capital and share of local partners in paid-up capital.

The motivation for using shares of Japanese parent companies and of local partners in paid-up capital separately is that the total is not equal to 100%. Older, established Japanese subsidiary companies in Hong Kong, Singapore and Taiwan (and in Thailand and Malaysia in later years) also contribute as investors and, therefore, as shareholders to financing the creation or expansion of new Japanese subsidiaries. This is explained to a large extent by the comparatively high level of corporate taxation in Japan that leads Japanese MNCs to rely on the cash flow available in foreign subsidiaries for the purpose of funding the expansion of their operations in other countries, such as China and more recently in India.[5]

Across host countries, MNCs face different levels of risk. Several indicators of country risk are readily available for the purpose of analysing the impact of perceived risk on expatriation and these have been used in multi-country studies, as mentioned above. Another example is the Organization for Economic Cooperation and Developments (OECD's) classification of country risk. As noted, there are several problems with these indicators. For example, the OECD's classification is explicitly intended for export insurance agencies and reflects the perceived risk to international payments. It is based on the payment experiences of OECD countries with partner countries, as well as indicators of the financial and economic situation in these countries. Other composite indicators are based on publicly available financial and economic data, aggregated with arbitrary weightings. Hence, the choice of country risk indicator, therefore, impacts on the results. To avoid the possible complications caused by the choice of a highly aggregated composite indicator in this paper, we use indicators that capture factors relevant to FDI decisions, obtained from the World Bank's *Governance* and *Doing Business* databases.[6]

The *Governance* indicators are measured in units, with higher values corresponding to better governance outcomes. Unlike the *Governance* indicators, the *Doing Business* variables are not available for each year of our database. For estimation purposes, these *Doing Business* variables are, therefore, regarded as constant for 1999–2004. We use the following indicators:

World Bank *Governance* variables:

- political stability and absence of violence,
- regulatory quality,
- rule of law,
- control of corruption.

World Bank *Doing Business* variables:

- number of procedures necessary to enforcing contracts,
- number of procedures necessary to start a business.

The level of competitive risk that firms face varies across manufacturing industries. Steel producers face different competitive challenges than textile and garment producers. The Tōyō Keizai database identifies 18 manufacturing industries: food processing; textiles; wood and furniture; pulp and paper; publishing and printing; chemicals and medicines; petrochemical; rubber, leather and plastics; ceramics, stone and glass; steel; non-ferrous metals; non-ferrous metal products; machinery; electrical and electronic equipment; automotive and parts; precision tools; transport machinery and shipbuilding; and other manufacturing. Industry-level indicators of competitive risk across industries are unavailable; we include industry dummy variables in our regressions in an attempt to capture the competitive risk factors in these different industries.[7]

The descriptive statistics given in Table 1 show that 25% of the firms in the sample are located in China, almost 16% in Thailand, 11% in Hong Kong, 10% in Taiwan, 9% in Malaysia and 7% in Indonesia. On average, firms in China, Vietnam and India are younger than their counterparts in other countries, reflecting the fact that these countries opened up to FDI later than others. In terms of size, the subsidiaries on average have about 300–500 employees. In South Korea, Hong Kong, Singapore and Taiwan, firms have fewer employees on average, which is most likely a reflection of the higher degree of skill and technology intensity in the production activities in those countries.

The average share of Japanese expatriate employment is 7.4%, which is higher than the averages in several countries, such as 3.4% in Indonesia. The share is relatively high in Hong Kong (23.4%) and Singapore (20.8%), which may reflect the fact that many firms in those countries are relatively small operations with their main manufacturing activities located in China in the case of Hong Kong, or elsewhere in Southeast Asia in the case of Singapore. The ratio of capital and employment indicates that capital intensity of production is significantly higher in Hong Kong, Singapore and Taiwan than in other countries. This suggests the use of more advanced and more capital-intensive production technologies. The share of Japanese partners in the subsidiary firms was on average 93% in

Table 1. Descriptive statistics, annual averages for 1999–2004.

Variables	China	Indonesia	Philippines	Thailand	Vietnam	Malaysia	South Korea	Hong Kong	Singapore	Taiwan	India	Pakistan	Sri Lanka
Number of firms	1421	395	253	886	103	515	213	603	690	541	66	6	11
Av. total employment	306 (848)	443 (682)	454 (1345)	312 (743)	283 (678)	322 (683)	222 (559)	116 (562)	85 (252)	171 (375)	531 (1053)	461 (450)	1400 (2546)
Av. Japanese expatriate employment	4 (8)	4 (4)	4 (5)	4 (5)	3 (3)	4 (5)	2 (3)	4 (5)	4 (7)	3 (4)	3 (4)	3 (3)	4 (4)
Av. ratio of Japanese expatriates and employment	0.054 (0.095)	0.0345 (0.056)	0.053 (0.081)	0.067 (0.107)	0.046 (0.078)	0.075 (0.119)	0.091 (0.141)	0.234 (0.204)	0.208 (0.198)	0.105 (0.140)	0.043 (0.079)	0.008 (0.004)	0.049 (0.123)
Av. paid-up capital (1000 US$, 2000 prices)	8861 (25,497)	9482 (50,662)	4713 (9515)	5354 (22,989)	4662 (5495)	5947 (19,200)	9349 (38,495)	4225 (13,815)	10,205 (312,070)	8852 (34,471)	7245 (18,686)	3987 (3888)	23,379 (64,496)
Av. capital per employee (1000 US $, 2000 prices)	124 (1589)	45 (203)	37 (101)	43 (263)	59 (100)	40 (188)	58 (72)	224 (811)	243 (1293)	229 (4804)	38 (81)	13 (18)	67 (255)
Av. number of Japanese JV partners	1.5 (0.8)	1.6 (0.8)	1.4 (0.7)	2.2 (1.9)	1.6 (0.8)	1.3 (0.7)	1.2 (0.4)	1.2 (0.5)	1.2 (0.5)	1.2 (0.6)	1.5 (0.7)	1.4 (0.5)	1.3 (0.6)
Av. capital share of all Japanese partners	0.715 (0.250)	0.703 (0.254)	0.766 (0.282)	0.608 (0.255)	0.770 (0.241)	0.733 (0.299)	0.718 (0.269)	0.931 (0.173)	0.930 (0.168)	0.756 (0.257)	0.563 (0.269)	0.509 (0.297)	0.848 (0.269)
Av. capital share of local partners	0.231 (0.238)	0.228 (0.224)	0.193 (0.267)	0.245 (0.247)	0.188 (0.214)	0.194 (0.275)	0.257 (0.269)	0.042 (0.137)	0.040 (0.127)	0.208 (0.248)	0.390 (0.265)	0.440 (0.324)	0.095 (0.231)
Av. age (years)	6.8 (3.1)	11.7 (8.6)	9.5 (7.2)	12.5 (9.0)	5.2 (2.1)	11.7 (6.9)	12.0 (8.6)	14.6 (9.3)	14.4 (8.1)	14.8 (9.8)	7.7 (6.5)	16.9 (6.4)	13.6 (10.0)

Note: Standard deviation in parentheses.

Hong Kong and Singapore, compared to 77% in Taiwan, which indicates that most firms are majority-owned by Japanese parent firms.

For the analysis in the next section, we take the logarithms of some key variables and assume a non-linear relationship between the explanatory and dependent variables. Table 2 shows the pair-wise correlations. Capital intensity is defined as the ratio of capital and total employment. Except for the correlation between the share of Japanese parent firms and the share of the local partner firms in the capital of companies, the correlations between the explanatory variables are all low, which indicates an absence of multicollinearity problems. The difference between the share of Japanese parent firms and the share of the local partner firms in the capital of companies is that in several cases, third-country investment plays a role, as explained above.

The underlying equation used to investigate the determinants of the share of expatriate employment implies that total employment is on both sides of the equation because we hypothesize that capital intensity is a key explanatory variable. The justification is we are not seeking to explain the engagement of the absolute number of expatriates on the basis of specified explanatory variables. The specification we use is required because a number of variables identified as potentially explanatory are not expressed as a ratio to total employment, in particular the share of Japanese or local investors in social capital. In addition, a risk of endogeneity exists if we have both social capital and total employment as explanatory variables and the absolute number of expatriates as a dependent variable.

Data analysis

To analyse the data and test the validity of the hypotheses, we use multiple regression techniques (ordinary least squares (OLS) and random effects). The OLS results are shown in Table 3. As the *Doing Business* variables are constant for all years in the data-set, we checked the robustness of the fixed effect results by estimating the random effects, which are shown in Table 4. Both tables show very similar results. In all models, R^2 and the explanatory power of the models are high. Capital intensity has a positive sign and is statistically significant as an explanatory variable for the degree of expatriation, which confirms Hypothesis 1. The share of foreign parent firms in the capital of the capital of the subsidiary was statistically significant and has a positive sign in model (1), while the share of all local partners used in models (2)–(8) has a negative sign and is also statistically significant. This confirms Hypothesis 2 and suggests that MNCs skew the human resource policies of their foreign subsidiary firms towards employing home-country expatriates, most likely in key management positions. In all cases, the age of the subsidiary firm

Table 2. Pair-wise correlations.

	Mean	SD	1	2	3	4	5	6
1. Share of expatriates	0.100	0.150	1.000					
2. Capital intensity	125	1772	0.095	1.000				
3. Number of Japanese JV partners	1.5	1.0	−0.140	−0.019	1.000			
4. Share of Japanese JV partners	0.754	0.266	0.280	0.034	−0.195	1.000		
5. Age	11.3	8.1	−0.098	−0.026	−0.045	−0.036	1.000	
6. Share of local JV partners	0.184	0.241	−0.272	−0.029	0.043	−0.828	0.048	1.000

moderates expatriation, because the sign is negative and the coefficient is statistically significant, thus confirming Hypothesis 3. Hence, subsidiary firms that have been in operation longer are more likely to engage locals in senior management positions.

As for the indicators of country risk, in models (3)–(6) the *Governance* variables all have a positive sign and are statistically significant. This implies that a higher degree of political stability, regulatory quality, rule of law and control of corruption is associated with a higher degree of expatriation. Conversely, in countries with a more risky business environment, subsidiary companies are likely to depend to a greater degree on locally recruited senior staff members. Likewise, in models (7) and (8), the two *Doing Business* indicators have a negative sign and are statistically significant. This means that increased difficulties experienced in establishing a subsidiary venture, or higher risk, reduces reliance on expatriates, and by implication increases reliance on local senior staff. In both these models, we included the 'control of corruption' indicator to test for interaction with the 'enforcing contracts' and 'starting a business' procedures. The results are statistically significant. In the case of a country with more procedures to enforce contracts, better control of corruption enhances reliance on local senior staff. In the case of a country with more procedures to start a business, better control of corruption enhances reliance on expatriates. In all cases, Hypothesis (4) is confirmed: higher perceived country risk relevant to FDI-related decisions leads a firm to localize senior management.

Tables 5 and 6 show the results of further OLS and random effects analyses in order to distinguish between some firm-specific characteristics. The results in the table test whether there is any difference in expatriation strategies between different types of firms in the data-set. The reason for this additional analysis is that there could be country-specific differences between subsidiary firms that are not captured and revealed in Tables 3 and 4. These differences are in this case analysed only with the *Governance* indicator 'control of corruption' interacting with the two *Doing Business* indicators.

The first distinction is between firms that produce with advanced technologies and a high capital intensity of production and those that produce with simple technologies and a low capital intensity. The first may be more exposed to risk than the latter and more concentrated in one country than another, because there are differences in the average capital intensity shown in Table 1. It is significantly higher in Hong Kong, Singapore and Taiwan than elsewhere. However, models (1)–(4) in Table 6 show that the signs are all the same as in model (7) in Table 4, and significant, although the values of the coefficients are different, particularly for the 'share of all local partners' variable. In capital-intensive firms, a higher share of local partners decreases the rate of expatriation more than in capital-extensive firms. This indicates that local partners in a capital-intensive firm are in a better position to require the appointment of local staff members, because of their ownership rights. While in capital-extensive firms, local partners are less likely to use their ownership rights to require the appointment of local staff members.

Second, Tables 5 and 6 distinguish between large and small subsidiaries in terms of the number of people employed. Table 1 showed that average total employment is relatively high in Indonesia, Philippines, India and Pakistan, as well as Sri Lanka, and on average relatively small in Hong Kong and Singapore. Models (5)–(8) in Table 6 show that the signs are all the same as in model (7) in Table 4, and significant, although the values of the coefficients are different, particularly for capital intensity. This indicates that large subsidiary firms that are capital intensive on average employ a greater proportion of expatriates than small subsidiaries that are capital extensive.

Third, Tables 5 and 6 exclude, respectively, China and Hong Kong and Singapore from the data-set. The reason to exclude China is that it hosts a relatively large number of

Table 3. Estimation results (OLS).

Variables:				Dependent variable: share of expatriates				
	(1)	(2)	(3)	(4)	(5)	(6)	(7)	(8)
Capital intensity	0.292***	0.295***	0.254***	0.244***	0.246***	0.242***	0.242***	0.249***
	(0.006)	(0.005)	(0.005)	(0.005)	(0.005)	(0.005)	(0.005)	(0.005)
Number of Japanese corporations	-0.007							
	(0.006)							
Share of total Japanese investment in the subsidiary	0.423***							
	(0.018)							
Age	-0.131***	-0.123***	-0.222***	-0.345***	-0.311***	-0.294***	-0.304***	-0.359***
	(0.011)	(0.010)	(0.010)	(0.011)	(0.011)	(0.011)	(0.012)	(0.012)
Share of all local partners in the subsidiary		-1.059***	-0.896***	-0.663***	-0.768***	-0.726***	-0.690***	-0.658***
		(0.030)	(0.030)	(0.031)	(0.030)	(0.031)	(0.033)	(0.033)
Political stability and absence of violence/terrorism			0.332***					
			(0.010)					
Regulatory quality				0.455***				
				(0.010)				
Rule of law					0.451***			
					(0.010)			
Control of corruption						0.330***	0.210***	0.168***
						(0.008)	(0.030)	(0.010)
Enforcing contracts							-0.640***	
							(0.149)	
Starting a business								-0.779***
								(0.032)
Constant	-2.117***	-2.351***	-2.078***	-2.097***	-2.117***	-2.351***	-0.071	-0.409***
	(0.035)	(0.032)	(0.034)	(0.034)	(0.035)	(0.032)	(0.520)	(0.108)
N	24,676	24,676	24,676	24,676	24,676	24,676	20,260	20,260
R^2	0.59	0.61	0.60	0.60	0.59	0.61	0.62	0.63

Notes: The following variables are expressed as logarithms in all regression models: share of expatriates, capital intensity, share of total Japanese investment in the subsidiary and age. The estimation of each model includes dummy variables for each industry and each year of observation. Robust standard errors are in parentheses. *Significant at 10%, **significant at 5%, ***significant at 1%.

Table 4. Estimation results (random effects).

Variables:	Dependent variable: share of expatriates							
	(1)	(2)	(3)	(4)	(5)	(6)	(7)	(8)
Capital intensity	0.411***	0.404***	0.389***	0.374***	0.377***	0.373***	0.371***	0.376***
	(0.008)	(0.008)	(0.008)	(0.008)	(0.008)	(0.008)	(0.008)	(0.008)
Number of Japanese corporations	−0.005							
	(0.005)							
Share of total Japanese investment in the subsidiary	0.151***							
	(0.024)							
Age	−0.082***	−0.092***	−0.107***	−0.157***	−0.123***	−0.123***	−0.184***	−0.195***
	(0.013)	(0.012)	(0.012)	(0.013)	(0.012)	(0.012)	(0.014)	(0.014)
Share of all local partners in the subsidiary		−0.450***	−0.446***	−0.360***	−0.435***	−0.377***	−0.306***	−0.333***
		(0.034)	(0.034)	(0.034)	(0.034)	(0.034)	(0.038)	(0.037)
Political stability and absence of violence/terrorism			0.174***					
			(0.012)					
Regulatory quality				0.422***				
				(0.014)				
Rule of law					0.282***			
					(0.014)			
Control of corruption						0.293***	−0.057**	0.066***
						(0.012)	(0.025)	(0.017)
Enforcing contracts							−2.451***	
							(0.144)	
Starting a business								−1.294***
								(0.061)
Constant	−2.059***	−2.015***	−2.074***	−3.850***	−3.675***	−3.645***	4.609***	−0.942***
	(0.226)	(0.223)	(0.198)	(0.250)	(0.247)	(0.240)	(0.537)	(0.247)
N	22,634	24,676	24,676	24,676	24,676	24,676	20,260	20,260
R^2	0.45	0.45	0.48	0.53	0.51	0.51	0.53	0.55

Notes: The following variables are expressed as logarithms in all regression models: share of expatriates, capital intensity, share of total Japanese investment in the subsidiary and age. The estimation of each model includes dummy variables for each industry and each year of observation. Robust standard errors are in parentheses. *Significant at 10%, **significant at 5%, ***significant at 1%.

Table 5. Estimation results for sub-samples (OLS).

	Dependent variable: share of expatriates											
	High capital intensity		Low capital intensity		Large subsidiaries		Small subsidiaries		Excluding China		Excluding Hong Kong and Singapore	
Variables:	(1)	(2)	(3)	(4)	(5)	(6)	(7)	(8)	(9)	(10)	(11)	(12)
Capital intensity	0.207***	0.204***	0.208***	0.212***	0.225***	0.221***	0.111***	0.110***	0.225***	0.220***	0.225***	0.266***
	(0.006)	(0.006)	(0.011)	(0.011)	(0.006)	(0.006)	(0.004)	(0.004)	(0.006)	(0.006)	(0.006)	(0.007)
Age	-0.315***	-0.322***	-0.282***	-0.294***	-0.079***	-0.094***	-0.191***	-0.194***	-0.339***	-0.364***	-0.339***	-0.363***
	(0.010)	(0.010)	(0.016)	(0.016)	(0.012)	(0.012)	(0.009)	(0.009)	(0.013)	(0.014)	(0.013)	(0.015)
Share of all local partners in the subsidiary	-1.197***	-1.198***	-0.482***	-0.481***	-0.749***	-0.754***	-0.914***	-0.912***	-0.570***	-0.584***	-0.570***	-0.556***
	(0.039)	(0.039)	(0.047)	(0.047)	(0.033)	(0.033)	(0.039)	(0.039)	(0.042)	(0.041)	(0.042)	(0.034)
Control of corruption	0.221***	0.252***	0.333***	0.287***	0.101***	0.111***	0.206***	0.208***	0.113***	0.204***	0.113***	0.141***
	(0.009)	(0.010)	(0.016)	(0.015)	(0.010)	(0.012)	(0.009)	(0.009)	(0.032)	(0.011)	(0.032)	(0.024)
Enforcing contracts	-0.220***		-0.124*		-0.400***		-0.057*		-1.043***		-1.043***	
	(0.037)		(0.070)		(0.052)		(0.033)		(0.160)		(0.160)	
Starting a business		0.021		-0.241***		-0.103***		-0.026		-0.664***		-0.734***
		(0.024)		(0.035)		(0.028)		(0.022)		(0.037)		(0.041)
Constant	-2.101***	-2.930***	-0.010	-1.189***	-1.464***	-3.599***	-0.873***	-1.010***	2.246***	-0.714***	-1.715***	-0.859***
	(0.148)	(0.088)	(0.284)	(0.086)	(0.184)	(0.071)	(0.113)	(0.055)	(0.546)	(0.126)	(0.616)	(0.097)
N	23,234	23,234	11,419	11,419	16,427	16,427	18,226	18,226	14,640	14,640	15,203	15,203
R²	0.53	0.53	0.57	0.58	0.43	0.43	0.37	0.37	0.63	0.63	0.53	0.54

Notes: The following variables are expressed as logarithms in all regression models: share of expatriates, capital intensity, share of total Japanese investment in the subsidiary and age. The estimation of each model includes dummy variables for each industry and each year of observation. Robust standard errors are in parentheses. *Significant at 10%, **significant at 5%, ***significant at 1%.

Table 6. Estimation results for sub-samples (random effects).

	Dependent variable: share of expatriates											
	High capital intensity		Low capital intensity		Large subsidiaries		Small subsidiaries		Excluding China		Excluding Hong Kong and Singapore	
Variables:	(1)	(2)	(3)	(4)	(5)	(6)	(7)	(8)	(9)	(10)	(11)	(12)
Capital intensity	0.343***	0.340***	0.387***	0.389***	0.360***	0.358***	0.219***	0.217***	0.342***	0.340***	0.401***	0.407***
	(0.009)	(0.009)	(0.014)	(0.014)	(0.009)	(0.009)	(0.007)	(0.007)	(0.010)	(0.010)	(0.010)	(0.010)
Age	-0.165***	-0.172***	-0.106***	-0.128***	-0.096***	-0.108***	-0.120***	-0.125***	-0.213***	-0.216***	-0.189***	-0.217***
	(0.012)	(0.012)	(0.021)	(0.021)	(0.017)	(0.017)	(0.011)	(0.011)	(0.017)	(0.017)	(0.017)	(0.017)
Share of all local partners in the subsidiary	-0.564***	-0.570***	-0.166***	-0.161***	-0.374***	-0.378***	-0.385***	-0.381***	-0.170***	-0.205***	-0.260***	-0.265***
	(0.047)	(0.048)	(0.050)	(0.050)	(0.043)	(0.043)	(0.047)	(0.047)	(0.044)	(0.043)	(0.039)	(0.039)
Control of corruption	0.189***	0.215***	0.273***	0.200***	0.077***	0.053***	0.140***	0.145***	-0.001	0.172***	0.075**	0.005
	(0.015)	(0.017)	(0.023)	(0.024)	(0.017)	(0.020)	(0.015)	(0.015)	(0.032)	(0.019)	(0.035)	(0.032)
Enforcing contracts	-0.776***		-0.754***		-0.590***		-0.385***		-2.043***		-1.125***	
	(0.082)		(0.137)		(0.105)		(0.072)		(0.175)		(0.252)	
Starting a business		-0.169***		-0.683***		-0.273***		-0.158***		-1.031***		-1.034***
		(0.048)		(0.066)		(0.056)		(0.040)		(0.076)		(0.083)
Constant	-0.933***	-3.301***	-2.451***	-3.334***	-2.461***	-3.917***	-0.131	-2.250***	3.388***	-1.393***	-0.184	-1.668***
	(0.313)	(0.165)	(0.509)	(0.232)	(0.432)	(0.272)	(0.282)	(0.825)	(0.634)	(0.260)	(0.911)	(0.289)
N	23,234	23,234	11,419	11,419	16,427	16,427	18,226	18,226	14,640	14,640	15,203	15,203
R^2	0.42	0.42	0.47	0.46	0.36	0.36	0.27	0.26	0.54	0.55	0.43	0.45

Notes: The following variables are expressed as logarithms in all regression models: share of expatriates, capital intensity, share of total Japanese investment in the subsidiary and age. The estimation of each model includes dummy variables for each industry and each year of observation. Robust standard errors are in parentheses. *Significant at 10%, **significant at 5%, ***significant at 1%.

subsidiaries for reasons that are not necessarily captured in the models in Tables 3 and 4. Excluding China in models (9) and (10) allows us to test for this. The results show that the signs remain the same as in model (7) in Table 4, but that the value of some coefficients changes. It decreases for the share of local partners in capital, which indicates that in China a higher share of local partners reduces the rate of expatriation to a greater degree than elsewhere. In model (9), the coefficient of 'control for corruption' is now statistically insignificant, which indicates that in combination with the 'enforcing contracts' variable, the role of the 'control for corruption' variable in explaining expatriation is particularly relevant in the context of China's business environment, not in the context of other Asian countries.

Lastly, the small average size of subsidiaries in Hong Kong and Singapore may be related to the possibility that manufacturing firms have regional headquarters in those city states, but production operations in sub-subsidiary firms in, respectively, neighbouring China and Indonesia or Malaysia. Excluding Hong Kong and Singapore does not change the sign of the coefficients in models (11) and (12), compared with model (7) in Table 4. The only key change is that the 'control for corruption' variable is statistically insignificant in model (12). This indicates that in combination with the 'starting a business' variable, the role of the 'control for corruption' variable in explaining expatriation is particularly relevant in the cases of the business environment in Hong Kong and Singapore, not in the context of other Asian countries.

In all, the signs of the coefficients remain the same as in model (7) in Table 4, which confirms Hypothesis (4). In other words, in countries with more risky business environments, subsidiaries of MNCs tend to rely to a greater degree on locally recruited senior staff rather than expatriates. This conclusion differs significantly from that of Gaur, Delios, and Singh (2007) who find that a greater institutional distance between home and host country leads firms to increase their reliance on expatriate managers. It confirms Ando and Paik (2013) who conclude the opposite. Arguably, the indicators of country risk in this study and of 'institutional distance' in other studies do not necessarily yield similar indications of distance between home and host countries. Nevertheless, both broadly point in the same direction. The key difference between this study and Gaur, Delios, and Singh (2007) is how it accounts for capital, as explained above. As a consequence of properly accounting for changes in the real value of capital since the establishment of subsidiary companies, this study finds that capital intensity is positively correlated and highly statistically significant, which impacts on the statistical significance of the coefficients of other explanatory variables.

Implications for theory and management practice

These findings advance the study of MNC responses to host-country risk, in terms of both methodology and theory. Our study argued that conventional indicators of host-country risk have been developed for portfolio investment and are not necessarily suitable for an assessment of the responses of MNCs engaged in FDI to risk in host countries. Using more appropriate risk indicators, our study found that host-country risk – keeping all else equal – is negatively correlated with the degree of expatriation, thus contradicting other studies that used conventional risk indicators for the same purpose. The corollary for international management theory is that MNCs engaged in FDI interact with country risk by localizing senior executive management positions to mitigate the consequences of risk.

Our study also found that, rather than host-country risk, firm-specific factors (particularly capital intensity, but also ownership share of parent firms in subsidiaries and the age of the venture) explain most of the variation in the degree to which subsidiaries rely on Japanese expatriates. By properly accounting for invested capital in subsidiaries, our study found that the capital intensity of production is a key explanatory firm-specific variable. It correlates positively with the degree of expatriation in subsidiary firms and contradicts findings in other studies. The corollary for international management theory is that MNCs are less likely to rely on expatriates to off-set host-country risk, but to mitigate risk to parent investment in subsidiaries.

The implications for management practice are that MNCs may consider offsetting perceived host-country risk to their foreign subsidiary firms by engaging host-country nationals in executive management positions. This strategy may be particularly relevant in the case of relatively low capital investment extended to subsidiaries. But in case of relatively high capital investment in foreign subsidiaries (possibly associated with the employment of proprietary technology and/or debt guarantees from their parent firms), MNCs may consider offsetting risk to such capital commitments by retaining home-country nationals in key executive positions.

Discussion and conclusion

This paper shows that firm-specific factors, particularly capital intensity, the ownership share of parent firms in subsidiary firms and the age of the venture, together explain a very large part of the variation in the degree to which subsidiary companies depend on expatriates, and that in host countries with more risky business environments, subsidiaries of MNCs tend to rely to a lesser extent on expatriates, and by implication to a greater degree on locally recruited senior staff. The paper shows that advancing age, as well as a higher degree of local participation, reduces the dependence of a foreign subsidiary firm on expatriate employees.

Further research should address the question why firms do this. It can be hypothesized that business success in a host country with a higher degree of perceived risk depends on a superior understanding of the idiosyncrasies of the business environment of the host country and possibly on local connections, both of which locally recruited senior staff may have. It could also be that a parent company is reluctant to expose expatriates and their families to the difficulties of living in a host country with a higher degree of perceived risk. Either way, localization of senior management is a strategy to minimize country risk.

By controlling for firm-specific factors, the paper also finds that the capital intensity of production of a subsidiary venture is positively correlated with the degree of expatriation and that this variable actually explains a large part of it. Further research should explain why this is the case. It can be hypothesized that MNCs maintain expatriates in their foreign subsidiary ventures as a consequence of company strategies aimed at maximizing control. The purpose of doing this is that a subsidiary firm needs to optimize its use of capital-intensive technologies, and also maximize the likelihood that it will be able to service its outside finance in the form of participations by parent firms as well as debt, especially if debt was guaranteed by parent MNCs. This will require data that allow the assessment of how Japanese foreign subsidiaries are financed.

Arguably, a shortcoming of this research is that it focuses on Japanese firms in an Asian context. Further research should also investigate whether the findings hold for non-Asian host countries with different business environments and levels of risk. Lastly, further research should compare the findings with those for earlier benchmark years to test whether Japanese firms have changed their expatriation strategies and assess the possible reasons for that.

Disclosure statement

No potential conflict of interest was reported by the authors.

Notes

1. METI (2003, 160) shows for example that in 1998 not only 72% of top executives were Japanese expatriates, but also that 63% of deputy top executives and 31–68% of personnel in key functional departments in Japanese subsidiary manufacturing companies in Asia were Japanese expatriates.
2. The database comprises the results of an annual survey undertaken by the Tōyō Keizai publishing company (Tōyō Keizai 2000–2005). It is published in Japanese as 海外進出企業総覧; *(Kaigai Shinshutsu Kigyō Soran)*. This source has been used in other studies, such as Tan and Mahoney (2006), Gaur, Delios, and Singh (2007), Wilkinson et al. (2008). But these studies did not make use of all relevant firm-specific variables in the source, nor of multi-year panel data.
3. The comparative study was limited to Asian countries for two reasons. These countries comprise a wide range of risk indicators, while such indicators vary less across European and North American countries. In 2004, 49% of Japanese subsidiaries were located in Asia, compared to 14% in Europe, 31% in Canada, the USA and Mexico and 6% elsewhere, while subsidiaries in Asian countries were across a greater range of e.g. size and industries than in the rest of the world.
4. Ideally, capital should be the total assets or total equity (paid-up capital plus retained earnings) of a subsidiary company. The database only gives paid-up capital, valued at the year in which the most recent addition was made to the equity of the subsidiary, generally the year of establishment (Beamish, Delios, and Lecraw 1997, 108). Consequently, the actual value of invested capital of older subsidiary ventures is underestimated, because of inflation since establishment and/or currency depreciation relative to the US$, and/or an accumulation of re-invested earnings. For that reason, paid-up capital data are converted for this paper to US$ in constant 2000 prices, calculated first by using the exchange rate (local currency unit per US$) in the year of establishment, and second by correcting for inflation with the Gross Fixed Capital Formation deflator (in US$, 2000 = 100) from the national accounts of the USA. Other studies, such as Gaur, Delios, and Singh (2007), also used capital as a control variable, but omitted this important correction.
5. For instance, in Thailand, Toshiba Semiconductors Thailand Co Ltd is a JV established in 1990 by Toshiba (Japan, holding 32.9% of the shares), Toshiba Electronics Malaysia Sdn Bhd (incorporated in Malaysia 45.6%) and Toshiba Electric Asia Pte Ltd (incorporated in Singapore 19%), along with a local investor (2.5%). Another example is Hitachi Chemical Shanghai in China, a wholly owned subsidiary established in 1998 by Hitachi Chemical Co Ltd, which is a JV incorporated in Hong Kong and controlled by Japanese parent company Hitachi Chemical (Japan, 88.6%) and Taiwan Hitachi Chemical (Taiwan, 11.4%).
6. See: http://www.worldbank.org/wbi/governance/data and http://www.doingbusiness.org.
7. In principle, the use of industry dummy variables identifies the difference between market-seeking firms focused on sales in the host country and requiring greater knowledge of the local market, and resource-seeking firms focused on exports.

References

Ando, Naoki, and Yongsun Paik. 2013. "Institutional Distance, Host Country and International Business Experience, and the Use of Parent Country Nationals." *Human Resource Management Journal* 23 (1): 52–71. doi:10.1111/j.1748-8583.2012.00201.x.

Baruch, Yehuda, and Yochanan Altman. 2002. "Expatriation and Repatriation in MNCs: A Taxonomy." *Human Resource Management* 41 (2): 239–259. doi:10.1002/hrm.10034.

Beamish, Paul W., Andrew Delios, and Donald J. Lecraw. 1997. *Japanese Multinationals in the Global Economy*. Cheltenham: Edward Elgar.

Beechler, Shon, and Jong Yang. 1994. "The Transfer of Japanese-Style Management to American Subsidiaries: Constraints, and Competencies." *Journal of International Business Studies* 25 (3): 467–491. doi:10.1057/palgrave.jibs.8490208.

Belderbos, René A., and Mariëlle G. Heijltjes. 2005. "The Determinants of Expatriate Staffing by Japanese Multinationals in Asia: Control, Learning and Vertical Business Groups." *Journal of International Business Studies* 36 (3): 341–354. doi:10.1057/palgrave.jibs.8400135.

Boyacigiller, Nakiye. 1990. "The Role of Expatriates in the Management of Interdependence Complexity and Risk in Multinational Corporations." *Journal of International Business Studies* 21 (3): 357–381. doi:10.1057/palgrave.jibs.8490825.

Chen, Edward K. Y. 1983. "Factor Proportions of Foreign and Local Firms in Developing Countries." *Journal of Development Economics* 12 (1–2): 267–274. doi:10.1016/0304-3878 (83)90044-5.

Click, Reid W. 2005. "Financial and Political Risks in US Direct Foreign Investment." *Journal of International Business Studies* 36 (5): 559–575. doi:10.1057/palgrave.jibs.8400157.

Downes, Meredith, and Anisya S. Thomas. 2000. "Knowledge Transfer Through Expatriation: The U-Curve Approach to Overseas Staffing." *Journal of Managerial Issues* 12 (2): 131–149.

Fang, Yulin, Guo-Liang Frank Jiang, Shige Makino, and Paul W. Beamish. 2010. "Multinational Firm Knowledge, Use of Expatriates, and Foreign Subsidiary Performance." *Journal of Management Studies* 47 (1): 27–54. doi:10.1111/j.1467-6486.2009.00850.x.

Gaur, Ajai S., Andrew Delios, and Kulwant Singh. 2007. "Institutional Environments, Staffing Strategies, and Subsidiary Performance." *Journal of Management* 33 (4): 611–636. doi:10. 1177/0149206307302551.

Gong, Yaping. 2003. "Subsidiary Staffing in Multinational Enterprises: Agency, Resources, and Performance." *Academy of Management Journal* 46 (6): 728–739. doi:10.2307/30040664.

Jaussaud, Jacques, and Johannes Schaaper. 2007. "European and Japanese Multinational Companies in China: Organization and Control of Subsidiaries." *Asian Business & Management* 6 (3): 223–245. doi:10.1057/palgrave.abm.9200222.

Jaussaud, Jacques, Johannes Schaaper, and Zhong-yu Zhang. 2001. "The Control of International Equity Joint Venture: Distribution of Capital and Expatriation Policies." *Journal of the Asia Pacific Economy* 6 (2): 212–231. doi:10.1080/13547860120059720.

Kawai, Norifumi, and Roger Strange. 2014. "Subsidiary Autonomy and Performance in Japanese Multinationals in Europe." *International Business Review* 23 (3): 504–515. doi:10.1016/j. ibusrev.2013.08.012.

Keeley, Timothy Dean. 2001. *International Human Resource Management in Japanese Firms: Their Greatest Challenge*. Basingstoke: Palgrave.

Konopaske, Robert, Steve Werner, and Kent E. Neupert. 2002. "Entry Mode Strategy and Performance: The Role of FDI Staffing." *Journal of Business Research* 55 (9): 759–770. doi:10. 1016/S0148-2963(00)00185-5.

Legewie, Jochen. 2002. "Control and Co-ordination of Japanese Subsidiaries in China: Problems of an Expatriate-Based Management System." *International Journal of Human Resource Management* 13 (6): 901–919. doi:10.1080/09585190210134273.

Ministry of External Trade and Industry. 2003. *White Paper on International Trade 2003*. Tokyo: Ministry of External Trade and Industry.

Oetzel, Jennifer M., Richard A. Bettis, and Marc Zenner. 2001. "Country Risk Measures: How Risky Are They?" *Journal of World Business* 36 (2): 128–145. doi:10.1016/S1090-9516(01)00049-9.

Paik, Yongsun, and Junghoon Derick Sohn. 2004. "Expatriate Managers and MNC's Ability to Control International Subsidiaries: The Case of Japanese MNCs." *Journal of World Business* 39 (1): 61–71. doi:10.1016/j.jwb.2003.08.003.

Peng, George Z., and Paul W. Beamish. 2014. "MNC Subsidiary Size and Expatriate Control: Resource-Dependence and Learning Perspectives." *Journal of World Business* 49 (1): 51–62. doi:10.1016/j.jwb.2012.11.001.

Selmer, Jan, ed. 1995. *Expatriates Management: New Ideas for International Business*. Westport, CT: Quorum.

Shiraki, Mitsuhide. 2007. *Role of Japanese Expatriates in Japanese Multinational Corporations: From the Perspective of the Multinational Internal Labor Market.* Creation of New Contemporary Asian Studies Working Paper No. 42. Tokyo: School of Political Science and Economics, Waseda University, http://hdl.handle.net/2065/12802

Tan, Danchi, and J. T. Mahoney. 2006. "Why A Multinational Firm Chooses Expatriates: Integrating Resource-Based, Agency and Transaction Costs Perspectives." *Journal of Management Studies* 43 (3): 457–484. doi:10.1111/j.1467-6486.2006.00598.x.

Tōyō Keizai. 2000–2005. 海外進出企業総覧 *Kaigai shushutsu kigyo soran 1999–2004* [Operations of Japanese-Controlled Firms in Overseas Markets]. Tokyo: Tōyō Keizai Shinpōsha.

Watson O'Donnell, Sharon. 2000. "Managing Foreign Subsidiaries: Agents of Headquarters, or an Interdependent Network?." *Strategic Management Journal* 21 (5): 525–548. doi:10.1002/(SICI) 1097-0266(200005)21:5<525:AID-SMJ104>3.0.CO;2-Q.

Widmier, Scott, Lance Eliot Brouthers, and Paul W. Beamish. 2008. "Expatriate or Local? Predicting Japanese, Subsidiary Expatriate Staffing Strategies." *International Journal of Human Resource Management* 19 (9): 1607–1621. doi:10.1080/09585190802294986.

Wilkinson, Timothy. J., George Z. Peng, Lance Eliot Brouthers, and Paul W. Beamish. 2008. "The Diminishing Effect of Cultural Distance on Subsidiary Control." *Journal of International Management* 14 (2): 93–107. doi:10.1016/j.intman.2007.08.003.

Yoshihara, Hideki. 2005. "Decline of Japan's Predominance in Asia." In *Japanese Firms in Transition: Responding to the Globalization Challenge*, edited by Tom Roehl and Allan Bird, 243–260. Amsterdam: Elsevier.

Yoshihara, Hideki. 2008. "Belated Changes in International Management of Japanese Multi-nationals." *Rikkyo Business Review* 1 (1): 4–15.

Zaheer, Srilata, Margaret Spring Schomaker, and Lilach Nachum. 2012. "Distance Without Direction: Restoring Credibility to a Much-Loved Construct." *Journal of International Business Studies* 43 (1): 18–27. doi:10.1057/jibs.2011.43.

Cross-national distance and insidership within networks: Japanese MNCs' ownership strategies in their overseas subsidiaries

Megan Min Zhang

Ivey Business School, Western University, London, Ontario, Canada N6G 0N1

This study investigates the controversial question about how cross-national distance influences MNCs' equity ownership in their overseas subsidiaries. Prior studies adopted aggregated constructs and time-invariant measures of cross-national distance, failing to capture the complexity of the phenomenon. Moreover, although 'insidership' within business networks may moderate the foreignness that MNCs confront in overseas markets, prior studies have not incorporated it into analysis. The present study confirms the explanatory power of multiple dimensions of cross-national distance and MNCs' insidership within networks. It also shows that cross-national distance and insidership within relevant works strengthen or weaken each other's influences on Japanese ownership strategies.

Introduction

The equity ownership strategy is critical for MNCs as it affects both the foreign affiliate's likelihood of success and its probability of survival (Dhanaraj and Beamish 2004; Li 1995; Stopford and Wells 1972). Meanwhile, the field of international business (IB) has paid much attention to the impact of cross-national distance on the various strategies of MNCs' operating in foreign countries (Werner 2002), including equity ownership. For decades of research, the most widely used approach to cross-national distance is based on Hofstede's four measures of culture, originally made available in his 1980 book *Culture's Consequences: International Differences in Work Related Values*. IB scholars find his approach appealing for two reasons. First, Hofstede (1980) proposes power distance, uncertainty avoidance, individualism and masculinity as the key distinguishing aspects of national culture, and compares these factors using a large sample of countries. Second, the emphasis on flows of information between the home and host countries lends itself to a conceptualization based on cultural and psychic differences, which increases the uncertainty, risk and, hence, the costs of entering foreign countries (Hennart and Larimo 1998).

Nevertheless, recent scholarship has pointed out the possible problems of using cultural distance as the proxy for cross-national distance. First, recent studies suggest that changes in economic conditions are the source of cultural dynamics, while the endurance of institutional characteristics provides the foundation for cultural stability (Tang and Koveos 2008). Since an aggregated and time-invariant measure on cultural distance is unable to capture these characteristics and dynamics, prior studies fail to

125

reflect sufficient complexity in their approaches to the phenomenon, and some even reach conflicting conclusions (Tihanyi, Griffith, and Russell 2005). For example, prior studies have been concerned with how MNCs' experiences influence their ownership strategies (Cho and Padmanabhan 2005; Delios and Beamish 1999; Jung, Beamish, and Goerzen 2010). However, they adopt static measures on cross-national distance that actually change over time. Therefore, it is difficult to identify how much variance in the phenomenon can be explained by accumulating experience and how much by changing cross-national distance.

Second, recent studies have extended cross-national distance from cultural distance to institutional distance, which is defined as the extent of similarity or dissimilarity between the regulatory, cognitive and normative institutions of two countries (Kostova 1996; Scott 1995). So far, the construct has been linked to two aspects of MNC operations: (1) the establishment of legitimacy in the host country (Kostova and Zaheer 1999), that is, local responsiveness; and (2) the transfer of strategic orientations and organizational practices from the parent firm to the foreign subsidiary (Kostova 1999), that is, internal consistency. Though the construction of institutional distance enriches implications of cross-national distance, the use of highly aggregated static measures still takes the 'distance' as a total sum of vectors, ignoring the possible conflicting influences of various institutions (Jackson and Deeg 2008).

Moreover, in addition to cross-national distance, equity ownership strategy may be leveraged by network characteristics (Johanson and Vahlne 2009; Scott and Davis 2007). As early as 1990, scholars suggested building a network theory of the MNC – such an entity can be conceptualized as an internal network that is embedded in an external network consisting of all other organizations, such as customers, suppliers, regulators (Bartlett and Beamish 2011; Dunning and Lundan 2008; Ghoshal and Bartlett 1990). For two decades, scholars have highlighted that collaboration within networks may provide opportunities for one partner to access the skills of the other, and thus improve its resource portfolio for coping with the liability of foreignness (Bartlett and Beamish 2011; Hamel 1991; Johanson and Vahlne 2009). Nonetheless, there is almost no study that empirically investigates whether and how MNCs' ownership strategies are affected by the insidership within networks, let alone by the potential interaction between the insidership and cross-national distance.

This exploratory study aims to investigate the above issues. First, by adopting Berry, Guillén, and Zhou's (2010) multidimensional and longitudinal measures on cross-national distance, the present study tries to unfold the diversity of how multiple dimensions of cross-national distance influence Japanese MNCs' ownership in their overseas subsidiaries. Second, it empirically examines the influences of business networks on Japanese MNCs' ownership strategies. And third, it investigates how insidership regarding networks interacts with cross-national distance to influence the ownership strategy of Japanese MNCs.

This study proceeds as follows. First, it reviews how aggregated and time-invariant constructs fail to capture the complexity about how cross-national distance influences MNCs ownership strategies. Next, it reviews the recent scholarship regarding cross-national distance and networks. Third, it describes general research setting for investigating research questions and explains reasons of using Japanese samples. It then develops hypotheses which posit that both multidimensional cross-national distance and insidership within business networks may independently, as well as interactively, influence Japanese MNCs' ownership strategies. The empirical results, implications for practice and suggestions for future research are also discussed.

Literature review

Cultural distance and ownership strategy

Two conflicting theoretical streams exist within the studies using cultural distance to address the influence of cross-national distance on equity ownership strategies. One stream posits that the higher the cultural distance between the home and the host country, the higher the level of equity ownership in the entry mode choice. According to this stream of literature, greater differences in cultures prompt MNCs to exert greater control in their entries so that they can minimize transaction costs (Hennart and Reddy 1997). Another stream explains ownership decisions by the risk-reduction rationale of MNC managers – greater cultural distance is associated with entry modes based on lower percentages of equity ownership (Barkema and Vermeulen 1998). Tihanyi, Griffith, and Russell (2005) conducted a meta-analysis with 66 independent samples and found that cultural distance does not significantly ($p = 0.416$) contribute to the prediction of ownership.

There are some potential explanations for Tihanyi, Griffith, and Russell's (2005) finding. One is that potential moderator effects might play a role in the relationship between cross-national distance and MNCs' ownership strategies (Hunter and Schmidt 1990). Another explanation is that cross-national distance is more than cultural distance (Berry, Guillén, and Zhou 2010). Hofstede (1980) reduces all cross-national differences to the dimension of culture, thus failing to capture the rich array of dimensions along which countries differ from one another (Ghemawat 2001). In particular, he neglects the critical role of societal institutions in articulating, disseminating and arbitrating cultural and social cues (Xu and Shenkar 2002). Additionally, scholars using Hofstede's cultural scores assume that cultural distance does not change over time (Cho and Padmanabhan 2005; Hennart and Larimo 1998; Kogut and Singh 1988; Tihanyi, Griffith, and Russell 2005). This assumption has been undermined by recent sociological research, which demonstrates that cultural distance, not to mention economic distance, can change quite rapidly over time (Inglehart and Baker 2000; Shenkar 2001). Especially in the era of globalization, a country's institutional environments coevolve with MNCs' cross-border activities (Cantwell, Dunning, and Lundan 2010). Given these issues, it should not be surprising that the empirical findings based on Hofstede's cultural scores can be ambiguous or contradictory. In summary, cultural distance tends to be one-dimensional and time-invariant in nature, and the measure does not entirely take into account the differences of countries (Berry, Guillén, and Zhou 2010).

Cross-national distance: multidimensional and longitudinal measures

Based on Jackson and Deeg's (2008) institutional theory, Berry, Guillén, and Zhou (2010) disaggregate the construct of cross-national distance by proposing a set of multidimensional measures. They base their institutional approach on three conceptualizations of cross-national institutions – national business systems, national governance systems and national innovation systems (Berry, Guillén, and Zhou 2010; Jackson and Deeg 2008). First, national business systems are 'particular arrangements of hierarchy-market relations becoming institutionalized and relatively successful in particular contexts' (Whitley 1992, 6). Countries differ in varying degrees in terms of the characteristics of their business systems, and these differences originate in cultural, economic, financial, demographic and geographic practices (Whitley 1992). Second, national governance systems refer to the set of incentives, safeguards and dispute-resolution processes used to order the activities of various corporate stakeholders (Kester 1996) and originate in administrative and political institutions

(Henisz 2000). Third, national innovation systems refer to the configuration of institutions that foster the development of technology and innovation (Nelson and Rosenberg 1993).

Within these systems, countries differ in their abilities to produce knowledge and the extent to which they can leverage that knowledge by connecting to other countries (Furman, Porter, and Stern 2002). Therefore, Berry, Guillén, and Zhou (2010) propose nine dimensions for cross-national distance, including cultural, economic, financial, demographic, geographic, political, administrative, knowledge and global connectedness distances. Moreover, they compute distance separately for each dimension based on various empirical indicators, thereby allowing researchers to utilize them theoretically to best fit their research questions. Further, the changes in MNCs' ownership strategy reflect the co-evolution of the firm and the context in which it operates (Cantwell, Dunning, and Lundan 2010; Hoffmann 2007). Studies that use time-invariant cross-national distance data suffer from spurious effects: it is difficult to identify whether the effects are caused by the change of cross-national distance, or by MNCs' accumulating experience. Berry, Guillén, and Zhou's (2010) longitudinal measures on multiple dimensions allow the study to distinguish between them empirically.

The present study uses these longitudinal dimensions of cross-national distance to address issues from prior studies. Table 1 provides a summary of these nine dimensions.

Insidership within networks

When investing abroad, MNCs not only confront cross-national distance, but also are embedded in networks (Johanson and Vahlne 2009). This study takes embeddedness as the same as insidership within certain networks, and both refer to the logic of exchange that promotes economics of time, integrative agreements and Pareto improvements in

Table 1.   Dimensions of cross-national distance.

Dimension	Definitions	Component variables
Economic	Differences in economic development and macroeconomic characteristics	Income, inflation, exports, imports
Financial	Differences in financial sector development	Private credit, stock market cap, listed companies
Political	Differences in political stability, democracy and trade bloc membership	Policy-making uncertainty, democratic character, size of the state, WTO member, regional trade agreement
Administrative	Differences in colonial ties, language, religion and legal system	Colonizer–colonized link, common language, common religion, legal system
Cultural	Differences in attitudes toward authority, trust, individuality and importance of work and family	Power distance, uncertainty avoidance, individualism, masculinity
Demographic	Differences in demographic characteristics	Life expectancy, birth rate, population under 14, population under 65
Knowledge	Differences in patents and scientific production	Patents, scientific articles
Global connectedness	Differences in tourism and internet use	International tourism expenditure, international tourism receipts, Internet use
Geographic	Great circle distance between geographic centre of countries	Great circle distance

Source: An institutional approach to cross-national distance (Berry, Guillén, and Zhou 2010).

allocative efficiency and complex adaptation (Uzzi 1997). In addition, the insidership of an MNC can be delineated by its position within relevant networks, such as degree, closeness, decay and betweenness (Jackson 2008). Because there is little literature about an MNC's insidership within networks, this study tentatively uses the degree, that is, the number of direct connections an MNC possesses within relevant networks (Jackson 2008), to represent the level of insidership.

Insidership within relevant networks may influence MNCs' ownership strategies in a more complicated way. On the one hand, a network form of organizing can allow firms to enjoy the benefits of flexibility, while at the same time gaining the economies of scale that are typically reserved for much larger organizations (Porter and Powell 2006). Moreover, by networking MNCs are able to access fine-grained information from partners and even solve problems jointly (Levitt and March 1988; Powell, Koput, and Smith-Doerr 1996; Uzzi 1997), making it possible to identify and exploit broader opportunities. In contrast, outsidership in relation to the relevant networks is the root of uncertainty, much more so than cross-national distance (Johanson and Vahlne 2009). Therefore, an MNC embedded in relevant business networks may need less ownership control when investing abroad. Further, insidership may even moderate the influence of cross-national distance on an MNC's ownership strategy.

On the other hand, insidership within networks can be a double-edged sword, as certain modality of networks may restrict the flow of information as well as the capacity to adapt (Porter and Powell 2006; Uzzi 1997), retarding MNCs from responding to local institutional environments. For example, if firms within networks are from the same country, they may have less institutional knowledge about a foreign country to share than those embedded in international networks. Under this situation, it is unclear how cross-national distance and insidership within networks independently and interactively influence MNCs' ownership levels. Extant studies have not yet examined this double-edged effect.

In brief, cross-national distance and the insidership within networks separately influence MNCs' ownership strategies. Moreover, they may also interact with each other to influence ownership strategies, a complexity that is further explored in this study.

Research setting

The present study focuses on the investments of Japanese MNCs in other countries and investigates their ownership strategies by simultaneously considering the influences of both cross-national distance and insidership within networks. Such a research setting naturally controls for confounding effects stemming from multiple home countries. One stream of institutional theory, the so-called 'national character theory', posits that countries vary systematically in psychological characteristics and that MNCs' ownership strategies in their subsidiaries will reflect the characteristics of the home countries in which they are domiciled (Hennart and Larimo 1998; Shetty 1979). It has been well documented that Japanese MNCs are likely to seek high ownership levels in their foreign subsidiaries because of their national character, which includes tendencies such as high uncertainty avoidance (Erramilli 1996; Hennart and Larimo 1998; Hofstede 1980). However, when involving multiple home countries, there might be an endogeneity issue in the research if their national characters conflict with each other. Focusing on one home country such as Japan allows this study to avoid this issue.

Moreover, Japanese industrial organization has long been characterized by inter-corporate linkages (McGuire and Dow 2009), and this alliance capitalism embeds firms in a broad home network of long-term relationships (Thomas and Waring 1999). Therefore, a Japanese overseas subsidiary is embedded in at least two types of business networks – home networks characterized by 'alliance capitalism' in Japan and the host networks formed by sibling subsidiaries operating in the same host country. Using Japanese samples provides two different types of networks, satisfying conditions that are necessary to investigate influences of insidership within relevant networks and their interactions with cross-national distance.

Further, it is difficult to incorporate all nine dimensions of institutional distance into theoretical analysis within one study. The present study tentatively concentrates on cultural distance and administrative distance, as they are closely associated with, yet distinct from, each other compared to the other seven dimensions (Berry, Guillén, and Zhou 2010). By focusing on these two associated dimensions of cross-national distance and two different types of networks, this study purports to reveal the complexity of the influence of cross-national distance and insidership within networks on MNCs' ownership strategies.

Theory and hypotheses

Cross-national distance

The influence of cultural distance on MNCs' ownership strategy has been well documented. Similar to Kogut and Singh (1988), Berry, Guillén, and Zhou (2010) suggest that cultural distance accounts for national differences in attitudes towards authority, trust, individuality and the importance of work and family. It is also similar to the construct cultural-cognitive distance that refers to the cross-national distance in cultural-cognitive rules that constitute the nature of reality and the frames through which meaning is made (Kostova 1996; Scott 1995; Xu, Pan, and Beamish 2004). Since holistic knowledge regarding local cultural-cognition may be too intangible to understand (Kogut and Singh 1988; North 1990; Peng 2003), MNCs usually adopt mimetic mechanisms such as shared ownership structure with local players to achieve legitimacy in cultural-cognitive pillar (DiMaggio and Powell 1983; Scott 1995). Therefore, greater cultural distance should be associated with MNCs' operation mode based on lower equity ownership in order to establish their legitimacy in host countries (Barkema, Bell, and Pennings 1996; Delios and Beamish 1999).

In contrast, administrative distance, which refers to differences in bureaucratic patterns due to colonial ties, language, religion and the legal system (Berry, Guillén, and Zhou 2010; Ghemawat 2001; Henisz 2000), has not been widely utilized by extant literature. However, according to its definition, administrative distance is similar to normative distance that refers to the cross-national difference in value and norms that designate social actors' appropriate behaviour (Kostova 1996; Scott 1995; Xu, Pan, and Beamish 2004). Moreover, just like cultural-cognitive and normative pillars are interdependent but different from each other (Scott 1995), cultural and administrative distances relate to but essentially differ from each other (Berry, Guillén, and Zhou 2010). For example, cultural rules as informal institutions are usually used to bridge institutional voids, which means relevant formal institutions (e.g., normative or administrative rules) do not exist (Khanna and Palepu 1997; North 1990; Peng 2003; Puffer and McCarthy 2011), making cultural and administrative distances are implicitly interlinked. The similarity between administrative and normative rules makes it possible for the present study to establish arguments based on literature about normative distance. Since holistic knowledge regarding normative practices in a foreign country may be too sophisticated and sticky to acquire (Kogut and Singh 1988; North 1990; Peng 2003), MNCs usually adopt normative mechanisms, such as higher involvement of the local partner to achieve local appropriateness (DiMaggio and Powell 1983; Scott 1995; Xu, Pan, and Beamish 2004).

The above analysis leads to following two hypotheses:

H1:   Cultural distance is negatively associated with a Japanese MNC's ownership level in its foreign investments.

H2:   Administrative distance is negatively associated with a Japanese MNC's ownership level in its foreign investments.

Insidership within networks

As aforementioned, a Japanese subsidiary is embedded in at least two types of business networks – home networks characterized by 'alliance capitalism' in Japan and the host networks formed by sibling subsidiaries operating in the same host country.

One distinctive feature of Japanese alliance capitalism is Keiretsu, which refers to established and commonly recognized networks of Japanese firms (McGuire and Dow 2009; Thomas and Waring 1999). Prior studies have considerably discussed interrelated benefits of Keiretsu structure including access to stable financing, insulation from market pressures, risk reduction, monitoring benefits and reduction of information asymmetries and mutual assistance (Gedajlovic, Yoshikawa, and Hashimoto 2005; Khanna and Yafeh 2005; McGuire and Dow 2009). As an extension of the Keiretsu heritage, a Japanese MNC may jointly invest in an overseas subsidiary with other Japanese partners (Makino and Beamish 1998). Under this situation, on the one hand a Japanese MNC may benefit from Keiretsu networks including access to fine-grained information about the host country (Levitt and March 1988; Powell, Koput, and Smith-Doerr 1996; Uzzi 1997), reducing its need to rely on indigenous players. On the other hand, joint problem-solving requires the focal Japanese MNC to achieve certain internal consistency with other Japanese partners (Kostova 1999; Levitt and March 1988; Powell, Koput, and Smith-Doerr 1996; Uzzi 1997). Both considerations result in higher Japanese ownership level when investing in a foreign subsidiary.

Moreover, the degree of insidership within the host networks represents how many direct information channels the focal MNC can access in the host country. Information flows within host networks improve the capability of realizing internal consistency by choosing appropriate partner firms, monitoring their behaviours and performance more efficiently (Jung, Beamish, and Goerzen 2010; Williamson 1985). Therefore, the higher degree of insidership within the host networks may encourage Japanese MNCs to afford overseas subsidiaries more autonomy, leading to lower Japanese ownership levels.

H3:   The level of insidership within the home networks positively relates to a Japanese MNC's equity ownership in its overseas subsidiaries.

H4:   The level of insidership within the host networks negatively related to a Japanese MNC's equity ownership in its overseas subsidiaries.

Interaction between cross-national distance and insidership within networks

Prior studies posit that the insidership within business networks may alleviate the liability of foreignness (Johanson and Vahlne 2009). This proposition is appropriate for the situation that networks are globally connected. However, when networks restrict to the same country, the information about institutional environments external to them are limited, resulting in the liability of insidership (Porter and Powell 2006; Uzzi 1997). Therefore, the insidership within networks can moderate the influence of cross-national distance on MNCs' ownership levels, vice versa. In this vein, moderation effects should be argued from both sides.

First, cultural distance may interact with insidership within home networks to influence MNCs' ownership strategies. On the one hand, as argued, the level of insidership within the home networks positively relates to a Japanese MNC's equity ownership level in its foreign investments. Nevertheless, Japanese MNCs embedded in their home networks may have less knowledge to share about the host country with greater cultural distance. In this vein, cultural distance negatively moderates the (positive) influence of insidership within home networks on MNCs' ownership strategies. On the other hand, since a Japanese MNC can access information from other Japanese partners and even solve problems jointly (Levitt and March 1988; Powell, Koput, and Smith-Doerr 1996; Uzzi 1997), the insidership within home networks may alleviate the (negative) influence of cultural distance on MNCs' ownership strategies (Johanson and Vahlne 2009). Both competing moderation effects may exist simultaneously. Nevertheless, as cultural knowledge is usually too intangible, sticky and sophisticated for MNCs to understand and utilize independently (Kogut 1988; North 1990; Peng 2003), this study argues that the moderation effect of cultural distance is stronger than the moderation effect of insidership within home networks.

Second, similarly, cultural distance may also interact with insidership within host networks to influence MNCs' ownership strategies. On the one hand, as argued, the level of insidership within host networks negatively relates to Japanese MNCs' equity ownership in their foreign investments because the access to information flows within networks reduces their needs to realize internal consistency by high equity control (Jung, Beamish, and Goerzen 2010; Williamson 1985). When an MNC invests in a more culturally distant country, it is more difficult to learn relevant cultural knowledge by itself. Under this situation, the influence of insidership within host networks should be even stronger. In this vein, cultural distance enhances the (negative) influence of host networks on the MNC's ownership level. On the other hand, the access to fine-grained information from host networks may reduce the need of a Japanese MNC to achieve necessary local responsiveness by lowering ownership control (Johanson and Vahlne 2009). Though both moderation effects may coexist, this study argues that cultural knowledge may be too tacit for MNCs to acquire and utilize independently. Therefore, the moderation effect of cultural distance may be more substantive than the moderation effect of insidership within host networks. The above analysis leads to following hypotheses.

H5:   Cultural distance weakens the positive influence of a Japanese MNC's insidership within home networks on its ownership levels in its foreign investments.

H6:   Cultural distance enhances the negative influence of a Japanese MNC's insidership within host networks on its ownership levels in its foreign investments.

Third, administrative distance may interact with insidership within home networks to influence MNCs' ownership strategies. Similarly to arguments for cultural distance, on the one hand administrative distance may negatively moderate the (positive) influence of insidership within home networks on MNCs' ownership strategies because Japanese partners may have less knowledge to share about the host country's administrative systems. On the other hand, the insidership within home networks may alleviate the negative influence of administrative distance on MNCs' ownership strategies because of the accessible information within networks (Johanson and Vahlne 2009). Although both moderations effects may exist, this study argues that administrative systems stemming from colonial ties, language, religion and legal systems are more codifiable than cultural systems, as they can be understood by internal or external accrediting bodies (Scott 1995). Therefore, the knowledge about administrative systems can be transferred relatively quickly (Kogut and Zander 2003). In this vein, the moderation of insidership within home networks should be stronger than the moderation effect of administrative distance.

Fourth, administrative distance may also interact with insidership within host networks to influence MNCs' ownership strategies. On the one hand, since it is more difficult for an MNC to independently learn administrative systems that they are unfamiliar with, it is more likely for them to rely on network ties within the host country to access relevant knowledge. Therefore, the (negative) influence of insidership within host networks may be stronger in the host country with greater administrative distance from the home country. On the other hand, insidership within host networks may weaken the (negative) influence of administrative distance on the Japanese ownership because the MNC can access relevant administrative knowledge from partners within host networks (Johanson and Vahlne 2009). Although both conflicting moderation effects may exist, this study argues that knowledge about administrative systems is more codifiable than knowledge of cultural systems, as it can be understood by internal or external accrediting bodies (Scott 1995). In this vein, the moderation of insidership within host networks should be stronger than the moderation effect of administrative distance.

H7: The Japanese MNC's insidership within home networks weakens the negative influence of administrative distance on its overseas ownership level.

H8: The Japanese MNC's insidership in the host network weakens administrative distance's negatively influence on its overseas ownership level.

Methodology

The present study adopts a multilevel and longitudinal approach. On the one hand, it investigates a cross-level phenomenon, for which multilevel research is one way to promote the development of a more expansive management paradigm for understanding organizational systems (Hitt et al. 2007). On the other hand, it uses a longitudinal regression model, reducing endogeneity issues caused by time-varying factors at subsidiary, MNC and country levels (Singer and Willett 2003).

Samples

This study combines data from merged Toyo Keizai and Needs data-sets (2012 Edition) and Berry, Guillén, and Zhou's (2010) longitudinal cross-national distance data-set. This study dropped subsidiaries invested in agriculture, forestry and mining industries, as these sectors usually have distinct industry-specific regulations. The study also dropped Japanese subsidiaries that function as local headquarters, since almost all of them are wholly owned subsidiaries. Moreover, to focus on strategic investments, the study dropped subsidiaries with less than 5% Japanese ownership during their lifetimes, since they were considered to be portfolio investments (Dhanaraj and Beamish 2009). Finally, the study dropped subsidiaries with missing data. With this careful screening, the final data-set consisted of 658 Japanese MNCs, 6463 subsidiaries in 40 foreign countries and a total of 45,087 observations during the period from 1990 to 2006.

Variables

The dependent variable of the study is the Japanese MNC's ownership level in its overseas subsidiary, measured by the Japanese equity percentage of the focal overseas subsidiary. Because of Keiretsu culture, usually several Japanese MNCs share partnership in one overseas subsidiary and the first owner is the dominant one. This study uses the ownership of the first one as the dependent variable.

For independent variables representing cross-national distance, this study focuses on cultural and administrative distances, longitudinal measures provided by Berry, Guillén, and Zhou's (2010) data-set.

For independent variables representing the degree of insidership within business networks, this study measures the level of insidership within the home networks measured by the number of Japanese MNCs investing in the same subsidiary, and the level of insidership within the host network measured by the number of sibling subsidiaries in the same host country. This study uses their *ln* values to cope with diminishing marginal utility of insidership (Delios and Beamish 1999; Dhanaraj and Beamish 2004). Further, the study includes the interaction items between focal dimensions of cross-national distance and the level of insidership within business networks.

In addition, this study controls for other variables that may influence Japanese ownership levels. First, it controls for influences stemming from the other seven dimensions of cross-national distance provided by Berry, Guillén, and Zhou (2010). However, demographic distance is highly correlated with knowledge distance and connectedness distance (their Pearson correlations are 0.636 and 0.672). Therefore, this study dropped demographic distance.

Second, this study adds industry and sector dummies. Following prior studies (e.g., Dhanaraj and Beamish 2004), this study includes eight industry and two sector dummy variables for the subsidiary level in order to remove the confounding industry and sector effects (the reference is manufacturing of electronics). This study does not use industry dummy variables for the MNC level because of the collinearity between the industrial categories of the subsidiary and its MNC parent. Nevertheless, an MNC from one sector may invest in other sectors in the host country (e.g., a Japanese manufacturer may invest in wholesale and retail sectors simultaneously). As such, this study includes two sector dummy variables for the MNC level (the reference is the manufacturing sector). However, based on a Pearson correlation test, an MNC from the service sector usually still invests in the service sector in foreign countries (correlation = 0.747). Therefore, the variable *subsidiary in service* is dropped to reduce multi-collinearity.

Third, this study controls for several subsidiary-specific factors. Prior studies suggest that the subsidiary's operating experience may strengthen its knowledge of institutional environments in the host country (Delios and Beamish 2001, 2004). Therefore, the study controls for the subsidiary's age. Considering a possible nonlinear effect, it includes the square of subsidiary age as well. Moreover, it controls for subsidiary size (measured by the *ln* function of the number of employees) representing the subsidiary resource commitment that may negatively relate to the MNC ownership level (Barkema, Bell, and Pennings 1996; Delios and Beamish 1999). The study also includes the percentage of Japanese expatriates in a subsidiary since it also represents the level of the MNC's control within the focal subsidiary (Delios and Bjorkman 2000; Gong 2003; Makino, Beamish, and Zhao 2004).

Finally, the study controls for MNC-specific factors. The study includes MNCs' asset specificity, measured by the advertising and R&D intensities (Chang, Chung, and Moon 2013; Delios and Beamish 1999; Hennart 1991). In addition, the study includes MNC size (measured by the *ln* function of the number of employees in the MNC), since large MNCs may have more flexibility in reallocating their subsidiary portfolio (Delios and Beamish 1999; Dhanaraj and Beamish 2004). Moreover, this study includes the MNC's profitability (measured by the annual return on assets, that is, ROA) that may represent the MNC's overall capability of making profit.

The study initially also included the MNC's host country presence, measured by the accumulation of subsidiary-year units, since accumulated operation within one country may provide a valuable local knowledge base (Delios and Beamish 1999; Dhanaraj and Beamish 2004). However, it was removed because of its high correlation with the insidership within host networks (0.699).

Descriptive statistics and correlation

This study centred all continuous independent variables and interaction items in order to reduce the multi-collinearity of the empirical model (Aiken and West 1991). Table 2 provides all the descriptive statistics of the variables and their Pearson correlation matrix. According to Table 2, the greatest correlation value is -0.621 (between *subsidiary size* and *MNC subsidiary expatriate ratio*). This study further evaluated the multi-collinearity of variables using variance inflation factor (VIF) tests and found that the maximum VIF value was less than 10, indicating that there is no serious multi-collinearity concern in the model (Neter and Michael 1990).

Data analysis

Based on unconditional modelling (that is, the regression on subsidiary performance using only information about analysis levels but without any independent or control variable), intra-class correlations (ICCs) are calculated for the constructed three-level model. ICC between the subsidiaries is 0.912, and the value between the MNCs is 0.062, indicating the need for three-level modelling (Singer and Willett 2003).

Table 3 provides a hierarchical regression process of a three-level longitudinal regression model. Model 1 includes control variables. In Model 2, cultural distance and administrative distance are included. Model 3 involves the subsidiary's insidership in the home and host networks. Model 4 includes the interaction items between cross-national distance and insidership within business networks.

Model 4 empirically examines the four hypotheses. First, cultural distance and administrative distance are negatively associated with Japanese ownership levels in overseas subsidiaries (coefficients are -0.041 and -0.086), supporting H1 and H2.

Second, the level of insidership within the home networks positively relates to the Japanese MNC's ownership level (coefficient $= 1.075$), supporting H3. In contrast, the level of insidership within the host networks negatively relates to the Japanese MNC's ownership level (coefficient $= -0.283$ with $p < 0.10$). Therefore, H4 is partially supported.

Third, cultural distance interacts with the insidership within networks to negatively influence a Japanese MNC's ownership level (coefficients are -0.143 and -0.027), supporting H5 and H6. Moreover, administrative distance interacts with the insidership within networks to positively influence a Japanese MNC's ownership level (coefficients are 0.053 and 0.033), supporting H7 and H8.

Discussion

Using multiple dimensions and longitudinal measures of cross-national distance, the present study investigates how cross-national distance and insidership within relevant

Table 2. Descriptive statistics and Pearson correlation.

Variable	Mean	SD	1	2	3	4	5	6	7	8	9	10	11	12	13	14
1 Japanese ownership level	82.754	26.023	1													
2 Insidership in home network	0.167	0.342	−0.206	1												
3 Insidership in host network	0.708	0.855	−0.198	0.071	1											
4 Cultural distance	16.474	8.136	−0.003	0.003	0.051	1										
5 Administrative distance	251.514	24.926	−0.155	0.139	0.028	0.078	1									
6 Economic distance	23.784	24.970	0.007	0.000	−0.094	0.208	−0.138	1								
7 Financial distance	11.604	11.919	0.046	−0.021	−0.207	0.490	−0.025	0.543	1							
8 Geographic distance	6953.336	3621.641	0.182	−0.087	−0.105	−0.353	−0.093	−0.516	−0.261	1						
9 Political distance	1405.512	1972.301	0.030	−0.026	0.166	−0.177	−0.024	0.032	−0.288	−0.032	1					
10 Knowledge distance	13.048	8.931	−0.154	0.111	−0.031	−0.148	0.051	0.352	0.046	−0.353	0.172	1				
11 Connectedness distance	3.238	2.713	−0.224	0.134	0.126	−0.063	0.191	0.188	−0.158	−0.352	0.269	0.435	1			
12 Manufacturing food	0.020	0.141	−0.054	0.055	0.015	−0.006	−0.001	0.000	−0.023	−0.030	0.014	0.006	0.026	1		
13 Manufacturing apparel	0.025	0.155	−0.055	0.145	0.088	0.035	0.102	0.007	−0.014	−0.063	−0.013	0.055	0.071	−0.023	1	
14 Manufacturing chemical and medical	0.067	0.250	−0.082	0.084	0.035	−0.027	0.048	0.031	−0.039	−0.053	0.038	0.057	0.082	−0.039	−0.043	1
15 Manufacturing transport	0.090	0.286	−0.172	0.126	0.006	−0.047	0.070	−0.082	−0.059	0.022	0.033	0.028	0.105	−0.045	−0.050	−0.084
16 Manufacturing machinery	0.056	0.230	−0.006	0.018	−0.010	−0.044	0.043	−0.035	−0.063	0.014	0.029	0.028	0.052	−0.035	−0.039	−0.065
17 Manufacturing metal	0.033	0.178	−0.076	0.165	0.062	0.007	0.006	0.011	−0.021	−0.019	0.008	0.029	0.049	−0.027	−0.029	−0.049
18 Manufacturing non-metal	0.029	0.167	−0.062	0.077	0.027	−0.017	0.025	−0.019	−0.026	−0.025	0.002	0.030	0.035	−0.025	−0.027	−0.046
19 Manufacturing other	0.018	0.134	−0.014	−0.015	0.000	0.003	0.021	0.006	0.001	−0.015	−0.007	0.012	0.017	−0.020	−0.022	−0.037
20 Subsidiary in wholesale or retail	0.387	0.487	0.273	−0.215	−0.169	0.007	−0.150	0.032	0.119	0.122	−0.032	−0.106	−0.250	−0.115	−0.127	−0.213
21 MNC in wholesale or retail	0.149	0.356	−0.041	−0.018	0.202	0.051	0.001	0.044	0.050	−0.034	0.038	0.047	0.011	−0.010	0.094	−0.035
22 MNC in service	0.108	0.310	−0.015	−0.058	−0.062	0.033	−0.014	0.026	0.035	−0.032	−0.017	−0.020	0.006	−0.050	−0.050	−0.093
23 MNC advertising intensity	0.459	1.270	0.040	−0.044	−0.030	−0.016	0.005	−0.018	0.019	−0.001	0.066	0.084	−0.026	0.113	0.013	0.103
24 MNC R&D intensity	1.038	1.923	0.042	−0.037	0.051	−0.016	0.044	0.021	0.005	−0.037	0.127	0.135	0.004	−0.030	−0.023	0.163
25 MNC size	8.949	1.486	−0.141	0.069	0.417	−0.084	0.001	−0.026	−0.001	0.048	0.031	0.129	0.037	−0.026	0.004	−0.076
26 MNC ROA	3.333	4.779	0.054	−0.052	−0.070	−0.017	0.010	0.025	−0.035	−0.001	0.249	−0.013	0.088	0.011	−0.052	0.074
27 Subsidiary age	12.590	9.843	0.107	−0.069	−0.099	−0.033	−0.107	−0.032	0.099	0.272	0.072	−0.083	−0.215	−0.019	0.013	−0.029
28 Subsidiary size	3.944	1.789	−0.241	0.197	0.186	−0.056	0.134	−0.037	−0.093	−0.085	0.037	0.128	0.214	0.056	0.152	0.043
29 Subsidiary expatriate ratio	0.136	0.210	0.277	−0.141	−0.159	−0.104	−0.111	−0.014	0.028	0.101	−0.048	−0.230	−0.189	−0.049	−0.088	−0.075

Variable	15	16	17	18	19	20	21	22	23	24	25	26	27	28	29
15 Manufacturing transport	1														
16 Manufacturing machinery	−0.077	1													
17 Manufacturing metal	−0.058	−0.045	1												
18 Manufacturing non-metal	−0.054	−0.042	−0.032	1											
19 Manufacturing other	−0.043	−0.033	−0.025	−0.024	1										
20 Subsidiary in wholesale or retail	−0.250	−0.193	−0.146	−0.137	−0.108	1									
21 MNC in wholesale or retail	−0.118	−0.091	−0.006	−0.033	−0.022	0.241	1								
22 MNC in service	−0.109	−0.081	−0.064	−0.052	−0.029	−0.265	−0.145	1							
23 MNC advertising intensity	−0.036	−0.035	−0.046	−0.030	0.058	0.042	−0.086	−0.058	1						
24 MNC R&D intensity	−0.062	0.001	−0.030	−0.001	−0.022	0.014	−0.214	−0.172	0.211	1					
25 MNC size	0.058	−0.033	0.022	0.004	0.017	−0.070	−0.088	−0.094	0.021	0.078	1				
26 MNC ROA	0.041	0.001	−0.030	−0.009	0.022	−0.030	−0.092	0.005	0.114	0.059	−0.117	1			
27 Subsidiary age	−0.097	−0.020	−0.020	−0.030	0.006	0.180	0.054	−0.008	0.069	0.016	0.102	0.005	1		
28 Subsidiary size	0.248	0.106	0.098	0.113	0.045	−0.401	−0.163	−0.100	0.060	0.050	0.344	0.018	0.161	1	
29 Subsidiary expatriate ratio	−0.135	−0.084	−0.073	−0.070	−0.028	0.263	0.087	0.027	−0.078	−0.052	−0.213	−0.022	−0.076	−0.621	1

Table 3. Three-level longitudinal regression.

	Model 1	Model 2	Model 3	Model 4
Cultural distance		−0.054(0.014)***	−0.053(0.014)***	−0.041(0.015)**
Administrative distance		−0.091(0.013)***	−0.093(0.013)***	−0.086(0.013)***
Insidership in the home networks			1.280(0.303)***	1.075(0.307)***
Insidership in the host networks			−0.259(0.147)†	−0.283(0.147)†
Cultural distance × home networks				−0.143(0.028)***
Cultural distance × host networks				−0.027(0.012)*
Administrative distance × home networks				0.053(0.012)***
Administrative distance × host networks				0.033(0.007)***
Economic distance	0.051(0.008)***	0.046(0.008)***	0.045(0.008)***	0.043(0.008)***
Financial distance	−0.005(0.006)	−0.003(0.006)	−0.003(0.006)	−0.004(0.006)
Geographic distance	0.001(0.000)***	0.001(0.000)***	0.001(0.000)***	0.001(0.000)***
Political distance	−0.000(0.000)	−0.000(0.000)	−0.000(0.000)	−0.000(0.000)
Knowledge distance	0.098(0.011)***	0.116(0.011)***	0.116(0.012)***	0.117(0.011)***
Connectedness distance	0.239(0.024)***	0.236(0.024)***	0.241(0.024)***	0.240(0.024)***
(Reference: manufacturing electronics)				
Manufacturing food	−1.942(1.756)	−1.955(1.753)	−1.934(1.755)	−1.906(1.755)
Manufacturing apparel	−4.294(1.274)**	−4.041(1.273)**	−4.075(1.274)**	−4.013(1.273)**
Manufacturing chemical and medical	−1.317(0.580)*	−1.286(0.580)*	−1.288(0.580)*	−1.300(0.579)*
Manufacturing transport	−3.994(0.525)***	−3.985(0.525)***	−3.992(0.525)***	−4.053(0.525)***
Manufacturing machinery	0.318(0.500)	0.366(0.499)	0.342(0.499)	0.356(0.499)
Manufacturing metal	−1.003(0.659)	−0.996(0.658)	−1.060(0.658)	−1.169(0.658)†
Manufacturing non-metal	−2.622(0.661)***	−2.631(0.660)***	−2.610(0.660)***	−2.638(0.660)***
Manufacturing other	−0.168(0.811)	−0.154(0.811)	−0.157(0.811)	−0.164(0.810)
Subsidiary in wholesale or retail	0.783(0.324)*	0.754(0.323)*	0.728(0.324)*	0.713(0.324)*
(Reference: manufacturing)				
MNC in wholesale or retail	1.027(0.706)	0.984(0.705)	0.987(0.705)	1.018(0.705)
MNC in service	−0.012(0.930)	−0.167(0.928)	−0.155(0.929)	−0.083(0.928)
MNC advertising intensity	0.183(0.057)**	0.180(0.057)**	0.183(0.057)**	0.181(0.057)**
MNC R&D intensity	0.073(0.033)*	0.069(0.033)*	0.072(0.033)*	0.078(0.033)*
MNC size	0.241(0.162)	0.226(0.162)	0.250(0.163)	0.250(0.163)
MNC ROA	−0.002(0.010)	−0.000(0.010)	−0.000(0.010)	−0.001(0.010)
Subsidiary age	0.230(0.017)***	0.217(0.017)***	0.222(0.017)***	0.224(0.017)***

Subsidiary age^2	$-0.001(0.001)^{***}$	$-0.002(0.001)^{***}$	$-0.003(0.001)^{***}$	$-0.003(0.001)^{***}$
Subsidiary size	$-0.676(0.077)^{***}$	$-0.661(0.077)^{***}$	$-0.662(0.077)^{***}$	$-0.697(0.078)^{***}$
Expatriate rate	$3.551(0.405)^{***}$	$3.548(0.406)^{***}$	$3.579(0.406)^{***}$	$3.543(0.405)^{***}$
Cons.	$84.813(0.554)^{***}$	$84.898(0.552)^{***}$	$84.914(0.553)^{***}$	$84.875(0.553)^{***}$
Log likelihood	-165347.78	-165315.26	-165304.69	-165268.28
Ward Chi^2	1717.83^{***}	1786.48^{***}	1807.06^{***}	1881.88^{***}

$^{***}p < 0.001$; $^{**}p < 0.01$; $^{*}p < 0.05$; $^{\dagger}p < 0.1$.

networks influence Japanese MNCs' ownership strategies. Empirical results support the proposed hypotheses, indicating that cross-national distance and MNCs' relevant networks not only independently influence, but also interact with each other to influence Japanese MNCs' ownership strategies in a more complicated way.

Contribution

The present study contributes to IB literature in a number of ways. First, the influence of cross-national distance on MNCs' ownership strategies has been an important theme in IB literature (Tihanyi, Griffith, and Russell 2005). Nevertheless, most prior studies used only one factor, or a few aggregated factors, with a single-level approach in their analysis, thus ignoring the complexity and rich implications of the phenomenon and even resulting in conflicting conclusions (Tihanyi, Griffith, and Russell 2005). The present study is one of the first papers that empirically investigate the necessity of using multiple dimensions of cross-national distance in IB research based on theoretical relevance, confirming the explanatory power of Berry, Guillén, and Zhou's (2010) work. According to Table 3, in addition to cultural and administrative distances, economic, geographic, knowledge and connectedness distances also influence Japanese MNCs' ownership levels. Failing to involve multiple dimensions can lead to the issue of endogeneity.

Second, this study is one of the first papers that explore the complicated interactions between cross-national distance and MNCs' insidership within networks. Theoretical analysis and empirical results indicate that not only the insidership within networks may moderate the influence of cross-national distance on MNCs' ownership levels, but also the cross-national distance may moderate the influence of insidership within networks. Nevertheless, the tacitness or codifiability of relevant knowledge of cultural and administrative systems determines which moderation effects may dominate. Because of the tacitness of cultural knowledge, cultural distance interacts with the insidership within networks to negatively adjust MNCs' ownership levels, improving local responsiveness (H5 and H6). In contrast, because of the codifiability of administrative knowledge, insidership within networks alleviates the influence of administrative distance on MNCs' ownership levels, improving internal consistency (H7 and H8).

Third, this study also contributes to the literature of Japanese MNCs since Keiretsu culture is deeply embedded in Japanese industrial organization and the Japanese business system (McGuire and Dow 2009). Extant studies have posited that traditional Keiretsu structure which fuelled Japan's post-war growth may be inappropriate and costly in the global business environment (Isobe, Makino, and Goerzen 2006; Lincoln and Gerlach 2004; McGuire and Dow 2009). Rather, Keiretsu ties may evolve to 'weak ties' that serve as a supporting or monitoring role for dyadic exchanges (Granovetter 1973; McGuire and Dow 2009). Nevertheless, prior studies have not examined whether and how Keiretsu networks play roles in Japanese MNCs' cross-border operations. The present study indicates that insidership within Keiretsu networks significantly and complicatedly influences Japanese MNCs' overseas strategies, confirming Keiretsu ties' supporting or monitoring roles.

Management implications

The present study provides a number of implications for managers too. First of all, it suggests that Berry, Guillén, and Zhou's (2010) multidimensional and longitudinal measures may provide a better toolkit for managers to understand cross-national differences. While some of them are difficult for MNCs to internalize such as the cultural knowledge, others might be relatively easy to codify and acquire, such as administrative knowledge. Therefore, managers need to consider the diverse natures of these multiple dimensions when formulating their international strategies. Moreover, though managers may employ network ties to proactively cope with the liability of foreignness, they also need to be careful of the double-edged effect of insidership within certain networks since the homogenous network ties may result in the liability of insidership, weakening the firm's local responsiveness.

Limitations and next step

As an exploratory study that incorporates multiple dimensions of cross-national distance and MNCs' insidership within networks into analysis, the present paper still has several limitations calling for future research. First, the study only tentatively focuses on cultural and administrative dimensions because of their close association. Future research may extend the focus to other dimensions.

Second, as aforementioned, MNCs are embedded in both internal and external networks. Because of data availability, the present study only focuses on internal networks based on equity relationships. Future research may take into account external networks such as customers and suppliers, investigating insidership within networks in a broader scope.

Third, ties among Keiretsu firms are complex (McGuire and Dow 2009), and degree of connectedness cannot fully address the level of insidership within networks. Future research may investigate whether and how other attributes of network position, such as closeness or 'betweenness', influence an MNC's cross-border strategies. Finally, it would be useful to extend the present study to MNCs from other countries.

Conclusion

This study shows that Japanese MNCs' ownership strategies in foreign countries are influenced by multiple dimensions of cross-national distance in complicated ways. Moreover, Japanese MNCs' insidership within relevant networks not only independently influences, but also interacts with cross-national distance to influence their overseas ownership strategies. While insidership within networks may moderate the influence of cross-national distance on Japanese MNCs' ownership levels in foreign countries, cross-national distance may moderate the influence of insidership too. This study provides a finer-grained picture to delineate the complexity of these interactions.

Disclosure statement

No potential conflict of interest was reported by the authors.

References

Aiken, L. S., and S. G. West. 1991. *Multiple Regression: Testing and Interpreting Interactions*. Thousand Oaks, CA: Sage.

Barkema, H. G., J. H. J. Bell, and J. M. Pennings. 1996. "Foreign Entry, Cultural Barriers, and Learning." *Strategic Management Journal* 17 (2): 151–166. doi:10.1002/(SICI)1097-0266(199602)17:2<151:AID-SMJ799>3.0.CO;2-Z.

Barkema, H. G., and F. Vermeulen. 1998. "International Expansion Through Start-Up or Acquisition: A Learning Perspective." *Academy of Management Journal* 41 (1): 7–26. doi:10.2307/256894.

Bartlett, C. A., and P. W. Beamish. 2011. *Transnational Management: Text, Readings and Cases in Cross Border Management*. 6th ed. Burr Ridge, IL: Irwin/McGraw-Hill.

Berry, H., M. F. Guillén, and N. Zhou. 2010. "An Institutional Approach to Cross-National Distance." *Journal of International Business Studies* 41 (9): 1460–1480. doi:10.1057/jibs.2010.28.

Cantwell, J., J. H. Dunning, and S. M. Lundan. 2010. "An Evolutionary Approach to Understanding International Business Activity: The Co-Evolution of MNEs and the Institutional Environment." *Journal of International Business Studies* 41 (4): 567–586. doi:10.1057/jibs.2009.95.

Chang, S. -J., J. Chung, and J. J. Moon. 2013. "When Do Wholly Owned Subsidiaries Perform Better Than Joint Ventures?" *Strategic Management Journal* 34 (3): 317–337. doi:10.1002/smj.2016.

Cho, K. R., and P. Padmanabhan. 2005. "Revisiting the Role of Cultural Distance in MNC's Foreign Ownership Mode Choice: The Moderating Effect of Experience Attributes." *International Business Review* 14 (3): 307–324. doi:10.1016/j.ibusrev.2005.01.001.

Delios, A., and P. W. Beamish. 1999. "Ownership Strategy of Japanese Firms: Transactional, Institutional, and Experience Influences." *Strategic Management Journal* 20 (10): 915–933. doi:10.1002/(SICI)1097-0266(199910)20:10<915:AID-SMJ51>3.0.CO;2-0.

Delios, A., and P. W. Beamish. 2001. "Survival and Profitability: The Roles of Experience and Intangible Assets in Foreign Subsidiary Performance." *Academy of Management Journal* 44 (5): 1028–1038. doi:10.2307/3069446.

Delios, A., and P. W. Beamish. 2004. "Joint Venture Performance Revisited: Japanese Foreign Subsidiaries Worldwide." *Management International Review* 44 (1): 69–91.

Delios, A., and I. Bjorkman. 2000. "Expatriate Staffing in Foreign Subsidiaries of Japanese Multinational Corporations in the PRC and the United States." *International Journal of Human Resource Management* 11 (2): 278–293. doi:10.1080/095851900339873.

Dhanaraj, C., and P. W. Beamish. 2004. "Effect of Equity Ownership on the Survival of International Joint Ventures." *Strategic Management Journal* 25 (3): 295–305. doi:10.1002/smj.372.

Dhanaraj, C., and P. W. Beamish. 2009. "Institutional Environment and Subsidiary Survival." *Management International Review* 49 (3): 291–312. doi:10.1007/s11575-009-0144-y.

DiMaggio, P. J., and W. W. Powell. 1983. "The Iron Cage Revisited: Institutional Isomorphism and Collective Rationality in Organizational Fields." *American Sociological Review* 48 (2): 147–160. doi:10.2307/2095101.

Dunning, J. H., and S. M. Lundan. 2008. *Multinational Enterprises and Global Economy*. 2nd ed. Cheltenham: Edward Elgar.

Erramilli, M. K. 1996. "Nationality and Subsidiary Ownership Patterns in Multinational Corporations." *Journal of International Business Studies* 27 (2): 225–248. doi:10.1057/palgrave.jibs.8490133.

Furman, J. L., M. E. Porter, and S. Stern. 2002. "The Determinants of National Innovative Capacity." *Research Policy* 31 (6): 899–933. doi:10.1016/s0048-7333(01)00152-4.

Gedajlovic, E., T. Yoshikawa, and M. Hashimoto. 2005. "Ownership Structure, Investment Behaviour and Firm Performance in Japanese Manufacturing Industries." *Organization Studies* 26 (1): 7–35. doi:10.1177/0170840605046346.

Ghemawat, P. 2001. "Distance Still Matters: The Hard Reality of Global Expansion." *Harvard Business Review* 79 (8): 137–147.

Ghoshal, S., and C. A. Bartlett. 1990. "The Multinational Corporation as an Inter-Organizational Network." *Academy of Management Review* 15 (4): 603–625.

Gong, Y. 2003. "Subsidiary Staffing in Multinational Enterprises: Agency, Resources, and Performance." *Academy of Management Journal* 46 (6): 728–739. doi:10.2307/30040664.

Granovetter, M. S. 1973. "The Strength of Weak Ties." *American Journal of Sociology* 78 (6): 1360–1380. doi:10.1086/225469.

Hamel, G. 1991. "Competition for Competence and Inter-Partner Learning Within International Strategic Alliances." *Strategic Management Journal* 12 (S1): 83–103. doi:10.1002/smj.4250120908.

Henisz, W. 2000. "The Institutional Environment for Multinational Investment." *Journal of Law, Economics, and Organization* 16 (2): 334–364. doi:10.1093/jleo/16.2.334.

Hennart, J. -F. 1991. "The Transaction Costs Theory of Joint Ventures: An Empirical Study of Japanese Subsidiaries in the United States." *Management Science* 37 (4): 483–497. doi:10.1287/mnsc.37.4.483.

Hennart, J. -F., and J. Larimo. 1998. "The Impact of Culture on the Strategy of Multinational Enterprises: Does National Origin Affect Ownership Decisions?" *Journal of International Business Studies* 29 (3): 515–538. doi:10.1057/palgrave.jibs.8490005.

Hennart, J. -F., and S. Reddy. 1997. "The Choice Between Mergers/Acquisitions and Joint Ventures: The Case of Japanese Investors in the United States." *Strategic Management Journal* 18 (1): 1–12. doi:10.1002/(SICI)1097-0266(199701)18:1<1:AID-SMJ862>3.0.CO;2-R.

Hitt, M. A., P. W. Beamish, S. E. Jackson, and J. E. Mathieu. 2007. "Building Theoretical and Empirical Bridges Across Levels: Multilevel Research in Management." *Academy of Management Journal* 50 (6): 1385–1399. doi:10.5465/amj.2007.28166219.

Hoffmann, W. H. 2007. "Strategies for Managing a Portfolio of Alliances." *Strategic Management Journal* 28 (8): 827–856. doi:10.1002/smj.607.

Hofstede, G. 1980. *Culture's Consequences: International Differences in Work Related Values.* London: Sage.

Hunter, J. E., and F. L. Schmidt. 1990. *Methods of Meta-Analysis: Correcting Error and Bias in Research Findings.* Newbury Park, CA: Sage.

Inglehart, R., and W. E. Baker. 2000. "Modernization, Cultural Change, and the Persistence of Traditional Values." *American Sociological Review* 65 (1): 19–51. doi:10.2307/2657288.

Isobe, T., S. Makino, and A. Goerzen. 2006. "Japanese Horizontal Keiretsu and the Performance Implications of Membership." *Asia Pacific Journal of Management* 23 (4): 453–466. doi:10.1007/s10490-006-9015-2.

Jackson, M. O. 2008. *Social and Economic Networks.* Princeton, NJ: Princeton University Press.

Jackson, G., and R. Deeg. 2008. "Comparing Capitalisms: Understanding Institutional Diversity and Its Implications for International Business." *Journal of International Business Studies* 39 (4): 540–561. doi:10.1057/palgrave.jibs.8400375.

Johanson, J., and J. -E. Vahlne. 2009. "The Uppsala Internationalization Process Model Revisited: From Liability of Foreignness to Liability of Outsidership." *Journal of International Business Studies* 40 (9): 1411–1431. doi:10.1057/jibs.2009.24.

Jung, J. C., P. W. Beamish, and A. Goerzen. 2010. "Dynamics of Experience, Environment and MNE Ownership Strategy." *Management International Review* 50 (3): 267–296. doi:10.1007/s11575-010-0039-y.

Kester, W. C. 1996. "American and Japanese Corporate Governance." In *National Diversity and Global Capitalism*, edited by S. Berger and R. P. Dore, 107–137. Ithaca, NY: Cornell University Press.

Khanna, T., and K. Palepu. 1997. "Why Focused Strategies May Be Wrong for Emerging Markets." *Harvard Business Review* 75 (4): 41–51.

Khanna, T., and Y. Yafeh. 2005. "Business Groups and Risk Sharing Around the World." *Journal of Business* 78 (1): 301–340. doi:10.1086/426527.

Kogut, B. 1988. "Joint Ventures: Theoretical and Empirical Perspectives." *Strategic Management Journal* 9 (4): 319–332. doi:10.1002/smj.4250090403.

Kogut, B., and H. Singh. 1988. "The Effect of National Culture on the Choice of Entry Mode." *Journal of International Business Studies* 19 (3): 411–432. doi:10.1057/palgrave.jibs.8490394.

Kogut, B., and U. Zander. 2003. "Knowledge of the Firm and the Evolutionary Theory of the Multinational Corporation." *Journal of International Business Studies* 34 (6): 516–529. doi:10.1057/palgrave.jibs.8400058.

Kostova, T. 1996. "Success of the Transnational Transfer of Organizational Practices Within Multinational Companies." Doctoral diss., University of Minnesota.

Kostova, T. 1999. "Transnational Transfer of Strategic Organizational Practices: A Contextual Perspective." *Academy of Management Review* 24 (2): 308–324.

Kostova, T., and S. Zaheer. 1999. "Organizational Legitimacy Under Conditions of Complexity: The Case of the Multinational Enterprise." *Academy of Management Review* 24 (1): 64–81.

Levitt, B., and J. G. March. 1988. "Organizational Learning." *Annual Review of Sociology* 14 (1): 319–338. doi:10.1146/annurev.so.14.080188.001535.

Li, J. 1995. "Foreign Entry and Survival: Effects of Strategic Choices on Performance in International Markets." *Strategic Management Journal* 16 (5): 333–351. doi:10.1002/smj. 4250160502.

Lincoln, J. R., and M. L. Gerlach. 2004. *Japan's Network Economy: Structure, Persistence, and Change.* Cambridge: Cambridge University Press.

Makino, S., and P. W. Beamish. 1998. "Performance and Survival of Joint Ventures with Non-Conventional Ownership Structures." *Journal of International Business Studies* 29 (4): 797–818. doi:10.1057/palgrave.jibs.8490054.

Makino, S., P. W. Beamish, and N. B. Zhao. 2004. "The Characteristics and Performance of Japanese FDI in Less Developed and Developed Countries." *Journal of World Business* 39 (4): 377–392. http://dx.doi.org/10.1016/j.jwb.2004.08.009.

McGuire, J., and S. Dow. 2009. "Japanese Keiretsu: Past, Present, Future." *Asia Pacific Journal of Management* 26 (2): 333–351. doi:10.1007/s10490-008-9104-5.

Nelson, R. R., and N. Rosenberg. 1993. "Technical Innovation and National Systems." In *National Innovation Systems,* edited by R. R. Nelson, 3–21. New York: Oxford University Press.

Neter, J. W., and H. K. Michael. 1990. *Applied Linear Statistical Models.* Boston, MA: Richard D. Irwin.

North, D. C. 1990. *Institutions, Institutional Change and Economic Performance.* Cambridge: Cambridge University Press.

Peng, M. W. 2003. "Institutional Transitions and Strategic Choices." *Academy of Management Review* 28 (2): 275–296. doi:10.5465/amr.2003.9416341.

Porter, K. A., and W. W. Powell. 2006. "Networks and Organizations." In *The Sage Handbook of Organization Studies,* edited by S. R. Clegg, C. Hardy, T. B. Lawrence, and W. R. Nord, 776–799. London: Sage.

Powell, W. W., K. W. Koput, and L. Smith-Doerr. 1996. "Interorganizational Collaboration and the Locus of Innovation: Networks of Learning in Biotechnology." *Administrative Science Quarterly* 41 (1): 116–145. doi:10.2307/2393988.

Puffer, S. M., and D. J. McCarthy. 2011. "Two Decades of Russian Business and Management Research: An Institutional Theory Perspective." *Academy of Management Perspectives* 25 (2): 21–36. doi:10.5465/amp.2011.61020800.

Scott, W. R. 1995. *Institutions and Organizations.* Thousand Oaks, CA: Sage.

Scott, W. R., and G. F. Davis. 2007. *Organizations and Organizing: Rational, Natural, and Open Systems Perspectives.* Upper Saddle River, NJ: Prentice Hall.

Shenkar, O. 2001. "Cultural Distance Revisited: Towards a More Rigorous Conceptualization and Measurement of Cultural Differences." *Journal of International Business Studies* 32 (3): 519–535. doi:10.1057/palgrave.jibs.8490982.

Shetty, Y. K. 1979. "Managing the Multinational Corporation: European and American Styles." *Management International Review* 19 (3): 39–48.

Singer, J. D., and J. B. Willett. 2003. *Applied Longitudinal Data Analysis: Modeling Change and Event Occurrence.* Oxford: Oxford University Press.

Stopford, J. M., and L. T. Wells. 1972. *Managing the Multinational Enterprise: Organization of the Firm and Ownership of the Subsidiaries.* New York: Basic Books.

Tang, L., and P. E. Koveos. 2008. "A Framework to Update Hofstede's Cultural Value Indices: Economic Dynamics and Institutional Stability." *Journal of International Business Studies* 39 (6): 1045–1063. doi:10.1057/palgrave.jibs.8400399.

Thomas, L. G. III, and G. Waring. 1999. "Competing Capitalisms: Capital Investment in American, German, and Japanese Firms." *Strategic Management Journal* 20 (8): 729–748.

Tihanyi, L., D. A. Griffith, and C. J. Russell. 2005. "The Effect of Cultural Distance on Entry Mode Choice, International Diversification, and MNE Performance: A Meta-Analysis." *Journal of International Business Studies* 36 (3): 270–283. doi:10.1057/palgrave.jibs.8400136.

Uzzi, B. 1997. "Social Structure and Competition in Interfirm Networks: The Paradox of Embeddedness." *Administrative Science Quarterly* 42 (1): 35–67. doi:10.2307/2393808.

Werner, S. 2002. "Recent Developments in International Management Research: A Review of 20 Top Management Journals." *Journal of Management* 28 (3): 277–305. doi:10.1177/014920630202800303.

Whitley, R. 1992. *Business Systems in East Asia: Firms, Markets, and Societies*. London: Sage.

Williamson, O. E. 1985. *The Economic Institutions of Capitalism*. New York: Free Press.

Xu, D., Y. Pan, and P. W. Beamish. 2004. "The Effect of Regulative and Normative Distances on MNC Ownership and Expatriate Strategies." *Management International Review* 44 (3): 285–307.

Xu, D., and O. Shenkar. 2002. "Institutional Distance and the Multinational Enterprise." *Academy of Management Review* 27 (4): 608–618. doi:10.2307/4134406.

Cultural determinants of alliance management capability – an analysis of Japanese MNCs in India

Sumati Varma[a], Richa Awasthy[b], Kalpana Narain[c] and Rishika Nayyar[d]

[a]Department of Commerce, Sri Aurobindo College (Eve), Delhi University, New Delhi, India; [b]Organizational Behaviour Area, International Management Institute, New Delhi, India; [c]Full Spectrum Consulting (A business and Strategy Consulting Firm), Gurgaon, India; [d]Department of Commerce, PGDAV College (M), Delhi University, New Delhi, India

This study examines the role of national and organizational culture in alliance management in the context of three prominent joint ventures between India and Japan, which reached diverse alliance outcomes. It uses the case study method as a tool for an initial rich exploratory analysis (Yin 2013) of alliance management capabilities that may later be tested on a larger dataset. The study finds that *national and organizational culture* is both important factors of alliance management capability. It highlights the specific role of *trust, consensus in decision-making, communication and relationship building as key constituents of alliance management capability*. This paper thus contributes to an important strand of literature on alliance management in the context of two important Asian players from the developed and emerging markets. Its focus on cultural factors as determinants of alliance management helps to establish a managerial blueprint leading to positive alliance outcomes for such ventures in future and to establish a roadmap for increased interaction between India and Japan.

Introduction

A strategic alliance, as a form of inter-organizational business collaboration, is a 'cooperative effort by two or more entities in pursuit of their own strategic objective' (Marks and Mirvis 1998, 9) and may involve equity participation. International alliances reside at the confluence of national, corporate and occupational cultures (Salk and Shenkar 2001) with varying degrees of cooperation and collaboration. In a dynamic business environment, strategic alliances are central to the success of organizations, and the 'capacity to collaborate' is a core competence of today's business since 'no company can go it alone' (Doz and Hamel 1998, ix).

International joint ventures (JVs) are one of the most important organizational forms in the context of market liberalization (Dussauge and Garrette 1999) carrying important strategic advantages of market entry and technology transfer (Kogut 1988a), supplementing capabilities (Hitt et al. 2000) and sharing costs (Glaister and Buckley 1996), with chances of failure on account of low profitability, control asymmetries, erosion of complementarities and strategic objectives, conflict between partners, and cultural differences (e.g. Buckley and Casson 1988; Contractor and Lorange 1988).

Cultural differences are an intrinsic element of international alliances and have been considered to wield immense influence on alliance outcomes. The impact of national culture difference on performance (Ariño 2003; Geringer and Hebert 1991; Park and Ungson 1997; Salk and Brannen 2000; Tihanyi, Griffith, and Russell 2005) has been documented as more important than organizational cultural difference (OCD) between parent firms, even though it may equally, if not more, influence a JV's performance (Fey and Beamish 2001; Meschi 1997; Pothukuchi et al. 2002; Sirmon and Lane 2004).

India and Japan are prominent global players and have recently renewed their economic engagement with the 'Look East' policy as a part of India's new economic reform programme of 1991 (Rajamohan, Rahut, and Jacob 2008), which identified Japan as one of the most important sources of investment and technology (Dixit 1996). Recent initiatives include the Comprehensive Economic Partnership Agreement 2011 as a step towards engagement between the two countries in a multitude of sectors and the Tokyo Declaration in September 2014 with promised investment of USD 33.5 billion into the development of economic corridors, infrastructure, transport system, smart cities, clean energy, skill development and food processing.[1]

The period 2000–2014 saw Japan emerge as the fourth largest contributor of foreign direct investment (FDI) to India, accounting for 7.46% of total FDI inflows, but India lags far behind China, USA and smaller Asian nations such as Thailand and Indonesia, which receive a greater magnitude of FDI from Japan.[2] There were 2542 Japanese business establishments in India in 2013,[3] which is an increase of 25.09% over the previous year. The drugs and pharmaceuticals and automobiles sector emerged as the highest recipients of Japanese FDI,[4] driven to an attractive emerging market with a high disposable income and expanding middle class. Japanese MNEs used JVs as the primary mode of entry into the Indian market given the policy framework and the institutional environment and pushed by the need for local experience to tap the Indian market (Horn, Forsans, and Cross 2010).

India's large population, expanding middle class and rising disposable income levels have all the features of an attractive investment destination for Japan. The two countries also have very distinct competitive advantages in manufacturing and services, which could prove to be sources of great synergy if combined efficiently. However, the size and heterogeneity of the Indian market, alongside divergent levels of subnational economic and infrastructure development and a huge number of marketing-related challenges, especially in relation to product positioning and market segmentation are challenges for any MNE (Horn, Forsans, and Cross 2010). The two countries also have diverse management styles and philosophy, which have often led to conflict in the operation of Indo Japanese ventures.[5]

In this context, this study examines the role of national and organizational culture in the development of alliance management capability of three prominent JVs between India and Japan, which reached diverse alliance outcomes. It thus contributes to an important strand of literature on alliance management capability (Doz 1996; Dyer and Singh 1998) that is linked to alliance outcomes (Schreiner, Kale, and Corsten 2009); in the context of the relatively scant literature on Japanese management in the developing country context (Horn and Cross 2009). At the alliance level, it focuses on skills relevant to all aspects of an individual alliance including formation, governance and management. Its focus on cultural factors as determinants of alliance outcomes helps to establish a managerial blueprint leading to positive alliance outcomes for such ventures in future and establish a roadmap for increased interaction between India and Japan.

The paper is organized as follows: Following the 'Introduction', the next section is a 'Literature review' on the subject, the next section contains the 'Theoretical framework', followed by the 'Methodology' and a 'Discussion of the results' and finally 'Conclusion'.

Literature review

Tracing the history of Japanese FDI into India, Buckley, Cross, and Horn (2012) use an institutional theory lens to relate FDI flows with the changing policy regime, while Nataraj (2010) highlights constraints like poor infrastructure, taxation issues and problems of red tapism and custom clearance. Comparing China and India as FDI destinations for Japan, Anand and Delios (1996) concluded that the two countries had unique country specific assets, which attracted Japanese FDI; Horn, Forsans, and Cross (2009) discovered that China was a preferred FDI destination compared with India – motivated by access to location-specific productive resources, it involved a high degree of technology, management skills and organizational knowledge transfer and Japanese subsidiaries in China were integrated with the network of international subsidiaries as a part of the MNC's global strategy. Japanese FDI in India, however, was motivated by the desire to access local markets, involved less transfer of technology and management skills, and Japanese subsidiaries in India operated independently as part of a multidomestic strategy.

Japanese firms reacted to institutional adjustments in India with an increase in investment activities, from the mid-1990s onwards. Existing firms extended their engagement either by establishing new production facilities, accompanied by an influx of *keiretsu* affiliated suppliers for the automobile industry (Horn, Forsans, and Cross 2010), or by increasing their equity share (Sharma 1999). Several studies have used a single case focus to discuss some prominent alliances such as Maruti Suzuki (Nayak 2005) and Honda Siel (Roychoudhary 2005). Sahoo, Banwet, and Momaya (2011) examine the role of effective technology management in the case of two JVs in the automobile and auto component sector, and Damanpour et al. (2012) study on the post-formation stage of Indo-Japanese JVs finds that communication, cooperation and conflict resolution play a key role in the implementation and management of JVs.

The resource-based view (RBV) of the firm considers a firm to be a bundle of resources and capabilities; its competitive advantages are based on access to idiosyncratic resources, especially tacit knowledge-based resources (Penrose 1959; Wernerfelt 1984; Conner 1991; Amit and Schoemaker 1993). Since it is not possible for any business to possess all the resources needed to grow (Commons 1934; Coase 1937; Barnard 1938; Simon 1957; Richardson 1972), firms use collaboration as a tool to access complementary resources for its survival and growth and to exploit new business opportunities. Strategic alliances are a popular form of collaboration, which enable market entry (geographic and technical) and increase the resource base of alliance partners through sharing of core competencies such as technology, R&D, manufacturing, sales and marketing. The constraints of the Indian policy framework and the imperatives of local experience led to Japanese MNEs using JVs as the primary mode of entry into the Indian market (Horn, Forsans, and Cross 2010).

Strategic alliances face a host of challenges as enumerated in the literature – these range from the problems in building relationships, developing mutual understanding, trust, collaboration, and successful implementation in such entities (Doz 1996; Doz and Hamel 1998; Fedor and Werther 1996; Ghosh 1996; Kanter 1994; Kumar 1998; Levinson and Asahi 1996). A key risk is opportunistic behaviour by one or more partners that can undermine trust and collaboration. Alliances use formal safeguards (contracts, agreements, and equity investments) and informal 'self-enforcing agreements' (Dyer and Singh 1998, 669) to protect the alliance and discourage opportunistic behaviour.

Alliance capability

A firm's alliance capability refers to the possession of certain superior organizational capabilities in managing alliances (Anand and Khanna 2000) leading to competitive advantage (Dyer and Singh 1998; Gulati 1998; Ireland, Hitt, and Vaidyanath 2002) and linked to diverse alliance outcomes for both the firm and the alliance (Schreiner, Kale, and Corsten 2009).

There are two broad strands of literature on alliance capability – the first focuses on the processes and mechanisms, which lead to the development of alliance capabilities (Anand and Khanna 2000; Kale, Dyer, and Singh 2002; Kale and Singh 2007). The second strand focuses on the elements that constitute alliance capabilities (Gulati 1998) and studies the phenomenon at two different levels. Studies at the micro level examine capabilities necessary for managing individual alliances (alliance management capability) (Doz 1996; Dyer and Singh 1998); as against studies that have a macro focus and examine skills vested in a firm's capability to manage its entire portfolio of the firm's capabilities (alliance portfolio capability) (Hoffmann 2007; Das and Teng 2002; Vapola, Paukku, and Gabrielsson 2010; Wassmer 2010).

A firm's alliance capability develops through structural mechanisms or organizational processes such as *alliance functions* to develop its alliance capability (Kale, Dyer, and Singh 2002; Hoang and Rothaermel 2005), through increased experiential knowledge of managing such relationships (Simonin 1997; Anand and Khanna 2000; Zollo, Reuer, and Singh 2002; Hoang and Rothaermel 2005); and by implementing alliance learning processes (Kale and Singh 2007) to learn and accumulate alliance management skills and best practices by carefully capturing, codifying, sharing and internalizing relevant alliance know-how.

The constituent elements of alliance capability have been studied at two different levels: at the micro level of each of a firm's individual alliance and from a more macro perspective through a study of the firm's entire portfolio of alliances. Within the micro perspective, studies have focused on capabilities at different stages of the alliance's life – the literature on formation has focused on issues of choice and suitability of an alliance partner (Hitt et al. 2000), complementarities and fit (Harrigan 1988; Geringer 1991; Park and Ungson 1997; Dyer and Singh 1998), coordinating tasks, sharing relevant know-how and information, resolving conflicts (Van de Ven and Polley 1992; Doz 1996; Ariño and De la Torre 1998; Kumar and Nti 1998; Madhok and Tallman 1998) through different stages of the alliance life cycle (Doz 1996; Gulati 1998).

Alliance portfolio capability on the other hand consists of a firm's ability to form new alliances, select partners compatible with existing alliances and develop mechanism for monitoring and coordinating knowledge and activity flows across different alliances in the portfolio (Hoffmann 2007).

Alliance outcomes

There are several different perspectives on alliance outcomes (Uzzi 1996; Gulati 1998), but two broad themes emerge in the literature (Dussauge, Garrette, and Mitchell 2000). Early studies on alliance outcomes linked alliance stability and duration to conditions surrounding the formation of the partnership. Several studies have investigated JV equity distribution between the parent companies (Janger 1980; Killing 1982, 1983; Beamish 1984, 1985; Beamish and Banks 1987; Geringer and Hebert 1989; Blodgett 1992), with somewhat contradictory results. Other studies (Harrigan 1988; Kogut 1988a, 1988b, 1989; Park and Russo 1996; Park and Ungson 1997) have focused on the influence of factors such as partner asymmetries, joint venturing experience, JV scope, industry structure, R&D intensity, inter-partner rivalry and governance structure on the duration and survival of the JV.

An alternate set of approaches examine the different forms of alliance termination and discriminate in particular between JV dissolution and acquisition (Park and Russo 1996; Reuer and Miller 1997; Dussauge and Garrette 1997). The focus of these studies is the effect of the alliance on parent firms and JV survival no longer stands as an implicit criterion of success. The second approach looks at alliance outcomes through a more evolutionary lens, as it focuses on collaborative processes and partner interaction as a factor in the dynamics and outcomes of alliances (Ring and Van de Ven 1994; Kumar and Nti 1998; Larsson et al. 1998). These studies focus on the consequences of allying for partner firms rather than the fate of the alliance itself. Using the RBV, many of these studies have insisted on the importance of learning and skill acquisition that tend to occur between the allied firms, especially in alliances among competitors (Doz 1988; Hamel, Doz, and Prahalad 1989; Hamel 1991; Kanter 1994). Some studies have used in-depth case analyses (Hamel 1990, 1991; Doz 1996; Ariño and de la Torre 1998), some of them have used larger sample studies to explore the impact of alliance activity on the ongoing financial performance and survival of the parent businesses (Berg, Duncan, and Friedman 1982; Hagedoorn and Schakenraad 1994; Mitchell and Singh 1996) and have found that parents often benefit from alliances, but that alliance activity also carries the risk of becoming dependent on a partner's capabilities.

Dussauge, Garrette, and Mitchell (2000) distinguishes between learning by alliance partners in link and scale alliances and using alliance outcomes as indicators of inter-partner learning it examines the impact of alliances on the partner firms by focusing on new capability acquisition.

Theoretical framework

Alliance capability in different phases of the alliance

Alliance management capability is a multidimensional construct that comprises skills necessary through different phases of an alliance's life. There are three different stages in the life cycle of an alliance (Doz 1996; Gulati 1998), viz. (a) the formation phase, wherein a firm evaluates its decision to form an alliance and selects an appropriate partner, (b) the design phase, wherein a firm sets ups an appropriate governance structure and design for the alliance and (c) the post-formation management phase, wherein a firm has to manage the alliance after it is up and running. Firms need different capabilities in each of these different phases (Kale and Singh 2009).

Alliance capability at the *formation* stage consists of three Cs: complementarity, commitment and compatibility (Shah and Swaminathan 2008). Partner complementarity is the extent to which a partner contributes exclusive resources to the relationship, with each partner contributing resources and capabilities to complement what the other partners can contribute (Dyer and Singh 1998; Harrigan 1988; Mowery, Oxley, and Silverman 1996). According to the RBV of the firm, a higher level of complementarity between partners increases the chances of alliance success. Partner compatibility refers to the fit between partners' working styles and cultures, whereas commitment refers to the willingness of a partner to make resource contributions required by the alliance and also to make short-term sacrifices to realize the desired longer term benefits (Gundlach, Achrol, and Mentzer 1995).

The *design* stage is crucial, since alliance success depends on appropriate choices about the structure (Pisano 1989; Oxley 1997; Gulati and Singh 1998; Hennart and Zeng 2005) and contractual terms (Mayer and Argyres 2004; Argyres and Mayer 2007; Reuer and Ariño 2007) of that alliance, and the flexibility to adapt them according to changing needs (Reuer, Zollo, and Singh 2002; Gulati, Lawrence, and Puranam 2005). Governance issues in an alliance may be addressed through formal measures such as equity ownership (Williamson 1985; David and Han 2004) and contractual provisions (Mayer and Argyres 2004; Poppo and Zenger 2002; Reuer and Ariño 2007) or through informal, self-enforcing or relational governance, relying on goodwill, trust and reputation (Granovetter 1985; Gulati 1995; Uzzi 1997).

Collaboration plays an important role in the governance of an alliance. Alliances use formal safeguards (contracts, agreements and equity investments) and informal 'self-enforcing agreements' (Dyer and Singh 1998, 669) to protect the alliance against the risk of opportunistic behaviour. In this context, informal self-enforcing mechanisms such as shared collaborative norms and trust are far more efficient and effective as measures of alliance governance and also become a key source of competitive advantage for an alliance as compared with formal safeguards, which are costly to write, monitor and enforce (Dyer and Singh 1998).

Collaboration is an effective way of combining resources that are subject to a high degree of knowledge-based market failure (Itami and Roehl 1987; Mitchell and Singh 1993, 1996; Gulati 1998). Moreover, collaboration provides a means for firms to protect the value of their resources through financial and organizational safeguards against opportunistic behaviour (Teece 1986; Hennart 1988; Bresser 1988; Kogut 1988a; Jorde and Teece 1990; Williamson 1991; Chi 1994).

Collaboration provides potential benefits to all partners through the creation of favourable conditions for inter-partner learning and thus may allow one partner to appropriate and internalize resources that another partner contributed (Balakrishnan and Koza 1993; Nakamura, Shaver, and Yeung 1996; Lane and Lubatkin 1998; Kumar and Nti 1998). Such appropriation is a particularly critical issue when alliances involve competing firms. When the partner firms in an alliance are also competitors in a product market, there will be many opportunities for inter-partner learning and major competitive consequences of such learning (Pucik 1988; Hamel, Doz, and Prahalad 1989; Hamel 1991). Alliances between competitors can lead to the loss of critical proprietary knowledge, to increased dependence of one partner vis-a-vis the other and even to the takeover of one partner by the other (Bleeke and Ernst 1995).

The post-formation stage

Alliance success is contingent upon capabilities in all three phases of the alliance's life. Capabilities in the post-formation stage include the ability of coordinating tasks, sharing relevant know-how and information, and resolving conflicts (Van de Ven and Polley 1992; Doz 1996; Kumar and Nti 1998; Madhok and Tallman 1998) through coordination, communication and trust between alliance partners.

Coordination is an important factor of successful alliance management (Schreiner, Kale, and Corsten 2009) in this phase. Since an alliance has a divided authority structure and there is often a great deal of physical, cognitive and cultural distance between partners, many alliances suffer from coordination lapses due to inappropriate interfaces and boundary-spanning mechanisms, as well as unclear roles, procedures, responsibilities and loci of control (Doz 1988; Bronder and Pritzl 1992; Larson 1992; Mohr and Spekman 1994; Park and Ungson 2001; Gerwin 2004; Luo 2006). These coordination failures lead to the alliance failing to fully use the unique potential vested in the specialized but interdependent activities of both partners (Thompson 1967, 55)

The classic coordination techniques include programming, hierarchy and feedback (Galbraith 1997). *Programming* involves developing clear guidelines on what specific tasks need to be carried out by each partner, who exactly is accountable for each task, and a timetable for implementing them. *Hierarchy* includes the creation of a formal role or structure with authority and decision-making ability to oversee ongoing interactions between partners and to facilitate information and resource sharing. To ensure information and resource sharing firms may use a dedicated alliance manager, an alliance review committee or joint teams and co-allocation mechanisms for more regular feedback.

Luo (2006) argues that firms need to have adaptable mechanisms in terms of formal and routine procedures, rules and policies to guide cooperation between partners and create an appropriate framework for their ongoing interaction. Thus, having relevant coordination know-how and skills is central to alliance management.

Communication

Communication and information sharing are essential elements of a successful alliance. Information asymmetries caused by a lack of information sharing and communication (Borys and Jemison 1989; Powell 1990; Anderson and Weitz 1992; Larson 1992; Mohr and Spekman 1994) prevent partners from gaining knowledge about each other's idiosyncrasies, building a shared understanding of their obligations and engagement rules, developing shared mental models of how to work together effectively (Klimoski and Mohammed 1994), mitigating potentially adversarial group dynamics (Hambrick et al. 2001) and preventing or managing conflict effectively (MacNeil 1981;Cummings 1984). Alliance management also needs lateral communication skills that enable a relationship to sustain through ongoing renegotiations of initial agreements and changing conditions (Osborn et al. 1998).

Relational capital

There is a similar advantage in building 'relational capital'. The goodwill and trust that partners accumulate in a relationship as they gain mutual confidence (Kale 1998) have a critical role in the success of an alliance. The development of mutual norms and trust leads to the development of relational capital (Kumar 1998) and helps to lower costs, increase productivity, and promote a sense of pride, belonging, vitality, well-being and satisfaction among members.

Shared norms and trust are the building blocks of a mutual alliance culture, which becomes the foundation for the partnership. Mutual culture evolves from a variety of factors, including a common understanding of, and respect for, each partner's business and strategic direction, and the creation of a joint strategic direction that creates synergy. Illuminating each partner's cultural assets can help promote the integration and success of the alliance. Such assets include each partner's history, heritage, processes, contributions and achievement (Marks and Mirvis 1998, 196, 205). When the partners appreciate each other's unique business philosophies, values and practices, they are more likely to leverage their respective strengths.

Methodology

Research objectives

The main objective of the study was to understand alliance management capabilities through the different phases of the alliance life cycle in the context of three Indo-Japanese

JVs with diverse alliance outcomes. In doing so, we restrict ourselves to understanding the main dimensions or skills that comprise a firm's capability to manage an individual alliance, similar to studies by Ring and Van de Ven (1994), Doz (1996), Ariño and De La Torre(1998), Dyer and Singh (1998) and Schreiner, Kale, and Corsten (2009).

Our main research questions are:

- What are the main skills that comprise a firm's capability to manage any individual alliance?
- How have these alliance management skills influenced the outcome of the alliance?

Research methodology

This study deals with a complex issue of alliance management and the research questions are characterized by description, interpretation and explanation. Because the research method needs the generation of rich data (Lee 1999), the case study approach was deemed fit. The multiple case study research method was found to be the most useful in this regard (Yin 2013), since it allows a detailed investigation of one or more organizations, with the view to providing an analysis of the context and processes involved in the phenomenon under study (Lincoln and Guba 1985; Eisenhardt 1989). It allows researchers to answer 'how' or 'why' questions, combine, develop and verify previously developed theories with new empirical insights and investigate complex phenomena within their real-life context (Eisenhardt 1989; Yin 1994; Welch et al. 2011).

The case studies are then supplemented with a content analysis of the interviews of key personnel from the four alliances. Content analysis is defined as 'a research technique for making replicable and valid inferences from data according to their context' (Krippendorf 1980). It is usually done at two levels – manifest content – where the material is coded into words or letters in written material, audio or visual material; and latent content – where the underlying or hidden meaning is inferred from sentences/paragraphs contained in letters, documents or press releases.

Sample selection

Following Eisenhardt (1991) and Miles and Huberman (1994), the paper focused on case studies of three Indo – Japanese JVs. Selecting a small number of cases may reduce the generalizability of results and increase observer bias (Voss, Tsikriktsis, and Frohlich 2002), but it allows retaining the depth of the study and the richness of results (Piekkari, Welch, and Paavilainen 2009). The use of purposeful sampling was done to find information-rich cases (Patton 2001). The sampling frame was defined following Miles and Huberman (1994) setting – event-actor-process parameter setting. Accordingly, we focused on Indo-Japanese JVs (setting), alliance outcome (event), on the top management team of these firms (actors) and the process of alliance management (process). Consistent with Eisenhardt's recommendation for a theoretical sampling strategy, we introduced variance along important theoretical dimensions by including firms from different industries, with varying life of the JVs and diverse alliance outcomes.

Data collection

Personal interviews were the main form of data collection. Using the key informant approach (Phillips 1981), interviews were held with key senior personnel from the three Indo-Japanese JVs. Most interviewees were director level technocrats, well-travelled and currently manage businesses upwards of USD 500 billion. They have successfully strategized various JVs and international partnerships.

Since a JV is a strategic issue, we interviewed personnel who were key decision-makers of the alliance. Data were collected through semi structured, face-to-face and phone interviews. All interviews lasted between an hour to two hours and were noted by two of the authors and later transcribed verbatim. The theme of the questionnaire was to trace the alliance management capability through the evolution of the alliance with particular emphasis on national, organizational and individual cultural facets. The key interview questions were sent to the interviewees a week prior to the interview, but additional questions were also asked during the course of the interview.

To safeguard the quality of the study, data collection followed the principles suggested by Yin (1989). Following the in-depth interview with key personnel, the transcript of the interview was sent back to the managers for validation. In all cases, interview data were substantiated with data from the firm's annual reports, marketing materials, website histories and financial databases to provide triangulation in validation of the interview material (Cresswell 2003), which contributes to a holistic view of the issue examined (Paul 1996). The collected data were then put through a content analysis.

Data analysis

Analysis was conducted in multiple steps, beginning with an overview of each case (Brown and Eisenhardt 1997), focusing on key central themes derived from the literature on alliance management capability and alliance outcomes. The identification of critical events helped to reconstruct the evolution of each alliance. A cross case comparison was then made and relevant literature was consulted to further explain the main findings.

Qualitative content analysis (Lincoln and Guba 1985) was the next step of analysis, which is 'a research method for the subjective interpretation of the content of the text data, through the systematic classification process of coding and identifying themes or patterns' (Hsieh and Shannon 2005). The first and second author separately analysed the interview transcripts, compared and contrasted the findings from each interview, independently derived themes and patterns, and collectively reconciled the same.

Case profiles (Table 1)

JV1

JV1 was established in 1987, with a state government of Karnataka enterprise, a leading Central Air-Conditioning and commercial refrigeration firm from India and a Japanese company expert in the field of industrial automation. The Japanese were keen to make an

Table 1. Case profiles.

JV	Year of JV	Industry	Purpose of JV	Life of JV	Outcome
JV1	1987	Industrial automation	Technology transfer	16 years	Successful conclusion through mutual consent
JV2	1985	Automotive industry	Technology transfer	Ongoing	Continuing as successful alliance
JV3	2008	Telecom industry	Technology and capital transfer	5–6 years	Early Termination

entry into the Indian market to establish their manufacturing presence in the country. India had become a strategic market for the Japanese company from their international business expansion point of view. Since the Indian partner had been representing them in India for over 10 years before the JV, they already had an established professional relationship with this company. Given that Japanese people prefer to stay with the relationships they have built over the years and trust in, the Indian partner was their obvious first choice. The Indian partner was keen on an association with the Japanese for technology. In an era of licencing and strict import control, partnership with a state enterprise was the only way to get a manufacturing licence. Thus, the JV was born. This was the first phase of the JV.

During the second phase of the alliance the state government enterprise exited the partnership as had been agreed earlier. The Indian partner bought out their stake. It took the Indian and Japanese partners 3 years to work out the modalities of alliance governance including shareholding patterns and technology sharing, which is typical of the Japanese style of functioning. The Japanese partner held 40% stake and extended support at all levels of operation including technology transfer and marketing, leading to a strong and dedicated workforce of skilled engineers, professionals and managers.

The JV concluded after a successful association of 16 years, with mutual consent of both the partners. Post-conclusion, the Indian partner continued to be the market leader in its core line of businesses, launching a host of new unique and innovative products and the Japanese partner set their independent business in India in the area of industrial autorotation.

JV2

JV2 was formed in 1985 as the technical JV in the Indian Automobile Industry. The Indian partner of the venture was a key supplier of auto components to another Indo-Japanese JV during that time. JV2 sought to primarily cater to the requirements of the existing JV. The terms of agreement called upon the Japanese partner to provide know-how, technical information, specification of machine tools, auxiliary equipment and technical support to the Indian partner for a period of 7 years from 1985 or 5 years from the commencement of commercial production whichever is earlier. During the initial years of the JV, the support from the Japanese partner was minimal as the Japanese partner had had a bad experience with another Indian partner. In addition, the Japanese are known to take time to develop trust in others.

The Indian partner's inclination towards Japanese manufacturing processes led them to design their processes and plant lay out in line with the Japanese practices and methodologies. They endeavoured to build trust with their Japanese partners by incorporating the Japanese culture in the company through implementation of management practices such as respect for the customer, promoting a team culture by wearing the same uniform and eating in same canteen and initiating weekly suggestion schemes. In most JV's challenges occur due to operational issues, which need to be resolved as they arise. Often they are allowed to linger on and become larger than life. In this JV, the partners set a system in place to address operational challenges. A steering committee with representatives of both partners met regularly to resolve issues and challenges. The agreement clearly stated that the CEOs of the two companies would meet outside of their offices at an offsite location to resolve such issues and challenges. They will not focus on any other business before the issue is resolved. This enabled the JV partners to arrive at amicable solutions whenever the situation arose, building trust and confidence in each other.

The protracted confidence building approach by Indian partners bore fruits in 1991 when Japanese agreed to share information and know-how on the implementation of

Unique Production System (Toyota production system) in the venture. By 1997, the Japanese partners had acquired 20.47% of the equity in the venture company.

The initiative resulted in valuable inter partner learning and significantly improved the efficiency of the company. The continued successful association of the venture partners in successive years is reflected in the milestones achieved by the company such as inclusion of the company in the cluster programme of total quality management (TQM) methodologies in 2002 and consequent development of capabilities (technical) of shop floor workers and engineers, ability to create new knowledge in the company resulting into grant of two patents during 2002–2006, receipt of Deming's Prize in 2003 and Bronze Trophy for Excellence in Technology (large category) from Automotive Component Manufacturers Association of India in 2013 for developing a patent in the USA.

The experiences and learning from this JV enabled the Indian company to sign six more JVs with other Japanese companies. In 2004, the company made its first international acquisition of 21% stake in a French auto Component Company and later also acquired stake in a precision forging company in Germany.

JV3

Formed in 2008, JV3 was the first investment made by a Japanese company in the Indian Telecom Market. As a technical and financial JV, JV3 was acknowledged as a partnership between two likeminded organizations, one being the market leader of Japan's telecom industry and another was an Indian company, which earned for itself a credible place in the Indian telecom industry. The two partners saw JV as a means of accessing complementary resources wherein the Japanese company was looking for the growing Indian market, which had become second largest wireless network in the world after China, and the Indian partner was seeking access to technology and capital.

The terms of the JV agreement involved the acquisition of 26% equity stake by the Japanese partner in the Indian company and extending support in the area of marketing, handset development and technology. The acquisition of stake was completed in 2009 and Japanese partner nominated three executives to the Board of Directors of the venture. The JV agreement also had a provision for the Japanese partner to increase its equity stake in the company to 35% in 2012 and further to acquire controlling interest of 51% in 2014. It could also sell its 26% stake back to Indian partner at a negotiated price if it did not exercise these call options.

Soon after the formation, in mid-2009, the venture moved a step ahead and unveiled a new brand for GSM services in India reflecting the strong partnership and commitment of JV partners. It also introduced a number of innovative schemes in the market. With an expectation of turning profitable in three years, the Japanese partner extended full support to the venture by proactively participating in the management of Indian company through varied means like provision of human resources and technical assistance to help realize improved network quality and introduction of leading edge value added services.

However, Japanese partners were dismayed for the first time in the year 2010 when the company was denied the 2G spectrum licence for the lucrative Delhi circle. This was a cause of grave concern for the Japanese who expressed their concerns over the non-transparent allocation policy of the Indian Government. In 2012, they declined to exercise the call option of raising their stake in the venture to 35% on the account of regulatory overhang following which a flexible option of increasing the stake directly to 51% in the year 2013 was incorporated into the JV contract. The venture's net worth was completely eroded, and it turned into a loss making entity by the year 2014 largely due to cancellation of its three licences following the ruling of the country's apex court. The Japanese partner then decided to offload its stake from the venture at a price to be negotiated as per the terms of agreement, while allowing the Indian partner to retain the brand name for at least 1 year in lieu of marginal royalty.

Cross case analysis

Formation of the alliance

It was evident in all cases studied that the national policy environment dictated the choice of mode of entry of the Japanese MNEs into India and also the choice of alliance partners. JV was the only viable entry mode for all three alliances, and JV1 initially included a state government entity as an alliance partner in order to adhere to the licencing policy in effect at that time.

The strategic intent of the alliances for all the Indian partners was technology transfer, and for the Japanese partners, alliance formation was the only route to the Indian market at that time. The Japanese partners were keen to establish a manufacturing foothold in India in the form of a 100% subsidiary, but had to opt for a JV due to the policy framework existing at that time meant to boost India's economy. The alliance partners in all three cases had unique resources and capabilities that they contributed to the alliance.

The Japanese had a long-term view and pursued their goals with a pragmatic approach. They realized the importance of the Indian partner for market entry and market existence in the long run, and treated the alliance with due respect. They understood that both partners had unique strengths that complemented each other and were necessary for the success of the alliance. All decisions and actions were taken in the interest of the alliance.

In case of JV1, the Indian partner was a better-known brand than the Japanese brand, which was lesser known in India. The Indian partner also had an extensive reach across the country. The Japanese partner had state-of-the-art technology, and the Indian partner was the right launching pad for them to establish base in India. Therefore, it was a win-win situation and a mutually beneficial JV for both. During the period of representation both entities won – Japanese got a new market and the Indian partner got a new business area.

All firms in the study emphasized the role of trust as a major factor, which helped to establish the alliance. JV1 had a prior relationship as a distributor with its Japanese partner that established trust and JV2 had to work for over 5 years to convince the Japanese partner and establish a position of trust. In the case of JV1, trust and relationship were built across levels during the years that the Indian partner represented the Japanese partner while they operated out of the same office in India.

Governance of alliance

The study found that the alliances used both formal and informal tools of governance. The study clearly illustrates that both JV1 and JV2 had an amicable life and final outcome since they were governed as per contract and by mutual trust. The alliance partners honoured the contractual commitments such as the exit of the state government entity in JV1 as per the terms of the initial contract. The Indian partners reposed complete trust in the Japanese since they honoured all their commitments completely and in time. The Japanese on the other hand had trust in their Indian partners based on prior experience and a continued commitment to work and quality. Deep mutual trust was visible in the case of JV1, where the Japanese partner agreed to let the Indian partner appoint the managing director and manage the operations.

The post-formation stage

The study found that JV1 and JV2 had successful outcomes due to the following factors in the post-formation phase:

Clear roles. The alliance partners had very clear roles. The Japanese were the dominant partners in the alliances and major contributors of technology know-how and management practices. The Indian partner provided manpower, infrastructure and an understanding of the Indian landscape.

Consensus and consultation in decision-making. Consensus and consultation in decision were found to be important factors that contributed to the success of the alliances. All the JVs had an interactive and participatory style of work, where consultation was the path towards consensus in decision-making, even though this sometimes led to delays. Consensus building is easy if there is a given framework of values. From the Japanese point of view, the service to the customer is the centre of all activity and becomes the central focal point of all decision-making.

Mutual understanding of differences in culture. The alliance partners in JV1 and JV2 exhibited a mutual understanding of the differences in culture – both national and organizational. For instance Japanese organizations are very transparent and all information is shared with concerned parties in a transaction. At a time of transition or a new alliance they seek information from all those who have had a prior working relationship with the alliance partner.

As individuals the Japanese took their time to reach decisions, and were process oriented, analytical and organized. They did not like situations that were unexpected and found it difficult to react to anything unplanned. Even when decision-making was long and arduous, it was always in the interest of the JV. The Indians on the contrary, were often less organized and disciplined and failed to 'walk the talk'

Japanese management style. Adherence to the Japanese style of management was an important factor in the success of all alliances. Trust, transparency in operations, consensus in decision-making and relationship building were key traits, which were of consequence in the two successful alliances. The Indian alliance partners admitted that their management vision and style were either similar to the Japanese or were adapted to ensure the success of the alliance.

In contrast JV3 faced difficulties and was terminated due to differences in management styles and vision. The two alliance partners had divergent views on the time horizon needed to break even and establish themselves and on issues of discipline and commitment.

Communication. The Japanese generally have an agreement at two levels – one which is known and open to all (legal agreement) – called the *Tattami* and the other, which is between two people, based on the relationship they develop – called the *Honne*. The latter stems from an understanding and emotional connect between two people. It is not always possible have a formal agreement on all aspects of work, but they share information as per their perception of the best interest of the business. For example, in JV2 the chairman of the Indian partner was worried about his company's manufacturing capability given the lack of infrastructure in those years. During an informal session, his Japanese counterpart invited him to visit their testing equipment the following day. During the visit, the team was given the freedom to observe and make notes. These actions are based on trust and relationship and cannot be documented in any agreement for various reasons. The Japanese are often known to allow such liberties to their partners, once a strong relationship based on trust has been built.

Alliance outcomes

All alliances examined here have reached diverse outcomes in terms of their conclusion/ continuity/termination.

JV1 reached a successful conclusion through mutual consent, when the Japanese partner wanted to convert this alliance into a subsidiary, which is their global policy. In addition, both the entities believed that the JV had run its course successfully and it would be mutually beneficial to conclude the partnership. As a gesture of goodwill, the Indian partner transferred the employees of the JV to the Japanese partner at the time of conclusion. The alliance experience was described as 'very successful and satisfying and providing both entities an exposure to the other one's cultures and geographies'.

JV2 has a continuing relationship and business. The trust developed with the Japanese during the first JV enabled the Indian partner to establish itself as a company that the Japanese would like to do business with. This alliance helped the Indian partner enter into six other alliances with different Japanese firms. The Chairman of the Indian partner has a vision to become world-class manufacturing company that provides support to the global network of their JV partner. They have also established a positive image about India through their commitment to quality, prompt payments of royalty in their interaction with the Japanese counterpart.

JV3 had an early termination as per the agreement due to differences in the alliance partners' vision, strategic intent and expectations from the alliance. There was a lack of fit arising out of different perceptions of the regulatory environment of the industry, differences in strategic vision and risk perception of the top management, and cultural differences.

- *Industry issues*: The industry climate was very competitive and unregulated and the two alliance partners had very different visions and perception of this scenario. In a difficult industry, what becomes important is the risk appetite of the senior Management as well as their patience with a new market. The Japanese senior management did not seem aligned with the market in this aspect.
- *Lack of alignment between foreign and local partners*: The alliance partners had a different perception of the time horizon for establishing themselves and for the business to break even. The Indian time horizon was long term, but the Japanese partner wanted profits more quickly and was unwilling to wait.
- *Local cultural issues acted as barrier*: Differences in cultural issues became a barrier in the alliance. For instance, the Japanese felt that Indians were unable to 'Walk the Talk' – they generally over committed and under delivered. The Japanese are extremely committed and deliver as promised. Over a period in time, they learnt to discount Indian commitments made by almost 30%. Discipline was another contentious issue – generally Indians and Japanese have very different ways of managing time. Indians generally accept 10–15 minutes delay in arrival or starting a meeting. The Japanese on the other hand an extremely punctual – almost to the last second!

Discussion of results

The findings of this study validate findings from earlier studies (Horn, Forsans, and Cross 2010), which have emphasized the importance of *national policy* as a key compulsion which dictated the JV as the only possible mode of entry for foreign enterprises into India. Japanese MNEs usually prefer high equity ownership when the market environment is opaque and there is a perception of expropriation-related hazards (Delios and Henisz 2000), to be able to control the quality and image of the brand and the organization and to be able to keep the focus on key issues such as customer satisfaction. It also corroborates the findings of earlier studies, which opined that Japanese firms pursue JVs driven by the need to tap into local experience (Belderbos, Capannelli, and Fukao 2000; Kiyota et al. 2005). It also provides evidence that alliances are vehicles of knowledge acquisition and learning (Hamel 1991) and an appropriate mode of market entry and market penetration.

It also lends credence to the theories on Latecomer MNEs from the peripheries that leapfrog to advanced technological levels and leverage their way into new markets through partnerships and JVs (Mathews 2006, 6).

In the specific context of this study, *Trust* has been an important component of alliance management capability in all stages of the alliance. It is a key determinant of the Japanese willingness to do business and is the basis of the key value of relationship building. The Japanese were desirous of a long-term commitment to India and took whatever time was necessary to establish trust before proceeding at any stage of operation. The Japanese have an intermediate position on the power distance scale (Hofstede 1980); therefore, they take time to establish trust. This finds credence in the findings of this study, which shows that Japanese companies in India took time to establish trust, but once they had established trust they allowed their alliance partners many privileges, which were not part of their formal agreement. The Japanese are often known to allow such liberties to their partners, once a strong relationship based on trust has been built.

Consensus through consultation emerged as the basis of all decisions regardless of the time it took to reach a decision. The Japanese style of functioning is extremely process oriented and planned, and the smallest details are carefully worked out. Data gathered for this study reveals that Japanese plan the minutest of details in advance. This corroborates Japan's high ranking on the uncertainty avoidance ranking. According to Hickson and Pugh (1995), the Japanese feel that uncertainty can be controlled by orderliness and diligent attention to details and, 'if anything might go wrong, it must not'.

Cultural issues both at the national level and the organizational level played an important role in alliance management. Cultural compatibility and an understanding of the alliance partner's cultural background emerges an important aspect of alliance management capability. It thus augments the findings of earlier studies that have found that cultural differences among partners influence the interpretation and responses to strategic and managerial issues affecting partner trust and creating transactional difficulties (Park and Ungson 1997; Pothukuchi et al. 2002). Successful alliances were the result of mutual respect and understanding of differences in national and organizational culture. This finds support in Awasthy and Gupta (2009), Hickson and Pugh (1995), Hofstede (1980) that the Japanese understand Indian culture.

Unsuccessful alliances failed because of a competitive and unregulated industry environment, differences in perception and the inability to come to terms with cultural differences between alliance partners. The alliances also contributed to inter-partner learning which translated into the inception of many new alliances for the Indian partner.

Cultural differences between the Indian and Japanese partners and its influence on alliance management capabilities can be explained using Hofstede's (1980) cultural framework, which is a comprehensive framework of analysis of national culture along five major dimensions.

Japan has been seen as a collectivist society (Hofstede 1980; Schwartz 1999; Trompenaars 1993). This explains the importance of consensus and collective decision-making, since collectivist cultures control their members more through external pressure (shame) and they tend to push employees by introducing work practices such as quality circles and appointing different committees to look after issues related to maintenance, canteen and cultural activities. This study also reveals that consensus and collective decision-making were the guiding principles in all cases.

According to Hofstede's ranking Japanese display greater long-term orientation, which is reflected in their work practices such as high concern for quality, 'Just in Time' practices, quality circles and intensive planning. This study also confirms these findings.

In terms of degree of masculinity (MAS) rankings as per Hofstede, the Japanese fall on the masculine side. In more Masculine countries, the focus is on success and achievements, validated by material gains. Work is the centre of one's life, and visible symbols of success in the work place are very important. Japan is one of the most masculine societies in the world. However, in combination with their mild collectivism, this does not result in assertive and competitive individual behaviours that we often associate with masculine culture. It is manifested as severe competition between groups, which is inculcated from a very young age. What you also see as an expression of MAS in Japan is the drive for excellence and perfection in their material production (*monodukuri*), which has made the Japanese notorious as workaholics.

Managerial implications

This study provides some important lessons for the successful management of cross border alliances. It highlights the importance of trust and cultural compatibility, both at the organizational and national level, as the primary factors that determine the success or failure of an alliance.

Trust has emerged as the single most important factor that determined alliance outcome. The issue of building trust is a key factor in any working relationship in the Japanese context and is built over a long period of time. Trust cannot be built overnight. It takes time and is based on experiences and past behaviour. Often, relationships begin on basic trust and faith. However, the best way to build trust is to consistently deliver on promises. From the practitioner's perspective, one way to quickly build trust is to use a 'connector' who is known to and deeply trusted by both parties, a technique used by many Asian cultures.

Japanese society is known to be a web society, driven by consensus, and therefore decision-making is often slow. Yet, collaboration and open communication such as encouraging ideas from the shop floor level, which is a characteristic feature of Japanese management culture, can lead to consensus and expedite decision-making. Other differences in cultural perception such as Indian managers being seen as not 'Walking the Talk' and the Japanese being oriented towards delivering on promises can become a huge management challenge. Setting realistic expectations or goals that are achievable and time bound ensure that managers and team members are clearly working towards well-defined goals. The achievement of short and medium term milestones enhances the confidence and trust of both parties in each other. The study also highlighted the lack of a shared vision as the reason for alliance failure. Shared vision is generally an outcome of expectation alignment, which finds its foundation in open communication. While the Japanese are a closed society they believe in open communication within the community as a tool to align differences in partner expectations.

Conclusion

This study makes a contribution to the understanding of alliance management capabilities with a specific focus on India and Japan. It is a valuable blueprint for management, as it specifies the constituents of successful alliance management capability, especially as the two countries seem to be on the threshold of renewed economic engagement.

The paper examines the cultural aspects of alliance management capabilities for three Indo-Japanese alliances with diverse alliance outcomes. It examines the role of national and organizational culture as a critical determinant of alliance management through the different stages of its life. The study finds that complementary resources and capabilities coupled with the need for a trustworthy alliance partner formed the basis of all alliances. At the governance stage, both formal and informal tools ensured a stable structure with clear-cut roles and responsibilities for the alliance partners.

The success of the first two alliances were based on mutual trust, communication, consensus in decision-making, an understanding of differences in culture and an overall adherence to the Japanese style of management. It infers that trust and relational capital are important instruments of collaboration, and are assisted by communication and commitment as measures of alliance management.

Efficient management of the alliance requires a formal communication process and system, especially a process to resolve differences of opinion and arriving at solutions to challenges faced. In addition, transparent and clear communication forms the foundation of a long-term successful alliance. Many agreements may not necessarily documented, but once made must be followed through.

The failure of the third alliance to reach its intended goals was the outcome of cultural differences alongside differences in common vision and perception about the industry dynamics, differences in the time horizon of expected results and in the risk appetite of senior management.

The main limitation of the study is the small sample size, which precludes the general applicability of results into theory, and has the dangers of researcher bias. Its findings are also restricted since they are specific to a single alliance for a firm and may not be amenable for generalization. The study may be extended to compare the alliance management capability of the firms with their portfolio management capabilities. It may also be extended to compare alliance management capabilities with alliance partners from different countries for a multicultural comparison.

Acknowledgements

The authors are grateful to all contributors to this study, many of whom preferred to remain anonymous. We specifically thank the Senior Management, Bluestar India Ltd, Mr Sudhir Gera, Director, Full Spectrum Consulting and our friends from the Japanese fraternity in India for their valuable inputs for this study. We would also like to thank the reviewers of this paper for their comments.

Disclosure statement

No potential conflict of interest was reported by the authors.

Notes

1. http://economictimes.indiatimes.com/news/economy/policy/industry-ministry-sets-up-japan-plus-team-to-fast-track-investments/articleshow/44755280.cms.
2. https://www.jetro.go.jp/en/reports/statistics/.
3. http://www.in.emb-japan.go.jp/PDF/J_C_list_2012_%20(rev).pdf.
4. http://dipp.nic.in/English/Investor/Japan_Desk/FDI_Synopsis_Japan.pdf.
5. http://economictimes.indiatimes.com/industry/et-auto/news/industry/are-japanese-manufacturers-not-able-to-address-labour-concerns/articleshow/32764621.cms.

References

Amit, Raphael, and Paul J. H. Schoemaker. 1993. "Strategic Assets and Organizational Rent." *Strategic Management Journal* 14 (1): 33–46. doi:10.1002/smj.4250140105.

Anand, J., and A. Delios. 1996. "Competing Globally: How Japanese MNCs Have Matched Goals and Strategies in India and China." *Columbia Journal of World Business* 31 (3): 50–62. doi:10.1016/S0022-5428(96)90040-X.

Anand, Bharat N., and Tarun Khanna. 2000. "Do Firms Learn to Create Value? The Case of Alliances." *Strategic Management Journal* 21 (3): 295–315. doi:10.1002/(SICI)1097-0266 (200003)21:3<295:AID-SMJ91>3.0.CO;2-O.

Anderson, Erin, and Barton Weitz. 1992. "The Use of Pledges to Build and Sustain Commitment in Distribution Channels." *Journal of Marketing Research* 29 (1): 18–34. doi:10.2307/3172490.

Argyres, Nicholas, and Kyle J. Mayer. 2007. "Contract Design as a Firm Capability: An Integration of Learning and Transaction Cost Perspectives." *Academy of Management Review* 32 (4): 1060–1077. doi:10.5465/AMR.2007.26585739.

Ariño, A. 2003. "Measures of Strategic Alliance Performance: An Analysis of Construct Validity." *Journal of International Business* 34 (1): 66–79.

Ariño, A., and J. De La Torre. 1998. "Learning from Failure: Towards an Evolutionary Model of Collaborative Ventures." *Organization Science* 9: 306–325.

Awasthy, R., and R. K. Gupta. 2009. "Indian Executives' Perceptions of Expatriate Managers." *International Journal of Indian Culture and Business Management* 2 (2): 164–184. doi:10.1504/IJICBM.2009.022342.

Balakrishnan, Srinivasan, and Mitchell P. Koza. 1993. "Information Asymmetry, Adverse Selection and Joint-Ventures." *Journal of Economic Behavior and Organization* 20 (1): 99–117. doi:10.1016/0167-2681(93)90083-2.

Barnard, Chester I. 1938. *The Functions of the Executive*. Cambridge: Harvard University Press.

Beamish, P. W. 1984. "Joint Venture Performance in Developing Countries." PhD diss., The University of Western Ontario.

Beamish, P. W. 1985. "The Characteristics of Joint Ventures in Developed and Developing Countries." *Columbia Journal of World Business* 20: 13–19.

Beamish, Paul W., and John C. Banks. 1987. "Equity Joint Ventures and the Theory of the Multinational Enterprise." *Journal of International Business Studies* 18 (2): 1–16. doi:10.1057/palgrave.jibs.8490403.

Belderbos, R. A., G. Capannelli, and K. Fukao. 2000. "The Local Content of Japanese Electronics Manufacturing Operations in Asia." In *The Role of Foreign Direct Investment in East Asian Economic Development*, edited by T. Ito and A. O. Krueger, 9–47. Chicago, IL: University of Chicago Press.

Berg, Sanford V., Jerome Duncan, and P. Friedman. 1982. *Joint Venture Strategies and Corporate Innovation*. Cambridge, MA: Oelgeschlager.

Bleeke, Joel, and David Ernst. 1995. "Is Your Strategic Alliance Really a Sale?" *Harvard Business Review* 97–105.

Blodgett, Linda L. 1992. "Research Notes and Communications Factors in the Instability of International Joint Ventures: An Event History Analysis." *Strategic Management Journal* 13 (6): 475–481. doi:10.1002/smj.4250130607.

Borys, Bryan, and David B. Jemison. 1989. "Hybrid Arrangements as Strategic Alliances: Theoretical Issues in Organizational Combinations." *The Academy of Management Review* 14: 234–249.

Bresser, Rudi K. F. 1988. "Matching Collective and Competitive Strategies." *Strategic Management Journal* 9 (4): 375–385. doi:10.1002/smj.4250090407.

Bronder, Christoph, and Rudolf Pritzl. 1992. "Developing Strategic Alliances: A Conceptual Framework for Successful Co-operation." *European Management Journal* 10 (4): 412–421. doi:10.1016/0263-2373(92)90005-O.

Brown, S. L., and K. M. Eisenhardt. 1997. "The Art of Continuous Change: Linking Complexity Theory and Time-Paced Evolution in Relentlessly Shifting Organizations." *Administrative Science Quarterly* 42 (1): 1–34. doi:10.2307/2393807.

Buckley, Peter. J., and Mark Casson. 1988. "A Theory of Cooperation in International Business." In *Cooperative Strategies in International Business*, edited by Farok Contractor and Peter Lorange, 31–53. Lexington, MA: Lexington Books.

Buckley, Peter J., Adam R. Cross, and Sierk A. Horn. 2012. "Japanese Foreign Direct Investment in India: An Institutional Theory Approach." *Business History* 54 (5): 657–688. doi:10.1080/00076791.2012.683417

Chi, Tailan. 1994. "Trading in Strategic Resources: Necessary Conditions, Transaction Cost Problems, and Choice of Exchange Structure." *Strategic Management Journal* 15 (4): 271–290. doi:10.1002/smj.4250150403.

Coase, R. H. 1937. "The Nature of the Firm." *Economica* 4 (16): 386–405. doi:10.1111/j.1468-0335.1937.tb00002.x.

Commons, John R. 1934. *Institutional Economics; Its Place in Political Economy*. New York: Macmillan.

Conner, K. R. 1991. "A Historical Comparison of Resource-Based Theory and Five Schools of Thought Within Industrial Organization Economics: Do We Have a New Theory of the Firm?" *Journal of Management* 17 (1): 121–154. doi:10.1177/014920639101700109.

Contractor, Farok J., and Peter Lorange. 1988. "Why Should Firms Cooperate? The Strategy and Economics Basis for Cooperative Ventures." In *Cooperative Strategies in International Business*, edited by Farok J. Contractor and Peter Lorange, 3–28. Lexington, MA: Lexington Books.

Cresswell, John W. 2003. *Research Design: Qualitative, Quantitative, and Mixed Method Approaches*. 2nd ed. Thousand Oaks, CA: Sage Publications.

Cummings, T. G. 1984. "Transorganizational Development." *Research in Organizational Behavior* 6: 367–422.

Damanpour, F., C. Devece, C. C. Chen, and V. Pothukuchi. 2012. "Organizational Culture and Partner Interaction in the Management of International Joint Ventures in India." *Asia Pacific Journal of Management* 29 (2): 453–478. doi:10.1007/s10490-010-9204-x.

Das, T. K., and Bing-Sheng Teng. 2002. "The Dynamics of Alliance Conditions in the Alliance Development Process." *Journal of Management Studies* 39 (5): 725–746. doi:10.1111/1467-6486.00006.

David, R. J., and S. K. Han. 2004. "A Systematic Assessment of the Empirical Support for Transaction Cost Economics." *Strategic Management Journal* 25 (1): 39–58. doi:10.1002/smj.359.

Delios, A., and W. J. Henisz. 2000. "Japanese Firms' Investment Strategies in Emerging Economies." *Academy of Management Journal* 43 (3): 305–323. doi:10.2307/1556397.

Dixit, J. N. 1996. *My South Block Years: Memoirs of a Foreign Secretary.* New Delhi: UBS Publishers' Distributors.

Doz, Yves L. 1988. "Technology Partnerships Between Larger and Smaller Firms: Some Critical Issues." In *Cooperative Strategies in International Business*, 317–338. Lexington, MA: Lexington Books.

Doz, Yves L. 1996. "The Evolution of Cooperation in Strategic Alliances: Initial Conditions or Learning Processes?" *Strategic Management Journal* 17 (S1): 55–83. doi:10.1002/smj.4250171006.

Doz, Yves L., and Gary Hamel. 1998. *Alliance Advantage: The Art of Creating Value through Partnering.* Boston, MA: Harvard Business School Press.

Dussauge, Pierre, and Bernard Garrette. 1997. "Anticipating the Evolutions and Outcomes of Strategic Alliances between Rival Firms." *International Studies of Management and Organization* 27 (4): 104–126.

Dussauge, Pierre, and Bernard Garrette. 1999. *Cooperative Strategy Competing Successfully through Strategic Alliances.* West Sussex: John Wiley & Sons.

Dussauge, Pierre, Bernard Garrette, and Will Mitchell. 2000. "Learning from Competing Partners: Outcomes and Durations of Scale and Link Alliances in Europe, North America and Asia." *Strategic Management Journal* 21 (2): 99–126. doi:10.1002/(SICI)1097-0266(200002)21:2<99:AID-SMJ80>3.0.CO;2-G.

Dyer, Jeffrey H., and Harbir Singh. 1998. "The Relational View: Cooperative Strategy and Sources of Interorganizational Competitive Advantage." *The Academy of Management Review* 23 (4): 660–679.

Eisenhardt, Kathleen M. 1989. "Building Theories from Case Study Research." *The Academy of Management Review* 14 (4): 532–549.

Eisenhardt, Kathleen M. 1991. "Better Stories and Better Constructs: The Case for Rigor and Comparative Logic." *The Academy of Management Review* 16 (3): 620–627.

Fedor, Kenneth J., and William B. Werther. 1996. "The Fourth Dimension: Creating Culturally Responsive International Alliances." *Organizational Dynamics* 25 (2): 39–53. doi:10.1016/S0090-2616(96)90024-8.

Fey, C. F., and P. W. Beamish. 2001. "Organizational Climate Similarity and Performance: International Joint Ventures in Russia." *Organization Studies* 22 (5): 853–882. doi:10.1177/0170840601225005.

Galbraith, J. 1977. *Organization Design.* Reading, MA: Addison-Wesley.

Geringer, J. M. 1991. "Strategic Determinants of Partner Selection Criteria in International Joint Ventures." *Journal of International Business Studies* 22 (1): 41–62.

Geringer, J. Michael, and Louis Hebert. 1989. "Control and Performance of International Joint Ventures." *Journal of International Business Studies* 20 (2): 235–254. doi:10.1057/palgrave.jibs.8490359.

Geringer, J. Michael, and Louis Hebert. 1991. "Measuring Performance of International Joint Ventures." *Journal of International Business Studies* 22 (2): 249–263. doi:10.1057/palgrave.jibs.8490302.

Gerwin, Donald. 2004. "Coordinating New Product Development in Strategic Alliances." *The Academy of Management Review* 29 (2): 241–257.

Ghosh, I. 1996. "Jinxed Ventures." *Business World*, July 24th–August 6th, 54–60.

Glaister, Keith W., and Peter J. Buckley. 1996. "Strategic Motives for International Alliance Formation." *Journal of Management Studies* 33 (3): 301–332. doi:10.1111/j.1467-6486.1996.tb00804.x.

Granovetter, M. 1985. "Economic Action and Social Structure: The Problem of Embeddedness." *American Journal of Sociology* 91 (3): 481–510. doi:10.1086/228311.

Gulati, Ranjay. 1995. "Does Familiarity Breed Trust? The Implications of Repeated Ties for Contractual Choice in Alliances." *Academy of Management Review* 38 (1): 85–112. doi:10. 2307/256729.

Gulati, Ranjay. 1998. "Alliances and Networks." *Strategic Management Journal* 19 (4): 293–317. doi:10.1002/(SICI)1097-0266(199804)19:4<293:AID-SMJ982>3.0.CO;2-M.

Gulati, Ranjay, and Harbir Singh. 1998. "The Architecture of Cooperation: Managing Coordination Costs and Appropriation Concerns in Strategic Alliances." *Administrative Science Quarterly* 43 (4): 781–814. doi:10.2307/2393616.

Gulati, Ranjay, Paul R. Lawrence, and Phanish Puranam. 2005. "Adaptation in Vertical Relationships: Beyond Incentive Conflict." *Strategic Management Journal* 26 (5): 415–440. doi:10.1002/smj.458.

Gundlach, G., R. Achrol, and J. Mentzer. 1995. "The Structure of Commitment in Exchange." *Journal of Marketing* 59 (1): 78–92. doi:10.2307/1252016.

Hagedoorn, John, and Jos Schakenraad. 1994. "The Effect of Strategic Technology Alliances on Company Performance." *Strategic Management Journal* 15 (4): 291–309. doi:10.1002/smj. 4250150404.

Hambrick, Donald C., Jiatao Li, Katherine Xin, and Anne S. Tsui. 2001. "Compositional Gaps and Downward Spirals in International Joint Venture Management Groups." *Strategic Management Journal* 22 (11): 1033–1053. doi:10.1002/smj.195.

Hamel, Gary. 1990. "Competitive Collaboration: Learning, Power and Dependence in International Strategic Alliances." . PhD diss, University of Michigan.

Hamel, Gary. 1991. "Competition for Competence and Interpartner Learning within International Strategic Alliances." *Strategic Management Journal* 12 (S1): 83–103. doi:10.1002/smj. 4250120908.

Hamel, Gary, Yves L. Doz, and C. K. Prahalad. 1989. "Collaborate with Your Competitors – And Win." *Harvard Business Review* 133–139.

Harrigan, Kathryn. 1988. "Strategic Alliances and Partner Asymmetries." *Management International Review* 28: 53–73.

Hennart, Jean-François. 1988. "A Transaction Cost Theory of Equity Joint Ventures." *Strategic Management Journal* 9 (1): 36–74.

Hennart, Jean-François, and Ming Zeng. 2005. "Structural Determinants of Joint Venture Performance." *European Management Review* 2 (2): 105–115. doi:10.1057/palgrave.emr. 1500034.

Hickson, D. J., and D. S. Pugh. 1995. *Management Worldwide: The Impact of Societal Culture on Organizations Around the Globe*. London: Penguin.

Hitt, Michael A., M. Tina Dacin, Edward Levitas, Jean-Luc Arregle, and Anca Borza. 2000. "Partner Selection in Emerging and Developed Market Contexts: Resource-Based and Organizational Learning Perspectives." *Academy of Management Journal* 43 (3): 449–467. doi:10.2307/ 1556404.

Hoang, Ha, and Frank T. Rothaermel. 2005. "The Effect of General and Partner-Specific Alliance Experience on Joint R&D Project Performance." *Academy of Management Journal* 48 (2): 332–345. doi:10.5465/AMJ.2005.16928417.

Hoffmann, Werner H. 2007. "Strategies for Managing a Portfolio of Alliances." *Strategic Management Journal* 28 (8): 827–856. doi:10.1002/smj.607.

Hofstede, G. 1980. *Culture's Consequences: International Differences in Work Related Values*. Beverly Hills, CA: Sage.

Horn, Sierk A., and Adam R. Cross. 2009. "Japanese Management at a Crossroads? The Changing Role of China in the Transformation of Corporate Japan." *Asia Pacific Business Review* 15 (3): 285–308. doi:10.1080/13602380802667221.

Horn, Sierk A., Nicolas Forsans, and Adam R. Cross. 2010. "The Strategies of Japanese Firms in Emerging Markets: The Case of the Automobile Industry in India." *Asian Business & Management* 9 (3): 341–378. doi:10.1057/abm.2010.20.

Hsieh, H.-F., and S. Shannon. 2005. "Three Approaches to Qualitative Content Analysis." *Qualitative Health Research* 15 (9): 1277–1288. doi:10.1177/1049732305276687.

Ireland, R. D., M. A. Hitt, and D. Vaidyanath. 2002. "Alliance Management as a Source of Competitive Advantage." *Journal of Management* 28 (3): 413–446. doi:10.1177/ 014920630202800308.

Itami, Hiroyuki, and Thomas W. Roehl. 1987. *Mobilizing Invisible Assets*. Cambridge, MA: Harvard University Press.

Janger, A. H. 1980. *Organizations of International Joint Venture*. New York: Conference Board Report.

Jorde, Thomas M., and David J. Teece. 1990. "Innovation and Cooperation: Implications for Competition and Antitrust." *Journal of Economic Perspectives* 4 (3): 75–96. doi:10.1257/jep.4.3.75.

Kale, P. 1998. "Learning and Protection of Proprietary Key Assets in Strategic Alliances: Building Relational Capital." Paper presented at the meeting of the Academy of Management, San Diego, CA, August.

Kale, Prashant, and Harbir Singh. 2007. "Building Firm Capabilities Through Learning: The Role of the Alliance Learning Process in Alliance Capability and Firm-Level Alliance Success." *Strategic Management Journal* 28 (10): 981–1000. doi:10.1002/smj.616.

Kale, P., and H. Singh. 2009. "Managing Strategic Alliances: What Do We Know Now, and Where Do We Go from Here?" *Academy of Management Perspectives* August: 45–62.

Kale, Prashant, Jeffrey H. Dyer, and Harbir Singh. 2002. "Alliance Capability, Stock Market Response, and Long-Term Alliance Success: The Role of the Alliance Function." *Strategic Management Journal* 23 (8): 747–767. doi:10.1002/smj.248.

Kanter, Rosabeth Moss. 1994. "Collaborative Advantage: The Art of Alliances." *Harvard Business Review*, July 1, 96–108.

Killing, J. Peter. 1982. "How to Make a Global Joint Venture Work." *Harvard Business Review*, May 1, 120–127.

Killing, J. Peter. 1983. *Strategies for Joint Venture Success*. New York: Praeger.

Kiyota, K., T. Matsuura, S. Urata, and Y. Wei. 2005. "Reconsidering the Backward Vertical Linkages of Foreign Affiliates: Evidence from Japanese Multinationals." Discussion Paper Series 05-E-019 (Research Institute of Economy, Trade and Industry, RIETI). Accessed October 7, 2008. http://www.rieti.go.jp/jp/publications/dp/05e019.pdf

Klimoski, R., and S. Mohammed. 1994. "Team Mental Model: Construct or Metaphor?" *Journal of Management* 20 (2): 403–437. doi:10.1016/0149-2063(94)90021-3.

Kogut, Bruce. 1988a. "Joint Ventures: Theoretical and Empirical Perspectives." *Strategic Management Journal* 9 (4): 319–332. doi:10.1002/smj.4250090403.

Kogut, Bruce. 1988b. "A Study of the Life Cycle of Joint Ventures." *Management International Review* 28: 39–52.

Kogut, Bruce. 1989. "The Stability of Joint Ventures: Reciprocity and Competitive Rivalry." *The Journal of Industrial Economics* 38 (2): 183–198. doi:10.2307/2098529.

Krippendorf, Klaus. 1980. *Content Analysis: An Introduction to Its Methodology*. New York: Sage Publications.

Kumar, Rajesh. 1998. "The Development of Strategic Alliances in a Chaotic Environment: Lessons from the Power Sector in India." In *Europe in the Global Competition*, edited by S. Urban, 163–192. Wiesbaden: Gabler.

Kumar, R., and K. O. Nti. 1998. "Differential Learning and Interaction in Alliance Dynamics: A Process and Outcome Discrepancy Model." *Organization Science* 9 (3): 356–367. doi:10.1287/orsc.9.3.356.

Lane, Peter J., and Michael Lubatkin. 1998. "Relative Absorptive Capacity and Interorganizational Learning." *Strategic Management Journal* 19 (5): 461–477. doi:10.1002/(SICI)1097-0266 (199805)19:5<461:AID-SMJ953>3.0.CO;2-L.

Larson, Andrea. 1992. "Network Dyads in Entrepreneurial Settings: A Study of the Governance of Exchange Relationships." *Administrative Science Quarterly* 37 (1): 76–104. doi:10.2307/2393534.

Larsson, R., L. Bengtsson, K. Henriksson, and J. Sparks. 1998. "The Interorganizational Learning Dilemma: Collective Knowledge Development in Strategic Alliances." *Organization Science* 9 (3): 285–305. doi:10.1287/orsc.9.3.285.

Lee, Allen S. 1999. "Rigor and Relevance in MIS Research: Beyond the Approach of Positivism Alone." *MIS Quarterly* 23 (1): 29–34. Accessed October, 2014. doi:10.2307/249407.

Levinson, Nanette S., and Minoru Asahi. 1996. "Cross-National Alliances and Interorganizational Learning." *Organizational Dynamics* 24: 51–63.

Lincoln, Y. S., and E. G. Guba. 1985. *Naturalistic Inquiry*. Thousand Oaks, CA: Sage Publications.

Luo, Yadong. 2006. "Opportunism in Cooperative Alliances: Conditions and Solutions." In *Handbook of Strategic Alliances*, edited by Oded Shenkar and Jeffrey J. Reuer, 55–81. Thousand Oaks, CA: SAGE Publications. doi:10.4135/9781452231075.n4.

Macneil, Ian Roderick. 1981. "Economic Analysis of Contractual Relations: Its Shortfalls and the Need for a Rich Classificatory Apparatus." *Northwestern University Law Review* 75: 1018–1063.

Madhok, A., and S. B. Tallman. 1998. "Resources, Transactions and Rents: Managing Value Through Interfirm Collaborative Relationships." *Organization Science* 9 (3): 326–339. doi:10.1287/orsc.9.3.326.

Marks, Mitchell Lee, and Philip H. Mirvis. 1998. *Joining Forces: Making One Plus One Equal Three in Mergers, Acquisitions and Alliances*. San Francisco, CA: Jossey-Bass.

Mathews, J. A. 2006. "Dragon Multinationals: New Players in 21st Century Globalization." *Asia Pacific Journal of Management* 23 (1): 5–27. doi:10.1007/s10490-006-6113-0.

Mayer, Kyle J., and Nicholas S. Argyres. 2004. "Learning to Contract: Evidence from the Personal Computer Industry." *Organization Science* 15 (4): 394–410. doi:10.1287/orsc.1040.0074.

Meschi, P. X. 1997. "Longevity and Cultural Differences of International Joint Ventures: Toward Time-Based Cultural Management." *Human Relations* 50 (2): 211–227.

Miles, Matthew B., and A. Michael Huberman. 1994. *Qualitative Data Analysis an Expanded Sourcebook*. 2nd ed. Thousand Oaks, CA: Sage Publications.

Mitchell, Will, and Kulwant Singh. 1993. "Death of the Lethargic: Effects of Expansion into New Technical Subfields on Performance in a Firm's Base Business." *Organization Science* 4 (2): 152–180. doi:10.1287/orsc.4.2.152.

Mitchell, Will, and Kulwant Singh. 1996. "Survival of Businesses Using Collaborative Relationships to Commercialize Complex Goods." *Strategic Management Journal* 17 (3): 169–195. doi:10.1002/(SICI)1097-0266(199603)17:3<169:AID-SMJ801>3.0.CO;2-#.

Mohr, Jakki, and Robert Spekman. 1994. "Characteristics of Partnership Success: Partnership Attributes, Communication Behavior, and Conflict Resolution Techniques." *Strategic Management Journal* 15 (2): 135–152. doi:10.1002/smj.4250150205.

Mowery, D. C., I. E. Oxley, and B. S. Silverman. 1996. "Strategic Alliances and Inter-Firm Knowledge Transfer." *Strategic Management Journal* 17 (S2): 77–91. doi:10.1002/smj.4250171108.

Nakamura, Masao, J. Myles Shaver, and Bernard Yeung. 1996. "An Empirical Investigation of Joint Venture Dynamics: Evidence from U.S.-Japan Joint Ventures." *International Journal of Industrial Organization* 14 (4): 521–541. doi:10.1016/0167-7187(95)00508-0.

Nataraj, Geethanjali. 2010. "India-Japan Investment Relations: Trends & Prospects." *Indian Council for Research on International Economic Relations*, Working Paper No. 245.

Nayak, Amar K. J. R. 2005. "FDI Model in Emerging Economies: Case of Suzuki Motor Corporation in India." *The Journal of American Academy of Business*, March, 238–245. http://www.ximb.ac.in/~jcr/Suzuki.pdf

Osborn, Robert G., Charles D. Dieter, Kenneth F. Higgins, and Robert E. Usgaard. 1998. "Bird Flight Characteristics Near Wind Turbines in Minnesota." *The American Midland Naturalist* 139 (1): 29–38. doi:10.1674/0003-0031(1998)139[0029:BFCNWT]2.0.CO;2.

Oxley, J. E. 1997. "Appropriability Hazards and Governance in Strategic Alliances: A Transaction Cost Approach." *Journal of Law, Economics, and Organization* 13 (2): 387–409. doi:10.1093/oxfordjournals.jleo.a023389.

Park, Seung Ho, and Michael V. Russo. 1996. "When Competition Eclipses Cooperation: An Event History Analysis of Joint Venture Failure." *Management Science* 42 (6): 875–890. doi:10.1287/mnsc.42.6.875.

Park, S. H., and G. R. Ungson. 1997. "The Effect of National Culture, Organizational Complementarity, and Economic Motivation on Joint Venture Dissolution." *Academy of Management Journal* 40 (2): 279–307. doi:10.2307/256884.

Park, Seung Ho, and Gerardo R. Ungson. 2001. "Interfirm Rivalry and Managerial Complexity: A Conceptual Framework of Alliance Failure." *Organization Science* 12 (1): 37–53. doi:10.1287/orsc.12.1.37.10118.

Patton, M. Q. 2001. *Qualitative Evaluation and Research Methods*. 3rd ed. Newbury Park, CA: Sage Publications.

Paul, J. 1996. "Between-Method Triangulation in Organizational Diagnosis." *The International Journal of Organizational Analysis* 4 (2): 135–153. doi:10.1108/eb028845.

Penrose, Edith. 1959. *The Theory of the Growth of the Firm*. New York: John Wiley.

Phillips, Lynn W. 1981. "Assessing Measurement Error in Key Informant Reports: A Methodological Note on Organizational Analysis in Marketing." *Journal of Marketing Research* 18 (4): 395–415. doi:10.2307/3151333.

Piekkari, R., C. Welch, and E. Paavilainen. 2009. "The Case Study as Disciplinary Convention: Evidence from International Business Journals." *Organizational Research Methods* 12 (3): 567–589. doi:10.1177/1094428108319905.

Pisano, Gary. P. 1989. "Using Equity Participation to Support Exchange: Evidence from the Biotechnology Industry." *Journal of Law Economics & Organization* 5 (1): 109–126.

Poppo, L., and T. Zenger. 2002. "Do Formal Contracts and Relational Governance Function as Substitutes or Complements?" *Strategic Management Journal* 23 (8): 707–725. doi:10.1002/smj.249.

Pothukuchi, V., F. Damanpour, J. Choi, C. Chen, and S. H. Park. 2002. "National and Organizational Culture Differences and International Joint Venture Performance." *Journal of International Business Studies* 33 (2): 243–265. doi:10.1057/palgrave.jibs.8491015.

Powell, Walter W. 1990. "Neither Market nor Hierarchy: Network Forms of Organizations." *Research in Organizational Behavior* 12: 295–336.

Pucik, Vladimir. 1988. "Strategic Alliances, Organizational Learning, and Competitive Advantage: The HRM Agenda." *Human Resource Management* 27 (1): 77–93. doi:10.1002/hrm.3930270105.

Rajamohan, P. G., Dil Bahadur Rahut, and Jabin T. Jacob. 2008. "Changing Paradigms of Indo-Japan Relations: Opportunities and Challenges." *Indian Council for Research on International Economic Relations*.

Reuer, Jeffrey J., and Africa Ariño. 2007. "Strategic Alliance Contracts: Dimensions and Determinants of Contractual Complexity." *Strategic Management Journal* 28 (3): 313–330. doi:10.1002/smj.581.

Reuer, Jeffrey J., and Kent D. Miller. 1997. "Agency Costs and the Performance Implications of International Joint Venture Internalization." *Strategic Management Journal* 18 (6): 425–438. doi:10.1002/(SICI)1097-0266(199706)18:6<425:AID-SMJ878>3.0.CO;2-#.

Reuer, Jeffrey J., Maurizio Zollo, and Harbir Singh. 2002. "Post-Formation Dynamics in Strategic Alliances." *Strategic Management Journal* 23 (2): 135–151. doi:10.1002/smj.214.

Richardson, G. B. 1972. "The Organisation of Industry." *The Economic Journal* 82 (327): 883–896. doi:10.2307/2230256.

Ring, Peter Smith, and Andrew H. Van De Ven. 1994. "Developmental Processes of Cooperative Interorganizational Relationships." *The Academy of Management Review* 19 (1): 90–118.

Roychoudhary, S. 2005. "The Spillover Effect of Japanese Foreign Direct Investment in Human Resource Management: A Case Study of Honda Siel." . CSIRD Discussion Paper No. 8.

Sahoo, Tapan, D. K. Banwet, and M. Momaya. 2011. "Strategic Technology Management Practices in Select Auto Component Joint Ventures in India: A Case Study Using SAP-LAP Methodology." *International Journal of Engineering Management and Economics* 2 (2/3): 153–174. doi:10.1504/IJEME.2011.041994.

Salk, J., and M. Y. Brannen. 2000. "Research Notes. National Culture, Networks, and Individual Influence in a Multinational Management Team." *Academy of Management Journal* 43 (2): 191–202. doi:10.2307/1556376.

Salk, Jane E., and Oded Shenkar. 2001. "Social Identities in an International Joint Venture: An Exploratory Case Study." *Organization Science* 12 (2): 161–178. doi:10.1287/orsc.12.2.161.10111.

Schreiner, Melanie, Prashant Kale, and Daniel Corsten. 2009. "What Really Is Alliance Management Capability and How Does It Impact Alliance Outcomes and Success?" *Strategic Management Journal* 30 (13): 1395–1419. doi:10.1002/smj.790.

Schwartz, S. H. 1999. "A Theory of Cultural Values and Some Implications for Work." *Applied Psychology: an International Review* 48 (1): 23–47. doi:10.1111/j.1464-0597.1999.tb00047.x.

Shah, R., and V. Swaminathan. 2008. "Factors Influencing Partner Selection in Strategic Alliances: The Moderating Role of Alliance Context." *Strategic Management Journal* 29 (5): 471–494. doi:10.1002/smj.656.

Sharma, S. 1999. "Democracy, Neoliberalism and Growth with Equity: Lessons from India and Chile." *Contemporary South Asia* 8 (3): 347–371. doi:10.1080/09584939908719873.

Simon, H. A. 1957. *Administrative Behavior*. New York: Macmillan.

Simonin, Bernard L. 1997. "The Importance of Collaborative Know-How: An Empirical Test of the Learning Organization." *Academy of Management Journal* 40 (5): 1150–1174. doi:10.2307/256930.

Sirmon, D. J., and P. J. Lane. 2004. "A Model of Cultural Differences and International Alliance Performance." *Journal of International Business Studies* 35 (4): 306–319. doi:10.1057/palgrave.jibs.8400089.

Teece, David J. 1986. "Profiting from Technological Innovation: Implications for Integration, Collaboration, Licensing and Public Policy." *Research Policy* 15 (6): 285–305. doi:10.1016/0048-7333(86)90027-2.

Thompson, James D. 1967. *Organizations in Action; Social Science Bases of Administrative Theory.* New York: McGraw-Hill.

Tihanyi, L., D. A. Griffith, and C. J. Russell. 2005. "The Effect of Cultural Distance on Entry Mode Choice, International Diversification, and MNE Performance: A Meta-Analysis." *Journal of International Business Studies* 36 (3): 270–283. doi:10.1057/palgrave.jibs.8400136.

Trompenaars, F. 1993. *Riding the Waves of Culture.* London: Economist Books.

Uzzi, Brian. 1996. "The Sources and Consequences of Embeddedness for the Economic Performance of Organizations: The Network Effect." *American Sociological Review* 61 (4): 674–698. doi:10.2307/2096399.

Uzzi, Brian. 1997. "Social Structure and Competition in Interfirm Networks: The Paradox of Embeddedness." *Administrative Science Quarterly* 42 (1): 35–67. doi:10.2307/2393808.

Van De Ven, Andrew H., and Douglas Polley. 1992. "Learning While Innovating." *Organization Science* 3 (1): 92–116. doi:10.1287/orsc.3.1.92.

Vapola, T. J., M. Paukku, and M. Gabrielsson. 2010. "Portfolio Management of Strategic Alliances: An International Business Perspective." *International Business Review* 19 (3): 247–260. doi:10.1016/j.ibusrev.2009.12.004.

Voss, C., N. Tsikriktsis, and M. Frohlich. 2002. "Case Research in Operations Management." *International Journal of Operations & Production Management* 22 (2): 195–219. doi:10.1108/01443570210414329.

Wassmer, U. 2010. "Alliance Portfolios: A Review and Research Agenda." *Journal of Management* 36 (1): 141–171. doi:10.1177/0149206308328484.

Welch, Catherine, Rebecca Piekkari, Emmanuella Plakoyiannaki, and Eriikka Paavilainen-Mäntymäki. 2011. "Theorising from Case Studies: Towards a Pluralist Future for International Business Research." *Journal of International Business Studies* 42 (5): 740–762. doi:10.1057/jibs.2010.55.

Wernerfelt, Birger. 1984. "A Resource-Based View of the Firm." *Strategic Management Journal* 5 (2): 171–180. doi:10.1002/smj.4250050207.

Williamson, Oliver E. 1985. *The Economic Institutions of Capitalism.* New York: Free Press.

Williamson, Oliver E. 1991. "Comparative Economic Organization: The Analysis of Discrete Structural Alternatives." *Administrative Science Quarterly* 36 (2): 269–296. doi:10.2307/2393356.

Yin, Robert K. 1989. *Case Study Research: Design and Methods.* 2nd ed. Beverly Hills, CA: Sage Publications.

Yin, Robert K. 1994. *Case Study Research: Design and Methods.* Beverly Hills, CA: Sage.

Yin, Robert K. 2013. *Case Study Research: Design and Methods,* Applied Social Research Methods. 5th ed. Thousand Oaks: Sage Publication.

Zollo, Maurizio, Jeffrey J. Reuer, and Harbir Singh. 2002. "Interorganizational Routines and Performance in Strategic Alliances." *Organization Science* 13 (6): 701–713. doi:10.1287/orsc.13.6.701.503.

How have Japanese multinational companies changed? Competitiveness, management and subsidiaries

Robert Fitzgerald[a] and Chris Rowley[b,c,d]

[a]Royal Holloway, University of London, UK; [b]Cass Business School, City University, London, UK; [c]HEAD Foundation, Singapore; [d]Griffith Business School, Griffith University, Australia

Evidence on the strategies and capabilities of Japanese multinational companies (MNCs) and their subsidiaries points to aspects of established management practices (typically home-grown) that complicate or inhibit adaptation to the demands of global competition since the 1990s. Japanese MNCs have had to respond, amongst other trends, to the switch from production to buyer-driven global value chains, cross-border vertical specialization, global factory strategies and strategic alliances and cooperative relationships. Amongst the factors that might affect the ability of Japanese MNCs to make competitive and organizational transitions are: parental MNC intent and capability in the cross-border transfer of management practices; the impact of host country risk on investment, ownership and entry strategies; measures of institutional difference and the gap in economic development between home and host nations; parent firm–subsidiary and subsidiary–subsidiary power relations and knowledge boundaries; and the evolution of insider networks that might overcome institutional and cultural distances within an MNC.

Introduction

This collection outlined and analysed the emergence and evolution of Japanese multinational companies (MNCs) across a range of sectors in a variety of ways. These range from watches to textiles to electronics in terms of global value chains (GVC), vertical specialization, subsidiary evolution, localization, expatriation, cross-national distance and alliance management. We noted the historical and context-specific ebb and flow of MNC organization, structure and foreign direct investment (FDI) patterns. For example, that leading general trading companies (*sogoshosha*) were often the arms of business conglomerates (*zaibatsu* and *keiretsu*) and government sponsorship and contacts were central to their growth and success (see Fitzgerald 2015), a model that would be replicated in South Korea, with their general trading companies and *chaebol* (see Jun and Rowley 2014).

This sort of approach in turn answers the contemporary common clarion call for more grounded and contextualized research. This is from a range of journal editors, especially in core business and management areas, albeit one already actually undertaken some time ago (Fitzgerald and Rowley 1997) and in areas such as industrial sociology and industrial relations. Indeed, historical work ranges from the famous work of Roethlisberger and Dickenson (1939) to Abegglen's (1958) pioneering study of Japanese factories.

Taking the contributions herein together, what can we conclude? Triple themes emerge: long-term challenges, core capabilities and localization, and organizational problems and solutions. We detail these next.

Long-term challenges

The first three contributions to this volume all took a business history or long-term approach to analyse the challenges encountered by Japanese MNCs. Donzé demonstrated how Seiko began to build production facilities overseas in the 1960s, starting with low-valued activities in assembly plants or in the manufacture of simple parts, in fulfilment of an efficiency-seeking FDI strategy. The company set the pattern for Swiss and US competitors, which copied Seiko's policy of utilizing cheaper labour and lower production costs overseas. The global watch industry witnessed the development of producer-driven value chains in which those firms owning core technologies in mass manufacturing watch movements controlled the chain. Change in the competitive environment was initially technology based and began from the 1980s with the arrival of electronic watches. As a consequence, key technologies became more easily replicable and traditional watch-makers lost their leading capabilities and source of sustained competitive advantage. As in the example of textile and apparel manufacturers, marketing emerged as the more important determinant of competition. Swiss and Hong Kong watchmakers adopted a strategy of investing in design and distribution, twinned with the internalization of design and marketing capabilities gained through the acquisition of companies.

Why did Seiko fail to adopt a new strategy and why, therefore, was it unable to replace its production-driven value chain overseas with one that was buyer-driven? Interestingly, Seiko has shown paradoxical tendencies since the 1980s. It had demonstrated a strong concern for marketing, design and distribution in its domestic market, while continuing to focus on the reduction of production costs abroad and on relocating output to China and East Asia. It founded in 1985 a subsidiary that acted as a retailer of watches in Japanese department stores. Overseas, Seiko had few luxury brands and no distribution-retail network until launching Seiko Boutiques in 2014. Seiko's strategic failing goes beyond technological issues or matching South Korean, Taiwanese or Chinese low cost competition. We might further venture that – given Seiko's marketing and branding strengths in its home market as developed since 2000 – it has had in principle the capabilities and experience to adapt to the watch industry's contemporary cross-border buyer-driven value chains. It appears to have been devoid of the capability to transfer capabilities overseas or lacked the strategic intent to do so. On the other hand, the Japanese market, with its high level of mechanical watch sales, had unique characteristics. Financial and human resources (HR) have remained with unprofitable divisions based in Japan. Critically, the engineering and production functions retained their hold over Seiko's strategy and organizational emphasis, a situation commonly associated with Japanese manufacturers and rooted in past commercial achievements and despite a critical shift in the nature of the industry's technology. Profits since the 1980s were to be found in marketing, distribution, branding and margins, not in suppressing costs. Seiko adhered to a stability and continuity-based strategy for its overseas operations. The company showed indications of a manufacturer that was able to transfer its capabilities in technology in production to overseas subsidiaries which catered for local markets, or supplied components to the parent MNC. Yet, Seiko lost ground from the 1980s, due to the expansion of global markets and to the failure of its parent–subsidiary structures to accommodate a less Japan-centric approach.

On the whole, Japanese manufacturing MNCs have coped with the reorganization of production at a regional level, notably in electronics and machinery. They transferred low technology output to East Asia and retained high value items in Japan, with China increasingly performing final assembly. Lehmberg revealed, nonetheless, the importance of differences between companies and industries and a mixed set of outcomes in the efforts of Japanese MNCs to meet challenges since the 1990s. He analysed over time vertical integration amongst Japanese electronics and IT firms making LCDs. As production volumes increased and technology improved, firms additionally experienced price swings. Product standardization, commoditization, new entrants and over-capacity put downward pressure on costs and favoured larger and specialist producers. Some Japanese electronics and IT firms responded with outsourcing and approaches stretching from full and partial de-integration; others kept full vertical integration. Firm- specific, industry-specific and time-specific factors were all influential in determining their responses.

Lehmberg argued that Japanese firms, which had historically favoured vertical integration strategies, were willing to adopt alternatives. In instances of quasi-integration approaches, Japanese MNCs transferred knowledge to non-Japanese businesses and signed outsourcing agreements, contradicting common perceptions of Japanese firms jealously guarding their technological and managerial secrets. Difficulties in copying needed components and inputs had once encouraged vertical integration in LCDs as a source of product quality and competitive differentiation. However, standardization and the lowering of industry entry barriers removed this strategic advantage and left in-house production with the disadvantage of higher costs. Some MNCs abandoned an established preference for wholly owned subsidiaries, control and expatriate staffing. To what extent was the growing reliance on some level of de-integration and alliance with non-Japanese firms the result of industry-specific factors in LCD production? Or, in other words, how willing have MNCs been to abandon the institutional norms of their home economy and to embrace the economic, technological and organizational realities of global competition? What can be observed is a number of influential and sometimes contradictory factors and the difficulties and managerial tensions involved in formulating viable strategic responses. While Japanese managers became more open to international cooperation, they continued to encounter particular difficulties when internationalizing. While accustomed to higher degrees of managerial homogeneity, they had to learn quickly lessons in managing diversity.

What our examples of the watch and LCD industries illustrate is the impact of technological change, although there were important differences in the nature of that change. In watch-making, Seiko failed to make the necessary transition in international strategy and organization, specifically the development of buyer-driven GVCs. There was a shift in one core technology in mechanical watches to the more easily replicable manufacture of electronic watches, switching the priority to marketing as a source of distinctiveness. In LCD production, it was the turn of the product life cycle that was more noticeable: it made LCDs subject to higher volume and more cost conscious, standardized and easily replicable manufacture, which pushed firms towards vertical de-integration and cooperative partnerships.

In contrast to watch-making and LCD production, however, Fitzgerald and Lai describe how Omron intensified the levels of cross-border integration between the main business in Japan, its subsidiary in China and its subsidiaries worldwide over two decades. Variations in economic development and technological advantage facilitated Omron's ability to transfer its capabilities from Japan to subsidiary operations in China.

Core capabilities and localization

The strategic motivation for the initial investment and founding of Shanghai Omron in 1993 was efficiency-seeking, with much of the output destined for export markets. It was obliged by institutional requirements at the time to adopt a joint venture with a state-owned enterprise (SOE). With the assistance of expatriate personnel, Omron Japan revealed a strong strategic intent to transfer practices to its subsidiary, with the notable and pragmatic exception of HR policies which were based on Chinese SOE traditions and left to Chinese managers. Institutional isomorphic pressures (if mainly in HR) existed alongside the MNC's need for cross-border symmetry (most obviously in production methods and quality standards). Given the joint venture arrangements, Omron was cautious about the transfer of its core technology and technological knowledge, and the localization of R&D in China was minimized. Institutional factors, nonetheless, did not prevent the parent MNC transferring its production and product quality systems to an effective degree, although some variations in processes and outcomes were detectable. As a result, the MNCs had been willing to continue the joint venture, although no longer required under revised institutional rules, but it ultimately accepted the need to convert Omron Shanghai into a wholly owned enterprise.

Changes in ownership at Omron Shanghai from 2005 encouraged the MNCs to accelerate the transfer of capabilities, including R&D and indicated a continuing ingrained caution commonly associated with Japanese businesses about the loss of proprietorial knowledge to strategic partners. The formation of a wholly owned subsidiary coincided with Omron's adoption of its global factory policy, with China as the low cost production centre manufacturing for world markets and the policy was based on the inculcation of international, as opposed to strictly Japanese, 'best practice'. To expand production capacity and to optimize product quality, the MNCs sought to enhance the role of local management and subsidiary capability, while integrating the Chinese operation more fully with its international networks and ensuring tight parent company involvement. Rather than being contradictory, strong parental control and enhanced subsidiary capabilities were complementary. Omron showed an ability to accept international standards and practices and to blend these with its own home-grown systems and managerial direction. In dealing with changes in the nature of global competition and MNC business structures from the 1990s, Omron was able to maintain its competitive position by merging international, home-grown and host country subsidiary practices and to pursue a 'global factory' strategy, while increasing the role of the parent firm within the MNCs. It was national institutional factors, more obviously in the host economy of the Chinese subsidiary, which gave way to cross-border integration and harmonization under the ambit of the MNCs. While Omron Japan retained leading capabilities that enabled it to achieve its strategic objectives, it showed itself adaptable enough to learn from and to absorb international best practices.

Hong and Snell similarly presented evidence on the localization of capabilities by Japanese MNCs in China. They conducted research into Toshiba TEC Information Systems (S.Z.) Co. Ltd (TESS). As in the case of Omron, TESS began as a joint venture (founded in 1993), initially as the Toshiba Copy Machine (Shenzen) or TCOS, which specialized in the production and assembly of copy machines for both worldwide exports and host markets. The subsidiary came under the control of the parent MNC (in 1996) and it was renamed TESS (in 2007) in recognition of its expanding manufacturing activities. Again, as in the example of Omron, this case revealed how parent MNCs sought to retain control over core competencies in R&D, creating a 'pragmatic boundary' as well as a 'knowledge boundary' for subsidiary management by keeping these functions in Japan. The headquarters R&D function would in addition have to sanction any product modifications. Close supervision of production methods through expatriates denied local management opportunities to adapt to local circumstances and preferences. As Toshiba's Chinese subsidiary grew in importance as a production base, the dysfunctional consequences of geographically and managerially separating R&D and production increased, yet uncertainty avoidance blocked any change of policy. Toshiba seemed more willing to allow local managers to cross pragmatic boundaries in what they perceived as non-strategic capabilities such as component sourcing and environmental protection.

Both Toshiba and Omron in China show the value of looking at differing business functions, which reveal differing levels of localization and subsidiary empowerment. In applying the ideas of pragmatic and knowledge boundaries, Hong and Snell detected how power relations, internal politics and the wariness of parent MNC management shaped the transfer of organizational capabilities. The impact on the transfer of R&D was evident. Production methods were transferred, but with adaptations, such as high levels of monitoring and control. This pointed to the managerial and technological asymmetries between home and host economies. It argued for the parent MNC creating in such circumstances joint activities through which home country managers can de-programme their uncertainty avoidance and any sense of cultural superiority and through which host country employees could acquire knowledge and express their ideas. Yet, Toshiba – as with Omron – associated its core capabilities and competitiveness with its parent business and home-grown practices and the legacy placed barriers on its development as a global company and on the adoption of federative cross-border organization.

Organizational problems and solutions

Bassino, Dovis and van der Eng continued with the theme of uncertainty avoidance or risk aversion by Japanese MNCs. Specifically, they asked to what extent these issues were connected to the use of expatriates and the transfer of capabilities to subsidiaries. The 'coordination and control' approach suggested that experienced expatriates could oversee the implementation of practices in host countries. Alternatively, in the notion of a 'transitory phase', expatriates took on the role of training local management, who understood local conditions more thoroughly and proved less expensive in the long run. To assess both schools of thought, the authors focused on the risks posed in host economies to MNC proprietorial capabilities, HR and financial assets. They utilized a database of Japanese subsidiaries in Asian countries. Rather than home and host institutional difference leading to a higher usage of expatriates, they concluded that in risky host environments in Asia, MNCs tended to rely more on local management. Firm-specific factors – capital intensity, percentage of ownership in a subsidiary and age of the venture – were also relevant and produced variations in outcome. Advancing subsidiary age allowed expatriates to train and empower local managers. Host country personnel had the connections to reduce political or regulatory risk and localization and market awareness could increase the efficient use of capabilities, especially relevant in large or capital intensive investments. Greater levels of ownership allowed more opportunities to control the activities of subsidiaries and might reduce the need to send large teams of expatriates abroad.

Similarly, Zhang analysed the relationship between home and host country factors and the internal dimensions of management, organization, knowledge and power relations within an MNC. She used large data-sets to test how cross-national distance and networks within Japanese MNCs interacted with each other and determined ownership strategies and acknowledged the influence of many factors. Zhang believed that the cultivation of insider networks within the company could help overcome problems of cross-border distance. Japanese companies could build on their existing capabilities to overcome divisions within MNCs and between home and host countries. Zhang's work indicated that 'insidership' within networks could moderate the influence of cross-national distance on the MNCs' ownership levels, but that cross-national distance could moderate the influence of insidership within networks. Due to the tacitness of cultural knowledge, cultural distance interacted with insidership within networks to negatively adjust MNCs' ownership levels, creating diversity in practice. In contrast, because of the codifiability of administrative knowledge, insidership within networks alleviated the influence of administrative distance on MNCs' ownership levels, improving internal cross-border consistency. It could assist in the transfer of knowledge and capabilities.

In contrast, Varma, Awasthy, Narain and Nayyarm investigated three cases of Japanese joint ventures in India and noted that, as in China in the 1990s, national policy dictated the nature of entry strategy (for the evolution over stages of people management and human capital development in Indian IT, see Malik and Rowley 2015). The need to access local markets and connections was an additional motive and alliances facilitated knowledge acquisition. As might be expected from their home nation practice, Japanese management was slow to develop trust relationships with host country partners, but eventually established valuable trusting working relationships. They could utilize, nonetheless, techniques for consultation and consensus formation and planning and an emphasis on process helped deflate uncertainty in their dealings. Successful alliances were the result of mutual respect and understanding of differences in national and organizational culture. In their analysis of the cultural aspects of alliance management capabilities, the authors detected diverse outcomes. The success of two of the alliances was founded on mutual trust, communication, consensus in decision-making, an understanding of differences in culture and, critically, an overall adherence to the Japanese style of management. It inferred that trust and relational capital were important instruments of collaboration and that communication and commitment were central to alliance management. Efficient management of the alliance required a formal communication process and system, especially a process to resolve differences of opinion and to arrive at solutions to challenges faced. In addition, transparent and clear communication formed the foundation of problem resolution and a long-term successful alliance. The failure of one joint venture to reach its intended goals was the outcome of cultural differences not being overcome by a common vision, varying perceptions of industry dynamics and differences in time horizons and risk appetites.

Implications

Key implications from our collection and analysis revolve around the analytical usefulness of historical perspectives. Several contributors to this volume take a long-term or business history approach to reveal how the international competitive landscape has changed for Japanese business in general and for specific Japanese industries and they assess how effectively Japanese MNCs have responded since the mid-1990s.

Overall, the authors looked at a number of significant changes in the nature of cross-border competition and identified topics of strategy and capability by which to assess the nature and extent of the response by Japanese MNCs. They emphasized instances of a clash between established Japanese management practices (typically home-grown) and the new demands of global competition for MNCs. By locating such developments, along with others, within a rich historical and country context, they provide a refreshing retort to the ahistorical, dry and anodyne nature of too much so-called international business and management research and publication infatuated and over-influenced by spurious American 'scientificism' and its implied 'one best way' universalism.

Conclusion

In summary, the contributions noted the Japanese manufacturing emphasis on production and process and the switch from production to buyer-driven GVCs; firm-level and management responses to the growing incidence of cross-border vertical specialization, when Japanese firms had frequently built their success on integration and homogeneity; the emergence of global factory strategies and the movement of production to foreign location, when Japanese MNCs had relied on home country capabilities and strong parent firm control; and the growing need for strategic alliances and cooperative relationships. The authors evaluated the factors that might affect the ability of Japanese MNCs to make competitive and organizational transitions: parent MNC intent and capability in the cross-border transfer of management practices; degrees of host country risk that influence investment, ownership and entry strategies; levels of institutional difference; gaps in economic development between home and host nations; and parent firm–subsidiary and subsidiary–subsidiary power relations and knowledge boundaries.

Nonetheless, there is evidence in this volume that Japanese MNCs can adapt their traditional management strengths and capabilities and find practical solutions to new demands and approaches to global competition. Dominant parent firm capabilities and cross-border control have been blended with global factory strategies and the enhancement of subsidiary capabilities; insider networks and transnational spaces can be developed to overcome perceptions of cultural distance and administrative difference between parent MNC and subsidiary; and traditional Japanese strengths in consensus building, planning and process have in noted cases been used in the management of strategic alliances, joint ventures and subsidiaries.

Disclosure statement

No potential conflict of interest was reported by the authors.

References

Abegglen, J. C. 1958. *The Japanese Factory: Aspects of Its Social Organization*. Glencoe, IL: Free Press.
Fitzgerald, R. 2015. *Rise of the Global Company: Multinationals and the Making of the Modern World*. Cambridge: Cambridge University Press.
Fitzgerald, R., and C. Rowley, eds. 1997. *Human Resources and the Firm in International Perspective*. Cheltenham: Edward Elgar.

Jun, W., and C. Rowley. 2014. "Change and Continuity in Management Systems and Corporate Performance: Human Resource Management, Corporate Culture, Risk Management and Corporate Strategy in South Korea." *Business History* 56 (3): 485–508. doi:10.1080/00076791. 2013.809522.

Malik, A., and C. Rowley, eds. 2015. *Business Models and People Management in the Indian IT Industry*. Abingdon: Routledge.

Roethlisberger, F. J., and W. J. Dickenson. 1939. *Management and the Worker*. Cambridge, MA: Harvard University Press.

Index

179

For Product Safety Concerns and Information please contact our
EU representative GPSR@taylorandfrancis.com Taylor & Francis
Verlag GmbH, Kaufingerstraße 24, 80331 München, Germany